Praise for *The God That Did Not Fail*

The project of remaking the world without God—the Enlightenment—
has failed. A powerful intellectual movement has arisen, a self-confident
movement of believing Jews and Christians, to do better what the Enlightened proved incapable of doing. Robert Royal is wondrously informative
on the intellectual bases of this new religious criticism, and is himself one
of its leaders.

Michael Novak

American Enterpris

The unsecularization of the world is the most important social
about the twenty-first century and the third millennium. Robert Royal's
exploration of the interaction of biblical faith and culture will help readers of all religious persuasions and none wrestle with the implications of
this momentous reality thoughtfully.

George Weigel

Ethics and Public Policy Center

As Robert Royal demonstrates in this elegant and lucid book, we now face
a new era in Western history—an era in which the long-predicted obso-
lescence of religion is itself being rendered obsolete, and a fresh, post-sec-
ular understanding of the future is emerging into view. The rough
arguments both learned and wise, Royal contends that the various "liberations" of modernity have been doomed to lose their meaning, because
they fail to acknowledge their own grounding in the transcendent dignity
of the human person and the necessity of ordered liberty—two proposi-
tions that depend in turn on belief in a God who has not failed, and who
awaits the return of his modern prodigals.

Wilfred M. McClay

University of Tennessee at Chattanooga

and Woodrow Wilson Center

THE GOD THAT DID NOT FAIL

THE GOD THAT DID NOT FAIL

Robert Royal

ENCOUNTER BOOKS

NEW YORK · LONDON

First paperback edition published in 2010 by Encounter Books, an activity of
Encounter for Culture and Education, Inc., a nonprofit, tax exempt corporation.

Encounter Books website address: www.encounterbooks.com

Manufactured in the United States and printed on acid-free paper.
The paper used in this publication meets the minimum requirements of
ANSI/NISO Z39.48 1992 (R 1997) *(Permanence of Paper).*

PAPERBACK EDITION ISBN 978-1-59403-517-3

THE LIBRARY OF CONGRESS HAS CATALOGUED
THE HARDCOVER EDITION AS FOLLOWS:

Royal, Robert
The God that did not fail: How religion built and sustains the West/Robert Royal
p. cm.
ISBN 1-59403-145-2
1. Civilization, Christian. 2. Civilization, Western. 1.Title.
BR115.C5R68 2006
200.9182'1—dc22   2006012548

10   9   8   7   6   5   4   3   2

For wherever one has fallen, it is there that he must apply himself,
in order that he may rise again.

Augustine, *De vera religione* XXIV.45

Contents

The Gods That Have Failed

> The religious impulse, the quest for meaning that transcends the restricted space of empirical existence in this world, has been a perennial feature of humanity. (This is not a theological statement but an anthropological one—an agnostic or even an atheist philosopher may well agree with it.) It would take something close to a mutation of the species to extinguish this impulse for good.
>
> Peter Berger[1]

ALL people by nature search for meaning and even for truth, and almost all of them, today as in the past, conduct that search through some form of religion. Historically, of course, this is a simple fact. The native peoples of the Americas, the various civilizations of Asia and Africa and Oceania, and the multiple cultures, ancient and modern, that gave rise to the modern West disagree about many things. But about religion, individually and in groups, with very limited exceptions, human beings show a remarkable similarity across cultures. All ask questions such as: Who am I? Where do I come from and where am I going? Why does evil exist? What exists after this life?[2] The answers to these questions, to put it mildly, vary. Still, all human cultures have taken seriously the obvious truth that everyday life as we live it on the practical level is not enough to satisfy the deepest questions we find within ourselves—or our longing towards truth, goodness, and beauty. Wherever human beings exist, these human aspirations will as well, even in such inhospitable habitats as Manhattan or Malibu, or modern departments of comparative literature. That we need to restate this truth is one indication of the odd position in which we find ourselves at the beginning of the twenty-first century.

For a good portion of the nineteenth and twentieth centuries, partly owing to the rise of science and technology and partly under the influence of naturalist psychologies like Freudianism, which classify religion as a neurotic illusion, certain sectors of Western high culture viewed continuing religiosity with what can only be called contempt. This view went hand in hand with an uncritical condemnation of the religious past of the human race as the source of much evil. For the partisans, the future of this particular illusion seemed assured.[3] As enlightenment and rationality spread, religion would weaken and disappear. Mature men and women would increasingly reconcile themselves to "ordinary unhappiness," as Freud called it, and the race would leave religion behind as it has other discredited practices like astrology and magic. This has not happened, however, and now appears as if it never will. Religion remains deep, widespread, and persistent, to the surprise and irritation of those who claimed to have cast aside illusion—and thought they could read the future.

Furthermore, believers themselves have obstinately begun to refuse—in public forums and at the voting booths—to accept denigration of their beliefs. Indeed, they have organized countermovements that not only defend the fact that religion has done much good in the world, but assert that modern democratic societies need transcendence in order to give an adequate account of themselves and the values they hold most sacred. In a surprising turnabout, it is now quite common to find secularists, bewildered at this unexpected religious vitality, who have come to feel themselves under siege. Even in France, the prototype of the modern secular state, the interior minister and likely presidential candidate, Nicolas Sarkozy, published a book in 2004 calling on the French to acknowledge the importance of religion to public life and to amend the unfair anticlerical laws of 1905.[4]

The story line they projected for religion has begun to crumble and it may be useful for us to get a clearer understanding of what that means by becoming reacquainted with and re-evaluating our religious history in the

West. The European model—secularization occurring in parallel with modernization—was once assumed to be the future for the rest of the world as well. We can now see that Europe was the exception, not the rule.[5] Indeed, secularization has stimulated a counterwave of desecularization as people threatened by rapid changes seek roots and foundations for personal identity in historic faith. Hindu computer programmers in India, evangelical entrepreneurs in Guatemala, Muslim factory workers in Indonesia, and large percentages of the population in the United States—in several ways the most modernized nation of all—find no great difficulty in being modern and religious. Even the exception has not entirely remained the exception. In the twenty-first century, while many Europeans are no longer strongly attached to the traditional Christianity and Judaism of the past, all but a small percentage of them are believers of some kind. So few are not that a European sociologist of religion has claimed, "There are not enough of them to be used for sociological research."[6] For the moment, the Europeans talk more of "spirituality" than of religion. But the same analyst believes that in the long run, the major world religions will very likely show their staying power even in Europe.

Science, too, has proven itself to be an uncertain factor in these matters. Another part of the secularists' projected story line claimed that scientific enlightenment would make belief unbelievable. But people of a philosophical bent, both scientists and nonscientists, have always known that science—properly understood as a value-free investigation of the physical world—by definition cannot pronounce on issues involving values and realities that transcend the physical world. The alleged war between science and religion, which historians now know is largely fiction, can be maintained only by deliberate misunderstandings. Scientific atheism, strictly speaking, is itself a kind of faith since science itself has nothing to say about God one way or the other. That faith's simple and unconscious adherents have been surprised lately when they are accused of doing what they believe the unenlightened are guilty of: trespassing in a realm that is not theirs. In this regard, the current debate over Darwinism and intelligent design has been revealing. The British neo-Darwinian biologist Richard

Dawkins has publicly admitted: "I believe, but I cannot prove, that all life, all intelligence, all creativity and all 'design' anywhere in the universe, is the direct or indirect product of Darwinian natural selection."[7] This profession of faith makes admirably clear that the old opposition of reason to belief is not as watertight as some people once thought, and—surprisingly—it puts Dawkins and others like him among the believers, albeit of a peculiar, modern kind.

Yet Dawkins is not wholly ready to accept even his own arguments. He seems quite pointlessly enraged at the beliefs of religious people, who in his system are only the necessary products of blind natural forces. And his belief faces a further challenge from within: why do human beings show a near-universal disposition to believe something that neo-Darwinism claims is unreal? Nowhere else does a false picture of the world in which we live aid our chances of survival. Some scientists have simply asserted that there must be some adaptive, evolutionary value in belief, which is "hard-wired" into our brains and may even stem from a "God Gene."[8] Perhaps so, but like the genes that enable us to do science and mathematics, the God Gene alone cannot tell us whether or not its products are true—a question that amidst the countless entities in a vast cosmos is asked only by human beings. Something else, an intellectual component that we know is not reducible to chemical reactions in our brains, and perhaps even a supernatural element, is needed for that. The dog-chasing-its-tail quality of arguments by neuroscientists and other strict naturalists about human consciousness is a sign that we cannot entirely understand ourselves in the terms we use to understand the rest of the world.

There is much more at stake in these debates than esoteric questions about human history and the origins of consciousness. We in the modern West are the heirs of a long religious and philosophical tradition that sees the human person as a free and rational being. Indeed, the whole complex of modern views on human rights, free economies, and democratic liberty depends on an almost dogmatic assertion that, whatever physical elements shape us, we are something more and quite different than the unbreakable chain of causal necessity that we observe in nature.[9] This sense is so deeply ingrained in us that it is hard for a Westerner to believe that the very notion of free will did not exist until it emerged under Christian auspices with Saint Augustine in the fourth century.[10] The full realization of what that view of the human person means for social organization took more than a thousand years to come to fruition. Even then, it was not clear that freedom was up to the task. Alexander Hamilton notes in the very first of the *Federalist Papers* a common argument in the period of America's founding: "It has been frequently remarked that it seems to have been reserved to the people of this country, by their conduct and example, to decide the important question, whether societies of men are really capable or not of establishing good government from reflection and choice, or whether they are forever destined to depend for their political constitutions on accident and force."

The modern West is currently engaged in a deeply incoherent and, in multiple ways, dangerous experiment. On the one hand, some sectors of our society have chosen to push the old Christian insight about human freedom to absurd lengths. In this view, human beings are radically free—from God, from history, from nature, even from "human nature," which is now often believed to be an ideological "construct" that is invoked for repressive purposes. But what is this radical autonomy if not a modern dogma, conceived in the face of overwhelming evidence to the contrary? Centuries of human experience show that human beings are not free in this way. Radical freedom is a raw political ideology that has already begun to reveal itself to be of very limited utility at best. It preserves human freedom at the cost of making that freedom ultimately empty and, in a very real way, self-defeating. If we have no nature and no need to act according to the order of the world and of truth, we may be able to do whatever we want. But what we want will have little meaning indeed and will make a human community all but impossible. As Tocqueville put it, "If each undertook himself to form all his opinions and to pursue the truth in isolation down paths cleared by him alone, it is not probable that a great number of men would ever unite in any common belief. . . . [W]ithout common ideas there is no common action, and without common action men still exist, but a social body does not."[11] Indeed, as we have seen since Tocqueville's day, it is even doubtful whether "men still exist" in any deep or substantial sense within this kingdom of radical autonomy.

On the other hand, many of us now believe that all previous arguments about human uniqueness and non-natural or supernatural dimensions to the human person have been exploded by scientific advances. All our vaunted independence of mind and spirit, our free political and economic institutions, our "lifestyle choices," and our pride in our artistic creativity in music, painting, sculpture, poetry, and architecture are an illusion. Some quite accomplished scientists and their followers in other sectors of society are not afraid to say precisely that.

A typical case is the distinguished Harvard biologist E. O. Wilson. No one will ever accuse Wilson of ignoring the implications of science, particularly the seamless procession, as he sees it, from subatomic quantum physics to DNA to every manifestation of human activity. Indeed, the sheer ambition with which he attempts to link everything in a causal chain is one of the most invigorating characteristics of his work. Yet there is something quite curious in his views nonetheless. When he tries to assess the notion of human freedom, he wants simultaneously to preserve the materialist explanation and to avoid falling into what he admits is a dispiriting determinism. The only way he can do so is to propose the following:

> The hidden preparation of mental activity [i.e., all the genetically programmed structures and processes of the brain] gives the illusion of free will. . . . The computer needed to track the consequences would have to be of stupendous proportions, with operations conceivably far more complex than those of the thinking brain itself. Furthermore, scenarios of the mind are all but infinite in detail, their content evolving in accordance with the unique history and physiology of the individual. . . . So there can be no simple determinism of human thought, at least not in obedience to causation in the way physical laws describe the motion of bodies and the atomic assembly of molecules. Because the individual mind cannot be fully known and predicted, the self can go on passionately believing in its own free will.[12]

But can even E. O. Wilson "passionately" continue to believe in his own freedom when he "knows" what he has expressed here? And can any society continue to believe in freedom as its foundation when its most distinguished scientists argue, as Wilson has elsewhere, that human behavior is roughly 60 percent the result of genes and the remainder "a complex algorithm of genes and environment"? An algorithm is not normally something we think of as a strong guarantee of our liberties.

Thomas Jefferson, hardly the most pious of the American Founders, nonetheless knew the source of a stable notion of liberty in a democratic republic: "Can the liberties of a nation be thought secure when we have removed their only firm basis, a conviction in the minds of the people that these liberties are the gift of God? That they are not to be violated but with his wrath?"[13] Yet very few voices even raise the question today when scientific determinism does precisely that and potentially much worse. In his famous "finest hour" speech, Winston Churchill remarked that Nazism threatened "a new Dark Age, made more sinister, and perhaps more protracted, by the lights of perverted science."[14] The perversion may not be so obvious among us now that Nazism is dead, but there are already worrying signs of its subtle survival in scientists dabbling in what amounts to a covertly totalitarian philosophy. This threat emerges most clearly in bioethics debates where "scientific views" of the human person threaten to undermine both human dignity and political liberty, to the renewed sorrow of the human race.

Strangely, E. O. Wilson and antiscientific thinkers such as the highly influential American philosopher Richard Rorty share a deep pragmatic streak here. Rorty is probably the best-known exponent of "anti-foundationalism" in modern American philosophy. But as someone committed to progressive politics, he has argued that we should simply ignore this lack of foundations and act to achieve the system we want.[15] His assumption also seems to be that since we cannot predict what human beings will do, we can simply go about our business as if we were free. In the great American pragmatic tradition, this argument first emerged with William James, who wrote in *The Varieties of Religious Experience:* "We can act *as if* there were a God; feel *as if* we were free; consider Nature *as if* she were full of special designs; lay plans *as if* we were to be immortal; and we find then that these words do make a genuine difference in our moral life."[16] James, of course, was more genuinely welcoming of older views of human freedom and of real religion, and his point is that belief *works*. Yet the fact that so many kinds of otherwise tough-minded pragmatists urge on us the uses of an illusion should warn us that something has gone astray along the way. If human freedom and dignity have really been exploded, along with the transcendent foundations on which they traditionally rested, then pretending that we can carry on without them may be the most damaging illusion of all.

Quite a different argument against incorporating religious values in our public lives stems from the allegedly evil consequences of religious belief throughout history. The terrorist attacks on the World Trade Center and the Pentagon on September 11, 2001, forcefully raised the specter once again, to some people living in the West, of the alleged opposition between civilization and religion. For them, the smoldering buildings provided a graphic confirmation of a longstanding view that religion has been the primary source of violence throughout history and needs to be carefully circumscribed by public authorities. For others, the murderous rage of the Muslim attackers reflected not so much their religious fanaticism as our own profound failures—moral, cultural, and political—as a civilization. In this view, the West, and particularly its leading nation the United States, has become an arrogant, violent, and callous empire, and not, as it often thinks itself to be, a universal civilization. The religious roots of the terrorists were much less important than their justifiable anti-Western rage.

For a much smaller number of people among the chattering classes, the outrages called for a rethinking of our complacent assumptions that all cultures and religions are basically the same (if we could only see it), and that there is no such thing as absolute good and evil, merely differing ethical "choices." It took large ideological blinders indeed to think that "America had it coming," as one British observer remarked. However much (or little) justice there may be in Islamic fundamentalist complaints, it used to be a universal assumption among civilized peoples that the behavior of a large country or civilization does not justify the murder of innocent people. Days after the attack, a writer in a prestigious journal argued that the events of

September 11 seemed to have destroyed in a single stroke the postmodern and postcolonial relativism and skepticism common among Western intellectuals, and to cry out for "some transcendent standard of good and evil."[17]

Of course, this suggests that we not only need some transcendent root, but need a root of a particular kind. Most Americans already believe it can be found in true religious teachings. This was a position missing from most of the post-9/11 controversy, yet was something taken for granted not all that long ago, at least in the United States. Religion has been a powerful energizing force in the very development of civilization. Religion—"organized religion," as the current intellectual etiquette often puts it—has been charged with various historical crimes. But the history of the nineteenth and twentieth centuries has shifted our perspective. Organized *irreligion* in the twentieth century committed atrocities on a scale that the fiercest religious wars never approached. The scientific racism of Nazi Germany killed forty million and attempted genocide against Europe's Jews. The scientific socialism of the Communist countries killed a hundred million (and still counting) people around the globe. As the Soviet dissident Vladimir Bukovsky has noted, people in the West routinely invoke the Spanish Inquisition as an example of religious horror. And they are right to do so. But the Inquisition, in the course of three centuries, and after legal procedures of a sort, killed fewer people—probably around three thousand—than the Soviet Union killed on an average day.[18] Callous, large-scale, extrajudicial slaughter of secular and religious figures for ideological reasons began soon after the French Revolution and continues in many countries around the world down to the present.[19] And European Christianity in the same period can point to humanizing features that several of the most prominent secular movements cannot.

In spite of all this mayhem, we often think of the past few centuries in the West as a period of enlightenment, beginning in the Renaissance and the Reformation, after a long medieval darkness. Several of the following chapters seek to revise this simplistic and misleading way of reading Western history. The Enlightenment itself in many ways can be understood only as an extension and development of certain religious values present in the

West, and could never have occurred without them. In addition, religion has often provided the moral fervor for needed reforms. The abolition of the slave trade, to take a glaring example, owes something to modern secular notions of human equality and dignity. But those notions have Christian roots and it was a British evangelical, William Wilberforce, who succeeded in convincing Parliament that it was England's duty to enforce developing moral perceptions by means of the Royal Navy. Similarly, it is impossible to understand the abolitionist and civil-rights movements in America without considering the energizing role of the churches and other religious institutions. Religious enthusiasms have often played a basic role in questions of poverty, war and peace, social reform, the environment, and a host of other issues.

There is much misunderstanding of the role of religion in the world even by intelligent and otherwise sympathetic people. One eminent British commentator, who in other moods would know better, rather typically put the situation like this: "Whereas religion demands unquestioning submission, the political process offers participation, discussion, and lawmaking founded in consent."[20] This sweeping and unhistorical generalization overlooks the religious tradition of ardent inquiry that we see in figures like Plato and Marcus Aurelius, Philo and Maimonides, Augustine, Aquinas, and Pascal, Spinoza and Kierkegaard, in favor of a highly idealized notion of democratic politics. Modern democracy has been a good thing by and large, but it contains its own degree of dogma, exclusion, majority tyranny, and submission—to say nothing of its historic tendencies towards demagoguery, superficiality, and self-destruction, absent the virtues that religion provides.

Further, it is good to remember that democratic moderation and consensus are good things where moderation and consensus are called for. Where passionate action to eliminate gross evils is required, democratic procedures need to be driven by something outside themselves. We see this most clearly in modern Europe, where dialogue and strict attention to procedure have become virtual ends in themselves, to the detriment of action when action is needed. At the deepest level, this is where America and Europe have begun to diverge. The law-abiding democratic nations of Europe were unable to act in 1995 even when a genocide was under way on their own continent in Bosnia.

The writer quoted above also says, "Religion is a static; politics a dynamic process." But this, too, is a failure to see some very large truths. Moses, Buddha, Jesus, and Mohammed have inspired very different religious currents over the centuries, but to call what followed their lives static is to be stone blind to one of the great dynamic forces in history. If none of them had ever lived, the entire history of the world would have been so different that it is impossible to imagine. By comparison, democratic deliberations are a hiccup in the history of humanity. Nor is it the case that once Judaism, Buddhism, Christianity, and Islam came into their classic forms, they were turned into merely status-quo institutions. They all have repeatedly generated fresh religious as well as social renaissances, reformations, refoundings, and renewals. It is a simple and verifiable historical observation that religion has been one of the most consistently—and profoundly—dynamic elements in human history.

Finally, it must be said frankly that many of the antireligious comments we meet with today are directed specifically at Christianity. Many intellectuals and other opinion leaders, for various reasons, would like to dismiss the whole of Christian history as an unfortunate interregnum between the supposed greatness of the classical world and the triumph of modernity, a historical caricature that began to take shape among the Renaissance humanists. No serious historian today would deny the importance of even the "Dark Ages" to the emergence of the West and the role of Christianity in preserving and developing what survived the collapse of the classical world. Today, we are much more aware of the roots of the New West in the Old West, and of the losses that have occurred in separating the two, for whatever current motivation. Perhaps the most naked manifestation of the impulse to deny Christianity's role in forming the West came during the debates over the European Constitution in 2003 and 2004. In early drafts of that document, a brief survey of the history of Europe jumped from the classical age to the Enlightenment, as if the entire continent were suffering from a collective and willful amnesia about its strongly Christian past. This comic and untruthful straining to avoid religion at all costs makes self-understanding about both the secular and the religious elements in Western culture impossible.

Ironically, the three primary architects of the post–World War II movement towards European unity—Robert Schuman in France, Konrad Adenauer in Germany, and Alcide De Gasperi in Italy—were deeply inspired by Christian personalism, a carefully elaborated view of the human person that sought to avoid the twin dangers of radical individualism and collectivism; their vision of Europe was very different from the one in evidence in recent decades. America is not quite as far along in this deliberate exercise in forgetfulness, but it too contains significant sectors in the media, the academy, and the arts who would like to promote the European understanding on these shores. In this perspective, religion—and specifically Christianity—is often seen as an amalgam of ignorance, bigotry, slavery, racism, oppression of women, Eurocentrism, rape of the environment, and a host of other sins, ancient and modern. To such critics, the kind of virtue rooted in religion that America's Founders recommended and its people practiced was essentially a confidence game intended to keep the people in theocratic chains, to the advantage of privileged individuals and classes. American history is not without blemishes—including the very large evil of slavery—and the spirit of truth should urge us to keep them in mind. But there is an entirely different spirit at work in the desire to invert our traditional understanding of the role of religion in American history. Indeed, from a merely practical perspective, it is difficult to imagine how American democracy, or any democracy, with its temptations to pander to popular passions, can survive absent religious principles.

The proper influence of religion in American society has been left theoretically vague because it is a balance that has to be worked out anew in every generation. Dwight Eisenhower is reported to have once said, "Our form of government has no sense unless it is founded in a deeply felt religious faith, and I don't care what it is." Unintended humor aside, Eisenhower had it just about right. Both the insistence on the necessity of religion and its democratic character have deep roots, primarily in Christianity, but by now in other major faiths of America too. Still, it is worth remembering the specifically Christian contribution. As a scholar of Late Antiquity characterizes it, "Christianity emerged as an unusually democratic and potentially wide-reaching movement. It takes some leap of the modern imagination (saturated as it is by later centuries of Christian language) to understand the novelty of seeing every human being as subject to the same universal law of God and as equally capable of salvation."[21]

The obstacles to believing that religion shapes and, in various ways, even lies at the heart of culture are multiple in the West today. What we now call culture provides the framework of all the other arguments and practices in our public life, even the arguments that are critical of that culture. In the United States, strong vestiges of that old insight persist and create tensions when people suspect that all opinions *except for religious ones* are welcome in the public square. To judge by surveys, 90 percent of Americans describe themselves as religious and the vast majority of those people also say they belong to specific Christian, Jewish, or other denominations. So at the most superficial level there is a large and widespread religious population in the United States whose beliefs should shape, to some degree, the current culture. Yet if we were to ask these same people whether contemporary American culture was informed by the *cultus*, they would rightly be skeptical.

Many people are quite content to have it that way. In the midst of the debates over domestic and international policies that constantly arise in America today, one member of the U.S. House of Representatives opined on the floor: "Religion is the last refuge of extremists."[22] Coming in a debate over the fitness of an openly Christian state attorney general to become a federal judge, this comment reflected a bias that surfaces in public with no little regularity. The accuser would have been ashamed to apply such a statement in blanket fashion to, say, Muslims. He and a significant portion of our cultural elites have no hesitation about doing so when it comes to traditional Christians and Jews. This is already bad enough in itself. But it is also leading to a conscious falsification of history. In the United States, this view is rapidly gaining ground in court decisions and political circles, as if the U.S. Constitution and American practice always aimed at eliminating religion from public life, but are only now coming into their true, purified form.

This book tries to look at religious developments at several stages in the history of the West that need to be better understood both for their own sake and as a means for responding to our present situation. That situation has seen the failure of several modern "gods" that offered themselves as candidates to replace the old Deity. Arthur Koestler and his colleagues were the originators of the phrase "the god that failed."[23] In the 1950s, it was Marxism that proved to be a quasi-religious illusion. We have witnessed similar failures by the other "masters of suspicion" in our own time—not only Marx, but in varying degrees, Darwin, Nietzsche, and Freud—because they too are unable to account for many elements of human nature traditionally associated with religion. The subject is large, and what appears here necessarily relies on specialized studies by many researchers and thinkers. Specialists may object, with some justice, to large assertions and broad generalizations here about complex matters. I am quite aware of the many objections that might be made to the argument at every point. But I am also aware of even more doubtful assertions that are currently quite commonplace. It would be a miracle if there were not much to debate in the following pages. Yet it would be a greater failure if the history of the West continued to be told as a story of liberation from religion or was not told at all, owing to a fixation on historical specialization that blinds us to a true account of some large realities about our culture.

We are at one of those periodic turning points in Western history that is too close to us to be entirely clear. The widespread notion that we live in a "postmodern" age captures both the sense of some major shift under way and the uncertainty about what exactly it amounts to. It seems that we no longer live in the old modernity of rationalism, democracy, and science, still less of Freud, Marx, and Darwin. The old modernity contained practices quite important to a fully human life, but we need to understand them in a new and more ample way to help them continue on in a very different age. This seems to be why we think of ourselves as postmodern, that is, still tethered to the modern though different from it. Yet there are many ways in which those practices and the major figures who advanced them now belong to an old pantheon in which we can no longer believe. They have shown themselves to have serious shortcomings that cannot be remedied from within because they offered us a relatively narrow and thin vision of human life. If those gods have failed, will the God of the Western faiths do any better?

If nothing else, real religion has survived vast changes in cultures around the world and even the birth and death of entire civilizations. Any attempt to understand the human past and future that neglects religion is doomed to failure, particularly in a civilization like the West that came into existence as the result of several religious currents. Three centuries of debunking, skepticism, criticism, revolution, and scorn by some among us have not produced the expected demise of religion and now are contributing to its renewal. I hope this book will help the reader understand why this is so, without indulging in the kind of partisanship that defends the historic Western faiths by making them appear to be the source of everything good in secular terms. Human life is more complex than that, and one of the benefits of a proper religious vision lies in constantly reminding us that reality transcends our capacity to grasp. Every human order, including the West, thus always remains open to greater truth and justice than it actually embodies, and can never claim finality. We cannot entirely predict, therefore, the future shape of religion in the West, but we can say with a high degree of confidence that whatever the postmodern West will be, it will find a central place for the God who did not fail.

THE GOD THAT DID NOT FAIL

CHAPTER 1

Greek Gifts

Zeus in Olympus is the overseer
Of many things. Many things the gods
Achieve beyond our judgment. What we thought
Is not confirmed and what we thought not god
Contrives. And so it happens in this story.

Euripides, *Medea* (conclusion)[1]

IN the most common contemporary accounts of our civilization, the ancient Greeks play a large and central role as the virtual originators of everything we believe to be distinctive about the West: democracy, philosophical speculation, economic efficiency, and physical science—in short, most of what we think of as rational. This is deeply misleading in several ways. The West did not begin in Greece, though some aspects of the West take their origins there. More importantly, to admire the Greeks because they are an early version of what some of us admire most about ourselves almost ensures that the Greeks will not be understood for themselves at all. We do the Greeks no favors by maintaining an anachronistic picture of them, and not solely because it has made them vulnerable to various forms of postmodern criticism—some justified, some not.[2] Ancient Greece was very different from the modern West, especially a West that thinks of itself as rationalist, and any account that neglects this "otherness" fails to come to grips with some fundamental truths. We would treat the Greeks more fairly—and understand ourselves more clearly—if we looked at the ways in which they are *different* from what some of us may think of as modern. After all, the greatest Greek philosopher, Plato, reports that his teacher, Socrates—both of them crucial to Western thought—regarded philosophy as a preparation for death so that the soul can go "into another place, which is, like itself, noble and pure and invisible, to the realm of the god of the other world in truth, to the good and wise God."*

We would see this quite clearly if we were not laboring under misimpressions. What we call Greek philosophy largely sought to lead its practitioners into a certain way of life that was more a religious path than mere intellectual analysis. Philosophers were supposed to live different and better lives than the average person because of their studies, which some modern scholars have compared to spiritual exercises, intended "to raise the individual from an inauthentic condition of life darkened by unconsciousness and harried by worry, to an authentic state of life in which he attains self-consciousness, an exact vision of the world, inner peace, and freedom."[3] That strain of Greek philosophy was far more influential for almost a thousand years in the ancient world and later in the Middle Ages and Renaissance than the Greek logic, science, and political theory emphasized in some quarters over the past two centuries. Modern reason is something quite different.

The rationalist Greece of the textbooks was created by people who could not take Christianity's God, let alone the pagan gods, seriously. But the Greeks were serious in their religious practices—at both the popular and the philosophical level—and did not typically see an essential conflict, like some modern philosopher, between religiosity and rationality. Almost all the ancient Greeks embraced a kind of rationality that could include religious beliefs, just as most believers do today. Even Aristotle, the most worldly of the prominent Greek philosophers, reasons towards an ultimately religious end.** This major fact has been overlooked in the desire to use the Greeks in modern debates. Even one of the better contemporary writers on

---

*Phaedo 80d. Plato shows Socrates making rational arguments at the end of his life about this religious belief, but in this he is more like other traditional religious thinkers than a modern rationalist. He even sees the possible need for revelation, because a philosopher must "take whatever human doctrine is best and hardest to disprove and, embarking upon it as upon a raft, sail upon it through life in the midst of dangers, unless he can sail upon some stronger vessel, some divine reason (λόγου) and make his voyage more safely and securely." 85c–d. (I have altered the standard Loeb translation from "revelation" to "reason" here because it unnecessarily introduces a later Christian concept. But the translator rightly felt the affinity.)

**Cf. Nichomachean Ethics X.viii.7: "the activity of God, which surpasses all others in blessedness, must be contemplative; and of human activities, therefore, that which is most akin to this must be most of the nature of happiness." The Greeks were closer to the medieval than the modern West in views such as these.

the importance of the Greek heritage for our culture has proposed the following experiment:

> Read at random a passage from Plato or Thucydides, and then one from the Bible. The mental outlook and sensibility of the former will be more familiar and comfortable to most of us than that of the latter. In Greece we will find, as [R. W.] Livingstone says, "people who think as we do." And if we are honest, we will admit as Livingstone does that "Most men would prefer to have been Greeks of the age of Pericles, rather than Jews in the prosperous days of the monarchy or under the Hasmoneans." For better or worse, the world we live in today prizes personal freedom, individual rights, material comfort, and a rational organization of life over obedience to the divine.[4]

This passage possesses a kernel of truth, though in its main contentions, particularly as most people would construe them today, it is also false and quite misleading.

Athens and Jerusalem

The opposition between a supposedly rational Greece and an uncritically religious Judeo-Christian tradition is, of course, a strong current in recent Western thought. As early as the second century A.D., the Christian writer Tertullian could famously ask from the other side of the supposed divide: *Quid Athenae Hierosolymis?* ("What has Athens to do with Jerusalem?"), though he meant something different by it than a conflict between reason and revelation. And the answer to his question, historically at least, proved to be: quite a lot, in spite of the different views of the world that arose in the two illustrious cities. Jerusalem gave Athens something that it conspicuously lacked: a popular conception of God worthy of the notable poetic and philosophical search of the Greeks. And Greece, as it did for many other cultures, gave Jerusalem singular intellectual tools, which proved their value in the Jewish and Christian thinkers in the centuries before and after Christ who, historical myths notwithstanding, used reason to analyze, expound, and advance revealed truths in ways that Socrates and Plato might well have appreciated.

That fruitful interplay was never wholly forgotten even after the collapse of the Roman Empire, though it sprang into new life in the High Middle Ages as soon as Greek authors became available in Latin translations. Another wave of Greek influence arose in the Renaissance with the recovery of the Greek language in the West, partly owing to Greeks fleeing the Muslim invasion of Byzantium after 1453. The discontinuity in the older tradition, however, led some later thinkers to see the Greek heritage not as something already partly incorporated into Western thought by way of Jewish and Christian speculation, but as a radical alternative to it. This reconceptualized Greece took on an idealized and highly selective form. By the eighteenth and nineteenth centuries, German scholars and romantics, especially the art historian Winckelmann and the poet Goethe, thought they saw in the Greeks the perfection of "nature" as opposed to a degenerate Christianity. This anachronistic view had no little influence in the nineteenth and twentieth centuries among people who thought Christianity was finished, and it even found its way into Anglo-American education until the mid-1960s:

> [A]ncient Greece as interpreted by the new scholarship became an ersatz religion. Greece was adopted by the modern West as, in part, a replacement for Christianity. This was not the actual Greece of two thousand five hundred years ago, however, but the Greece re-created by adoring scholars, mostly in Germany and England, starting around 1770.[5]

Arguments like this make many people nervous because they appear to join in the deconstruction of Greece and other Western foundations that has been a standard motif of feminist, Marxist, multiculturalist, postmodernist, postcolonialist, and other radical intellectual currents. But the ancient Greek legacy is quite strong enough to withstand all such assaults, and we need to be careful not to falsify the real historical achievements of the Greeks by recasting them in our own image.

To begin with, whatever we may prize today, it would be difficult to say that the list of Western traits proposed earlier ("personal freedom, individual rights, material comfort, and a rational organization of life over obedience to the divine") reflects the real Greek inheritance. It makes the ancient

Greeks sound like the modern European or American bourgeoisie, which is obviously wrong. Suppose that—to take up the challenge that accompanied this list—instead of the historian Thucydides and, presumably, the more rationalist passages in Plato, we chose to look at the dramatist Sophocles, from roughly the same period. In his *Antigone*, the title character opposes King Creon because he has given an order to leave a body unburied, which contradicts the fundamental rules of justice established by the gods. She argues:

> For me it was not Zeus who made that order,
>
> Nor did that Justice who lives with the gods below*
>
> mark out such laws to hold among mankind.
>
> Nor did I think your orders were so strong
>
> that you, a mortal man, could over-run
>
> the gods' unwritten and unfailing laws.
>
> Not now, nor yesterday's, they always live,
>
> and no one knows their origin in time.[6]

This passage has often been cited as evidence for natural law, the rationally discernible order of good and evil woven into the fabric of nature itself by God or the gods, which is to say the deep religious ground for the specific determinations of law in any given society. *Antigone* was probably produced in 441 B.C. Sophocles was a friend of Pericles and a contemporary of Thucydides. Why should we neglect him and focus solely on rationalist interpretations of the other two figures except that, in the West, some of us are currently trying to live with a purely secular order rather than the mixed rational-religious one that Greece and the West alike, until quite recently, believed better reflected the whole of reality?

The same might be said about the invocation of Plato in the challenge cited earlier. The phrase that the rationalizing interpreters have often repeated as reflecting the core of Greek thought is the Sophist Protagoras' saying: "Man is the measure of all things." And in line with the misleading claim for the Greeks as precursors of modern values, even this formula has been interpreted as somehow reflecting what a modern person might

---

* The realm of the dead here is thought of as "below" because after this life they are assigned to a different place, under different gods, than the high dwelling of the Olympians.

mean by it: that we each decide for ourselves what we believe is true. In the ancient world, there was some dispute about whether Protagoras meant this or rather that the whole human race judges. But there is no question that there also existed a long, rich, and powerful tradition in Greece pointing in a very different direction. Plato's *Republic* gives expression to what many other Greeks of various religious and philosophical schools thought: Since all of us are imperfect, it is difficult to find pure standards in ourselves, for "Nothing imperfect is the measure of anything."[7] And in a late work, *The Laws*, Plato is even more explicit in his opposition to Protagoras: "God is the measure of all things."[8] Plato's views, of course, do not simply negate a more rational current in ancient Greece, which found a place in Plato himself. But it would be a curious argument today to say that Protagoras truly represents Greece while Plato does not. There is strong rational analysis in Plato, for example, but there is also a strong and pure religious feeling that would inspire Jewish and Christian Platonism, and a mystical pagan Neoplatonism over many centuries.*

Historical Balance

Historical truth consists in giving various factors their proper proportions. In recent centuries, religion has been underemphasized as a feature of Greek society, while rationalism has been overemphasized. At the present moment, we need most to recognize that the Greeks were sincerely religious without being irrational[9]—a far cry also from the kind of fashionable scholarship that has recently emphasized "the Greeks and the irrational." One of the most eminent scholars of ancient Greek religion has warned us: "the adventures of ideas which mark the second half of the fifth century B.C. [the period we are examining here] and which so profoundly affected later European thinking should not lead us to think of the Greeks as being or becoming in any large measure like men of the Enlightenment." Pointing out that a lunar eclipse in 413 B.C. caused the Athenians to urge a change

---

*"We have to see Plato's rationalism, not as a cool scientific project such as a later century of European Enlightenment might set for itself, but as a kind of passionately religious doctrine—a theory that promised man's salvation from the things he had feared most from the earliest days, from death and time. The extraordinary emphasis Plato put upon reason is itself a religious impulse." William Barrett, *Irrational Man: A Study in Existential Philosophy* (New York: Anchor, 1962), p. 84.

in war plans, he continues that this political and military effect had parallels in other areas of Greek life that we think of as characteristic: "It is therefore most important to be reminded of the immense part which oracles and methods of divination played in Greek life. These things counted for so much. So did various forms of fear and superstition; as a rule they were not obsessive, but they were present and could make themselves felt. You cannot understand the Greek achievement in poetry and philosophy if you ignore its background in religion at a popular level."[10] The same might be said of Greek warfare, as in the passage above, and of Greek politics.

Perhaps the most famous event in Greek history to this day, the trial of Plato's teacher Socrates, helps us appreciate how deeply intertwined religion was with allegedly secular activities. There was some personal freedom in ancient Athens under Pericles, and any fair person has to give much credit to the unique and remarkable Greek discovery of democracy. But you do not have to be deep in Greek history to know that democracy meant participation in political decision making, not the vague and somewhat incoherent modern belief in personal liberty. Greek democracy was far more restricted than what we mean by that term today—and the author quoted above who claims we would prefer to have been "Greeks of the age of Pericles" elsewhere recognizes as much: "Athens exerted control over its citizens' lives in ways that we today would consider to be intolerable encroachments on private life."[11] The trial of Socrates reveals some of the deep problems in Athenian democracy, but also the complications introduced by religious considerations that need to be factored in when we think about it.

An Athenian jury voted to execute Socrates for two reasons, one religious and one secular. The first charge specified that Socrates was guilty of impiety because he did not worship the gods that the city worshiped; the second, that he was a corrupter of youth. Plato offered Socrates' reply to these two charges in his *Apology*. In Plato's view, the Athenians clearly did not understand what Socrates was doing. Instead of impiety and corruption, he had been trying to bring about a truer understanding of the gods and the moral life. Indeed, in Plato's telling, Socrates pursued this dual vocation in no small part because of a kind of religious revelation. A certain

Chaerephon, he says, went to the oracle at Delphi and was told that Socrates was the wisest of men. When Socrates heard this, he wondered: "What in the world does the god mean, and what riddle is he propounding? For I am conscious that I am not wise either much or little."[12] So he began questioning his fellow citizens and found that the only way in which he was superior to them was that he at least knew that he knew nothing.

Now, the larger meaning of this well-known story points in several directions simultaneously. For much of Western history, Socrates was regarded as a martyr for truth and his execution by Athens functioned almost as a secular counterpart of Christ's crucifixion. Since the Enlightenment, however, Socrates has been portrayed more as the rational inquirer, the forerunner of our own fearless investigation into how things stand, whatever moral and religious taboos it may break. But on Plato's showing, this was not bold impiety and irreligion, but a higher sort of piety misunderstood by the Athenian jury. A further paradox here for the view of Greece as ancestor of the secular West: The very democratic process we value so highly condemned this pious philosophical pursuit because it had different religious commitments. And the philosophers returned the favor. Socrates, Plato, and Aristotle—three generations of the very best philosophical minds—all expressed profound doubts about democracy. Aristotle, encountering popular criticism at one point and with Socrates' fate in mind, left Athens "lest Athens sin twice against philosophy." So those of us who want to draw a direct line from the Greeks to ourselves have to decide where the line should go: to the Athenian democracy as it actually existed, or to the great thinkers we rightly value, who had good reasons for doubts about the moral judgments of popular democracy?

And the grounds for deeper reflection do not end even there. Modern scholars allow that there is a certain case to be made for Socrates as a martyr for truth. But they also argue that another factor of equal or perhaps even greater importance was in play. Athens had recently been defeated by Sparta in the Peloponnesian War, in which Socrates had fought, and had to submit to the imposition of the "Thirty Tyrants," Athenians aligned with Spartan interests, on the conquered city. Several of Socrates' students were numbered among the Thirty. And they and their master himself (and presumably Plato, who reports on these views) were quite worried about the ways that material prosperity in Athens had sapped civic virtues. Socrates openly admires Spartan discipline and Spartan, in the modern sense, living arrangements (though he and Plato both deplored the tyranny imposed on Athens). And this view had a central resonance in Greek culture, because—as the renowned Greek historian Herodotus had argued—the Athenians and other Greeks believed they had been able to defeat the massive armies of the Persian Empire for the reason that they were free and virtuous citizen-soldiers uncorrupted by oriental tyranny and luxury.

The Athenians may also have been angry with Socrates because he was essentially right. After Athens defeated the Persians in 480–479 B.C., it was at its cultural height but started almost immediately into political decline. As the historian Arnold Toynbee has put it, "The Attic literature of the fifth and fourth century B.C. was unquestionably great, and so was contemporary Attic philosophy and visual art and architecture. On the other hand, the years 478–338 B.C. were the political nadir of Attic history and the history of the Hellenic world as a whole."[13] So here we come upon one of the common paradoxes of history: a period of high cultural achievement, which produces the Parthenon, Pericles, Thucydides, the Greek dramatists, Socrates, Plato, and Aristotle, at the same time as we observe steady political weakening. Thucydides and others attributed this to the foolishness of Athenians in reaching beyond what was just. Socrates and Plato saw the flaw as involving much deeper matters. To begin with, it stemmed from a wrong view of the gods as petty and vicious in Homer and the other poets, and was compounded by the bad example of the politicians who had been partly corrupted by materialism and sophistry, which led to disbelief and ethical relativism in some quarters and the breakup of such virtue as was able to survive Athenian democracy.

None of these criticisms detracts from the very real achievements of the Greeks, which later ages have rightly envied. But these kinds of complexities need to be factored into the picture when we assess the Greek heritage as if it fit comfortably with modern notions of "personal freedom, individual rights, material comfort, and a rational organization of life" rather than "obedience to the divine." Socrates, Plato, Aristotle, Isocrates, and many more of the philosophers we view as constituting the central intellectual legacy of Greece feared that "personal freedom" in their age tended towards the same kind of self-indulgence and irresponsibility that many people worry is leading to self-destruction in modern democracies today. And the other terms in the list above do not fare much better under careful scrutiny. The very notion of "rights" as personal or inherent in individuals did not appear until the late Middle Ages.[14] Material comfort, as we have seen, was not universally admired in ancient Greece: Socrates, Plato, the Spartans, the Stoics, and a variety of other individuals or groups were very wary about the effects of prosperity. And the notion that the Greeks, even of the brief Periclean age, pursued "rational organization" to the exclusion of religion is a modern myopia that traces its roots to several generations of classicists who themselves did not have much interest in religion, and therefore thought the Greeks must not have, either.

Greek Public Religion

Religion permeated Greek life, not only in personal devotion to the gods, but in a comprehensive set of social, civic, and cultural practices, from life in the family, up through local and regional groupings, to the *polis* as a whole: "for the *individual,* his or her additional obligations were manifold and mul-tivalent. Piety was judged to be displayed through participation in the city's cults, abundance of offerings in sanctuaries, devotion towards kindred dead and the family's guardian deities, financial generosity in enabling the most magnificent celebrations of public rituals (games, civic liturgies, sacrifices, and public banquets), and a host of other practical activities."[15] In Athens, all this was seamlessly integrated with democracy in gritty practice rather than in the idealized abstractions of admiring textbooks.

We have already seen that Greek drama at its height, for example, treated deep religious themes. But religion was present not merely in the dramatic material. Plays were offered only during a very few days a year, usually at a festival in honor of the god Dionysus at Athens. There are no exact equivalents for this in our culture, but it would not be out of order to say by way of range-finding that the typical Greek tragedy combined elements that we would associate with a secular activity like a modern play, the pageantry and emotion of grand opera, the religious resonance of a solemn High Mass, and the communal dimension of a religious festival. And we must remember that it was the Athenian state itself that organized these dramatic contests; the whole people and their culture gave rise to this curious amalgam of secular and religious components that we call Greek drama.

Since the Renaissance, we have looked at Greek temples as beautiful architectural achievements, which they indisputably were. But especially since the Enlightenment, we have tended to forget that the purpose of temples was to honor the gods, who typically were worshiped by the sacrificing of animals and the burning of their body parts on altars placed in front of the temples. So in their original uses, what have often been presented as constructions of a pure and austere aesthetic had large ash heaps before them from the many sacrifices offered and smoky altars sending the smell of burning fat continuously into the air. A visitor to Greece in the classical period like Saint Paul would not have seen "monuments of unageing intellect," but functioning places of worship—much more like a modern church, though the rituals took place on the outside of the structure—and ample physical signs of it.

Even Greek athletic contests honored the gods: the Isthmian games, Poseidon; the Pythian games, Apollo; and the Nemean and Olympic games were dedicated to Zeus. One hundred white oxen were slaughtered and burned as an offering to the king of the gods at the high point of the ancient Olympics. The religiosity, however, may also remind us of other ways in which the Greek games differed from the modern. A classical scholar observed at the time of the 2004 Olympic Games in Athens: "We may like to think of ourselves as Greek, but . . . everything about the ancient Olympics was darker, rougher, more brutal than its modern counterpart." The ancient games, like the heroic ethos of Homer, centered on individual glory. And with good reason. Since in the dominant archaic understanding there was no afterlife that punished or rewarded what was done on earth, "good and bad all went to the same gray, characterless, drizzly underworld after death, and that was that. In the absence of the post-mortem reward for moral goodness, the one thing you could strive for was immortal fame." It was for this reason that the ancient games were ruthlessly individualistic and gave rise to the saying "Victory or Death!" The most prized competition was the *pankration,* an all-out fight that, often enough, literally led to death.

Of course, the modern Olympic movement would be appalled by all this. It has grafted onto the Greek origins more recent Christian and Western notions of good sportsmanship and honorable competition. A French nobleman, the Baron Pierre de Coubetin, the force behind the renewal of the games in 1896, regarded them as "a 'religion' of sorts: its commandments were the 'spirit of friendship' that the Games would encourage and the idea that gentlemanly co-operation in sporting events would create (as he put it) 'chivalry,' all expressed in the athletes' creed 'of honor and disinterest.'" We award three medals to reflect the honor due to the top finishers, and even think highly of anyone who qualifies for a national team. The Greeks admired the remarkable bodies of the athletes training in the gym, but when it came to prizes they gave out only one—to the winner, who did not, like a modern athlete, at least pretend to show humility. In recent Olympics, the idealistic facade has been slipping a bit, but however battered, it reveals something: "even after all the amateur rules were abandoned—[it] looks, if anything, like the uncomfortable byproduct of our compensatory desire to graft Judeo-Christian values onto the irreducible, very ancient, and very ugly business of competitiveness."[16]

Differences and Resemblances

We should not be surprised to find by this example and others that the Greeks cannot be forced into a modern taxonomy, whether of a rationalist or a religious kind. Indeed, to underestimate the distance between the Greeks and ourselves is to risk a profound misunderstanding both of what we legitimately can admire in the classical heritage and of inescapable differences. The classical scholar Donald Kagan has formulated this quite clearly:

> To understand the ancient Greeks and Romans, we must be alert to the

great gap that separates their views, and those of most people throughout history, from the opinions of our own time. They knew nothing
of such ideals as would later be spoken in the Sermon on the Mount,
and they would have regarded them as absurd if they had. . . . Modern states, especially those who have triumphed in the Cold War . . .
are quite different. . . . The most important of these [differences] is the
Judeo-Christian tradition. . . . There are now barriers of conscience in
the way of acquiring and maintaining power and using it to preserve
the peace that would have been incomprehensible to the Greeks and
Romans.[17]

But if there are sharp differences that we should not overlook between
the ancient Greeks and ourselves, we also need to note some profound agree-
ments between Athens and Jerusalem that set them both in opposition to a
good deal of what we think of as distinctively modern. To begin with, almost all the ancient Greeks, even those who tended towards a more materialist view of the world, had a deep sense of the world's order and the need
to reflect that order in human life. In one crucial respect, then, the Greeks
resembled the ancient Hebrews more than they do a modern European or
American. The Jews believed that they had been given the Law—the factory instruction manual, so to speak, for how human beings ought to behave—by the Creator himself. The Greeks, it would be fair to say—and Saint
Paul said it more than once in his letters—believed that what constituted
the good life could be discovered through rational inquiry into the nature
of the gods, man, and the world. What Greeks and Hebrews agreed about,
above all differences, was that there is simply a common and fixed human
nature that sets a limit on the paths that lead to good human lives. In other
words, they denied what large numbers of people living in advanced societies think of as their rights or as their pursuit of happiness. And in both in-
stances, their view was rooted in a larger religious vision of the world.

On Deep Background

It is difficult to provide a brief summary of Greek religion and culture in the
more than one thousand years between the time the Homeric poems were

written down (probably in the eighth century B.C.) and the period in which Christianity started to replace the Olympic pantheon in the third and fourth centuries A.D. But if we want to understand the evolution of Greek religion and culture in broad outline, we can get a reasonable idea by looking at five stages that scholars have identified as marking some significant turning points in Greek history, namely the Homeric age, the time of the farmer/ poet Hesiod, the Ionian scientific revolution, the age of the dramatists, and the philosophical flowering.

The heroic ideals in Homer's *Iliad* become the background for virtually all of Greece in subsequent ages.[18] Later developments could introduce quite different beliefs and practices, but Homer remained the center of gravity. A modern person reading the *Iliad* in translation may at first be puzzled by the gods and their occasional interventions in human affairs. For us—influenced as we are, even when we are disbelievers, by the Old and New Testaments, which put forward a good Creator who wills a certain ethical behavior for human beings—these mythological figures who are easily slighted, revengeful, lusty (engaging in illicit affairs with other gods and even mortals), who commit abductions and rapes and outrages from spite, who at times appear ready to enforce justice but at others are simply unconcerned about the puny human race, hardly seem worthy to bear the term "god" at all. Even the greatest of them, Zeus, can behave like an abusive father.

The perplexity we feel in the face of these gods is just one indication of how far we are from the Homeric Greeks. The basic image of the Greek gods in all periods is intimately bound up with Greek society in Homer's time. It has been brilliantly characterized in this way:

> In the eyes of the warlike aristocracy gods and men together formed
> one society, organized on a basis of strongly marked class-distinctions
> as was the human society itself. The highest class of aristocrats were
> the gods; their relation to the whole of mankind is much the same as
> that of a king or chieftain (*basileus*) to the lower orders, and the analo-
> gy between the two—*basileis* and gods—is helpful in considering ques-
> tions of mutual relationships and obligations, and of morality.[19]

Moral questions, too, seem confused to us in the *Iliad.* To take only the most obvious point, the whole poem turns on the "rage" (the first word in the text) of the preeminent warrior among the Greeks, Achilles. He leaves the Greek host along with his men because the commander, Agamemnon, has asserted his authority and forced Achilles to turn over a captured girl, who will now presumably be a sexual slave. Separated from the grand reputation of Homer, the plot outline seems to us a sordid tale of slavery and rape and egotism. And the gods seem to be arranging—at times causing—all this behind the scenes to fulfill "the will of Zeus."

The Homeric hero does not listen to conscience in the way we think of it because of the Bible. He only fears the dishonor he will receive from the community. Gods and men alike act in ways that preserve their dignity as it is understood within a culture of aristocrats, which is to say a general adherence to social norms unless they wish to break the rules for some reason. The gods can do so with impunity since by definition a god is an immortal in this system. Aristocratic humans can as well, within limits: "when men are punished by the gods, it is not usually on moral grounds. They are punished for personal offense against the gods. The few who are condemned to eternal torment—Ixion, Tityos, Tantalos, Sisyphos—had personally affronted Zeus. . . . The only immorality involved was an infringement of Zeus' prerogatives."[20] Obviously, this is worlds away from our automatic assumption that God is intrinsically good, worthy of worship, and that morals reflect the design of the Creator.

In the archaic Greek system, the gods are not the creators; or if they are, there is not much emphasis on the fact. They are deathless creatures within a cosmos that came into being by some unclear mythological process. Zeus is often referred to in Greek literature as Father Zeus, but we should never read this in the same way we do the biblical God the Father. Zeus is literally, which is to say sexually, the father of certain gods and heroes; but the human race belongs to a lesser breed, though sometimes there is a kind of miscegenation when a god falls in love with a mortal. Achilles is the product of one such liaison. But even so, Achilles' plight is one all mortals face. Since he must die, he has the choice, as his divine mother tells him, between a long and pleasant life at home or a glorious death in battle. The only immortality possible for a human being is immortal fame. When he dies, his shade, a paltry shadow left after the destruction of the body, will descend into Hades to live a furtive, batlike, witless existence. Whatever power there is—fate or chance or, in a later development, a more powerful Zeus—has assigned mortals and immortals their respective places, and whether they are powerful kings or poor slaves, it matters little since for human beings there is one common end.*This pessimistic (for humans) view of the order of things dominated Greek culture over centuries because of Homer's prestige.

Inventing Theology

Since early Greek culture had no theologians (Plato invents the discipline centuries later in Book X of *The Laws*) and little in the way of defined religious teachings, poets provided much of what the Greeks thought about the nature of the gods. One current allowed for the possibility that human beings might approach the life of the gods. This typically appeared in two forms: the cult of heroes and the mystery cults.

The veneration of "heroes" who had become immortals—Herakles (Latin: Hercules) or Theseus—was quite common among the Greeks. For most modern readers, these appear to be merely persons who perhaps did great things and later had a mythological or spiritual significance attached to them. But in the casual and somewhat disorganized way of Greek cults, these heroes were more like the saints and martyrs of Catholic culture than anything else with which we are familiar. To the Greeks, some of them seemed to have special powers even in death, so that the oracle at Delphi might encourage their cults in the way that a pope might declare

---

*In the *Odyssey*, Odysseus descends into the other world on his way back home, and confirms this truth when he talks with the shade of Achilles:

> "Achilleus
> no man before has been more blessed than you, nor ever
> will be. Before, when you were alive, we Argives honored you
> as we did the gods, and now in this place you have great authority
> over the dead. Do not grieve, even in death, Achilleus."
> So I spoke, and he in turn said to me in answer:
> "O shining Odysseus, never try to console me for dying.
> I would rather follow the plow as a thrall to another
> man, one with no land allotted him and not much to live on,
> than be a king over all the perished dead." (*Odyssey* XI.482ff.)

someone a saint on the basis of miracles. A modern person may believe that the cults of heroes and saints are peasant superstitions or mere wishful thinking. But that the Greeks possessed and passionately adhered to such cults cannot be denied. Beliefs of this kind were also quite tenacious; some seem to have survived in altered form into the age of Christianity in Greece, down to modern times.[21]

But these pale in comparison with the influence of cults such as the Eleusinian mysteries.[22] One measure of the importance of these mystical rites is the fact that the Athenians held trials and executed anyone who profaned the mysteries. Another is that—like the times when the major athletic contests were held—the various Greek cities would call a truce to their perpetual fighting with one another during the period when the Eleusinian mysteries were celebrated. No one today knows exactly what these mysteries consisted in, perhaps because violation of the secret brought harsh penalties. But there was some revelation of something "to be seen," perhaps a symbolic representation of the cyclical renewal of life in the seasons. Prior to classical times, when the sense of the individual was still weak, the Eleusinian mysteries seem to have assured people of the worldly survival of their group. With higher consciousness of individual existence, the mysteries too seemed to change into an assurance of personal immortality. Plato's Socrates hints at this several times as he approaches death.

Hesiod's Cosmos

The poet Hesiod is far less well known than Homer, but in some ways he was as important to future Greek reflection on men and gods. On the one hand, he seems to gather up traditions that predate Homer's pantheon and gives us the best mythological account we have from the ancient Greeks on how things got started. (It's worth recalling that this question, which seems central to those of us who have been influenced by the biblical tradition, was not as lively a question for Homer or many other Greeks.) Hesiod's *Theogony* describes how the world and living beings came to be. But at the same time, and in ways that somewhat parallel the influence of the Bible, his vision of the difference between the creation and the gods opened up the possibilities of philosophical and scientific speculations that we see in the Pre-Socratic philosophers and even in the great Greek dramatists.

His poem tells of the cosmos prior to the birth of the Olympian gods. It begins with Chaos, here meaning something more like the void than disorder, which gives birth to Earth (Gaia) and Heaven (Ouranos). The mating of this female/male pair produces a first generation of gods, prominent among them Chronos. This inaugurates a series of struggles between succeeding generations involving violence, genital mutilation, sons supplanting fathers, unruly giants and threatening beasts, along with other unpleasant events until, with the birth of Zeus and the other Olympians, a stable world order comes into existence.

What this means for human beings is somewhat ambiguous. On the whole, Hesiod seems to reflect a peasant view that this orderly Zeus rewards order, industry, and right behavior by humans. But he sees the human generations mostly as a story of decline from a Golden Age, through Silver and Bronze, down to Iron (with a brief interlude for an Age of Heroes). This genealogy is accompanied by a kind of Greek Fall from the Garden of Eden as well, intimately tied to the story of Prometheus, which Hesiod relates twice. In most modern tellings, Prometheus is characterized as loving humans and opposing the tyranny of Zeus. The king of the gods banishes Prometheus to eternal torment for this *lèse majesté* (he is chained to a rock and his liver is eaten by an eagle, who returns the next day when it has grown back to repeat the torment). Humans get fire, which is a two-edged benefit: civilization will become possible, but unremitting toil will now be necessary. Finally, Zeus sends woman to man in the form of Pandora ("All Gifts"). The deep misogynistic strain of Greek culture appears here in the way that Zeus speaks of women as a punishment for men:

> "The price for the stolen fire will be a gift of evil
> to charm the hearts of men as they hug their own doom."
> This said, the father of the gods and men roared with laughter.[23]

(Works and Days, 58–60)

Out of curiosity, Pandora opens a jar that she has been forbidden to touch (a rough parallel to Adam and Eve in the Garden). All human ills fly out, and only Hope is left inside the jar. But is Hope really a consolation, or is it, too, just one more human evil in that it makes promises that keep the human race going, but never really delivers on them?

In spite of this melancholy feature of human life, Hesiod also displays a view of the universe more in keeping with the notion of a good Creator as found in the Bible. He has sometimes been compared to Amos, his rough contemporary, or the other Hebrew prophets. Though he laments that he lives in the Iron Age, the lowest of the ages of man, he still believes deeply in the justice of Zeus towards those who, unlike the Homeric heroes, work humbly, deal justly, and know their proper place in the universe. To his brother Perses he writes: "Lay up all this in your heart: give ear to justice and wholly forget violence. This is the way that Zeus has ordained for mankind. Fish and wild beasts and the winged birds shall eat one another, for there is no justice among them. But to man he has given justice, the highest good of all."[24] Though Homer was dominant in Greece's aristocratic culture, this strain of simple peasant piety must have resonated widely among the numerous Hellenes who lived close to the soil, unmindful of the prerogatives and pretenses of kings.

And amidst all that, Hesiod and the current of Greek culture of which he is a part make possible some further developments, primarily a distance between the divine and the human and a certain space for more specifically human activity and thought. And all this aligns Hesiod, for all his peasant virtue, with what we think of as a sophisticated scientific current:

> According to Aristotle, Greek archaic thought, that is, Pre-Socratic philosophy, consisted in speculation on principles, on the origins of things. From this perspective, one would have to include the poet Hesiod in the company of the Pre-Socratic philosophers since he too seems obsessed with the question of beginnings. Or, perhaps more accurately, one could consider Pre-Socratic thought as both a continuation and a response to the issues raised by Hesiod concerning the origins of the gods and the cosmos.[25]

It has been argued that Homer's aristocratic gods are only an interlude in a Greek religious culture that in its humbler day-to-day form more typically resembles Hesiod's vision.[26] This is an exaggeration and no account of Greek culture can minimize the influence of Homer on everything that followed him. But Hesiod, whether the originator or the first surviving proponent of this tradition, thus stands at the beginning of a long line of Greek thinkers who will start, on the coast of Ionia, to regard the world as something related to but different from the gods, and will ultimately lead to the remarkable reflections by Socrates, Plato, and Aristotle.

The Ionian Scientific Revolution

What came to be known as the Ionian scientific revolution began with Thales in the Greek colony of Miletus in Asia Minor towards the start of the sixth century B.C. and reached something of a climax with Democritus around the time of Plato. This current of Greek thought has rightly received much modern praise. But the person who goes back to it expecting science may be surprised at the degree to which real scientific speculation among this group is mixed up with philosophical and religious sentiments. It is difficult to say much definitively on it for two reasons. First, though we have many fragments from the so-called Pre-Socratic thinkers, we have little in the way of complete works that would allow us to make confident assertions about even the most basic matters. And second, what we do have does not provide a consistent view of how their speculations related to the traditional gods. There would be a revival and some truly stunning subsequent developments that made it possible for the old pantheon to survive down to the fifth century A.D., but for a time many thoughtful Greeks put more emphasis on finding what we would call more "natural" explanations for things.

It is difficult to say exactly why this happened. Some of the contemporary poets seem to give expression to a feeling of abandonment or unjust treatment by the gods. Others portray the bleakness of the human lot and lament that there are few good men in the world. Little trustworthiness, thus, exists between men and gods, or among human beings. Whatever the reasons for this widespread sensibility, the more vigorous minds of the age turned towards the regular patterns of nature and sought to explain them. The standard histories of the period describe the result, with some justice, as materialistic. But just as we have seen that the "gods" were not what we might anticipate from our own sense of the divine, "matter" has a somewhat different appearance to these Greek philosopher/scientists.

Thales, for example, who stands at the beginning of the movement (at least so far as it has come down to us, since we know he had "many predecessors" according to Plato), speaks at one point of soul being mixed up in everything and all things being "full of gods."[27] At the same time, he and many of the subsequent Ionians were looking for the "divine" principle that persisted beneath the appearance of change. The references to gods are less inconsistent with "science" than they look if we remember that the gods in Homer are not transcendent, ethical, or concerned with human beings, but are an immortal part of nature. So if Thales points to water as the divine element, he may be saying among other things that water is a constant, nonhuman determinant of what is, and he attaches some religious reverence to it. Indeed, this reverent sense of mystery about "natural" processes is a common feature of Greek scientific thought in this period.

Once this process got started, philosophers made the case for various other explanations. Anaximander, who seems to have been a student or associate of Thales, spoke of the basic principles as the "unbounded" (*to apeiron*); Anaximenes surmised that it was air. This last suggestion had considerable power because air appeared to be a universal and ubiquitous breath of life. When it left the human body, the body was dead, as anyone could see. This whole notion had a lasting grip on Greek culture. Comic poets made fun of the "airy" speculations of the philosophers. In the *Phaedo*, Plato's Socrates feels obliged to refute the argument for the benefit of his elderly friend Cebes, who was approaching the end of his life, by saying that their souls are immortal and will not be dispersed with the winds at the time of death.[28]

Almost anyone who has looked into early Greece has come across the sayings of Heraclitus that "Everything flows" and "You cannot step into the same river twice." Heraclitus, who was called "the obscure" by the ancients, seems to have held some mysterious, perhaps even mystical position. His guess at the elemental stuff—fire—comes closest, in a way, to the modern view. This fire was really a kind of universal energy, an incessant change that is the only real constant, which bears some similarity to our own notions of conservation of mass and energy.

Another contemporary, Xenophanes, is often cited as saying: "If cattle or lions had hands, so as to paint with their hands and produce works of art as men do, they would paint their gods and give them bodies like their own—horses like horses: cattle like cattle." Many assume that because Xenophanes denied the validity of anthropomorphic gods he was a nonbeliever. But in another fragment we find him saying something quite different: "God is one, supreme among gods and men, and not like mortals in body or mind."[29] And this, too, seems to be one of the results of the Ionian scientific revolution: a purification of thinking about the gods in the direction of monotheism. Indeed, Plato's Socrates laments that another Ionian, Anaxagoras, spoke of Mind (*Nous*) as the guiding principle of all things, but failed to develop this idea further, falling prey to the usual "materialist" explanations: "the man made no use of intelligence, and did not assign any real causes for the ordering of things, but mentioned as causes air and ether and water and many other absurdities."[30] This is no small matter for Socrates and Plato because they believe that a "materialist" view of the world leads to moral relativism and political disaster.

Socrates comments on Anaxagoras while he is in prison facing execution, and is discussing with some friends the immortality of the soul. Many of these friends are Pythagoreans, or followers of one of the most remarkable thinkers of the sixth century B.C. Every high-school geometry student down to this day still learns the Pythagorean theorem, and Pythagoras is regarded as one of the great early mathematicians. But like that of his contemporaries, his scientific work had a spiritual side as well. Pythagoras saw the numerical consistencies in the world as evidence of divine order and harmony. Musical tones such as octaves, fifths, and fourths, for example, show perfect ratios of 1:2, 3:4, and 4:5. Unlike modern mathematical physicists, Pythagoras, or the school he founded, developed this discovery into a whole system involving the eternity of the soul, its reincarnation in various forms, and a set of practices in a kind of monastic community. The system may have been influenced by thinkers from the Middle East and as far away as India. It has sometimes earned Pythagoras the label, among the rational-izers, of being very un-Greek. But that Pythagoras had many followers, not least among them Plato, leads us to expand our notion of Greekness, even in the representatives of its most scientific and rational age.

Greek Drama

The natural philosophers were also to have an influence on one of the great-est antique arts, the drama. The earliest Greek dramatist whose works we still have, though in fragmentary form, is Aeschylus. As best we can tell, he began his career in the decade prior to the Greek battles against the Persians and fought at Marathon. In other words, he both reflects and helps form the background atmosphere for the classical period of Greek democracy in the mid-fifth century B.C. A writer of tragedy in that period was not the moral equivalent of a modern playwright. As we have already noted, Athenian tragedies were performed only once a year, at the festival of the god Dio-nysus, and were attended by the whole city. The eminent classical scholar Werner Jaeger says of all this: "tragedy can be appreciated only if we start from the conviction that it is the highest manifestation of a type of human-ity for which art, religion, and philosophy still form an indissoluble unity."[31] Such tragedies were far distant from everyday life, "for every tragedy was played by characters of superhuman majesty in a strange world heavy with religious awe."[32] But at the same time, they revealed the profound spiritual roots that the Greeks, even after the Ionian scientific revolution and the rise of democracy, perceived as constituting the basic ground of life.

In a way, all Greek tragedies have a similar theme: the mystery of hu-man suffering and its relationship to the nature of gods and men. Tradi-tional Greek wisdom had produced a much-repeated saying: "By suffering comes understanding" (*toi pathei mathos*). Mostly the wisdom gained was, in the words of the Delphic oracle, "Know thyself," i.e., know that human beings are a humble, insignificant part of the universe and should not seek to overstep the limits assigned to them by Fate or the gods. That, as Aeschy-lus shows in his play *The Persians*, was why the powerful Persian Empire was defeated upon leaving its own territory by the weaker Greeks. The historian

Herodotus had made the same case. Why humans do such things is variously explained. At some points, it seems the major gods send the minor god Até, who blinds them or causes them to forget their place. At other points, human evil—often passed down imperceptibly from generation to generation, almost like the Christian notion of Original Sin—makes men vulnerable to Até. That is the situation in the *Oresteia*, where Agamemnon returns home and is murdered by his wife, partly for having sacrificed their daughter Iphigenia to obtain favorable winds for the expedition to Troy, partly because the whole house of Atreus, Agamemnon's father, is tainted by an outrage involving cannibalism from years earlier. Agamemnon's son, Orestes, is therefore put in the terrible situation of being able to avenge his father's death only by killing his mother. Athena herself has to intervene to resolve this problem. In any event, in Aeschylus and his successors, inexplicable misfortunes for the human race are usually the only way we learn our place in the universe.

These elements may be seen in starkest form in Aeschylus' play *Prometheus Bound.* We have already encountered the main outline of this story: Prometheus, a god, has taken the side of human beings against the decrees of Zeus by stealing fire from the gods and therefore making civilization possible. Since human life is ultimately miserable, the civilized arts are no small boon. But the drama hinges on the question of whether the will of Zeus represents the good and just, or whether Prometheus rightly rejects a tyrant's oppression. Modern readers, of course, are inclined to side with Prometheus. Ancient readers could not have been wholly indifferent to the rebel's favors. But we also know that a deep current in Greek culture emphasized the insignificance of human life and the hubris of trying to deny it. Even the gods must know their place in Zeus's order. When Oceanus comes to comfort Prometheus, he counsels the old Delphic exhortation to humility, "*Know yourself* and conform your ways to new ways" (line 311). And the Chorus goes still further:

> Kindness that cannot be requited, tell me,
>
> where is the help in that, my friend? What succor
>
> in creatures of a day? You did not see

the feebleness that draws its breath in gasps,

a dreamlike feebleness by which the race

of man is held in bondage, a blind prisoner.

So the plans of men shall never

pass the ordered law of Zeus. (lines 446–553)[33]

A modern reader has to be careful here not to confuse this "Promethe-an" protest against injustice, whether we think it just or not, with rebel-lion against God *tout court*. The existence of Zeus and the other gods is not in doubt. The justice of human and other suffering, a topic going back to Homer, remains an open question; it recurs in the two great successors to Aeschylus, Sophocles and Euripides, though in differing ways. We have al-ready seen Antigone's cry about the just laws as coming from beyond time and not by the decrees of men. Sophocles is a bit more distant from the dark furies of Aeschylus and gives fuller expression to a correspondence between the divine and the human. But as we see in his Oedipus plays, the just retribution of the gods passes by long paths that, to the human eye, seem to involve injustice to otherwise innocent individuals like Oedipus. In his blindness, Oedipus is led to kill his father and marry his mother, not by some dark unconscious impulse as in Freud, but in recompense for an out-rage perpetrated by his ancestors.

This pattern may persist even in Euripides. It used to be the fashion among modern scholars who were themselves growing skeptical about religion to see in these successive dramatists a growing skepticism during the fifth cen-tury in Athens. Nietzsche, for example, in *The Birth of Tragedy*, claims to see this process at work in Euripides and, though a secularist himself, dislikes it because he believes it shows "dramatic Socratism," or the dominance of a shallow rationalism over the powerful and profound combination of Diony-sian and Apollonian elements in earlier Greek drama. That might have been a problem in Greek culture if Euripides and Socrates were narrow rational-ists, but both of them (at least as Socrates is portrayed by Plato) mobilize immense daemonic forces of their own, which continue to fascinate us by their intellectual and their spiritual power, Nietzsche notwithstanding.

Indeed, in addition to the brilliance and charm of Plato's Socratic dialogues, some new spirit is coming into view amidst the turmoil at the close of the fifth century B.C. in Athens. Not only does Socrates defend himself by quoting the oracle of the god Apollo at Delphi that he was the wisest of mortals; in his final hours he speaks of a *daimonion,* a sign that comes to him when he may be about to do something wrong. A modern reader might view this, erroneously, as the voice of conscience; Socrates thinks of it as a divine visitor from outside himself. And like figures in the Bible, he even reports a prophetic dream as he nears his death: "a beautiful, fair woman, clothed in white raiment, came to me and called me and said, 'Socrates, on the third day thou wouldst come to fertile Phthia,"[34] meaning that after death he will be with the gods. The woman in white is quoting the *Iliad* and, historically, Plato here opened up some possibilities in the whole classical tradition at least as important to the subsequent development of the West as Greek democracy and science.

What concrete lesson might be drawn from these necessarily brief reflections on the religious dimension of ancient Greece? Perhaps the most important is balance and comprehensiveness. We rightly prize the unique rational developments within Greek culture, though as we have seen, these do not have the direct connection to modern rationality that is sometimes suggested. But we also need to learn a lesson that our ancestors once learned. As different as Greek religion and rationality are from the world figured in the Bible, they had similarities and have proven to lead to significant gains in dynamic interaction with one another. When we go in search of the origins of Western identity, we do not always have to seek entirely unique elements. That would be to say that what is particularly Western shares nothing with the rest of the human race. What must enter inevitably into the proper appreciation of Western identity are also common human elements, the universal tendency towards religious beliefs among them, configured in different ways and therefore bearing new fruits. In the next chapter, we will look at the particular contribution to that process of the other great classical civilization, Rome.

CHAPTER 2

Roma Aeterna

> Others will cast more tenderly in bronze
> Their breathing figures, I can well believe,
> And bring more lifelike portraits out of marble;
> Argue more eloquently, use the pointer
> To trace the paths of heaven accurately
> And accurately foretell the rising stars.
> Roman, remember by your strength to rule
> Earth's peoples—for your arts are to be these:
> To pacify, to impose the rule of law;
> To spare the conquered, battle down the proud.
>
> Virgil, *Aeneid* VI.846–853[1]

THESE verses are among the most famous in all of Latin literature, and almost every schoolboy who has studied Latin—in the West, this meant virtually every literate person for almost two thousand years—read them and often memorized them in the original language. Virgil was the greatest Latin poet, and the *Aeneid,* his epic poem about the distant events leading up to the founding of Rome, expresses, as only the greatest of poetry can, large dimensions of the whole Roman experience that would be difficult to catch a glimpse of otherwise. So it is no small matter that Virgil affirms here—during a conversation in the other world between Aeneas, the legendary ancestor of Rome, and the prophetic soul of his dead father—what many have said about Rome before and since. The Romans could not claim to be the greatest artists; clearly, the Greeks had cast bronze and carved marble with more grace. Nor did they rival Greek skills in argument, whether philosophy or courtroom oratory, though Cicero objected to this last point.[2] Similarly, Rome added little to the development of science, especially in the purer sciences like astronomy. But the Romans were pre-eminent in one area: they knew how to rule over human beings, and their rule at its best, as Virgil's otherworldly discourse made clear, had both moral and religious dimensions.

Early in the *Aeneid*, Zeus, chief among the Olympian gods, promises the Romans: "For these I set no limits, world or time, / But make the gift of empire without end." The Roman Empire influenced the Western world so deeply over the centuries that there have been widely divergent reactions to this claim. For those who think the Roman inheritance largely good, Virgil is profoundly prophetic. When the United States is compared to ancient Rome today, it is often this view of Rome—shared by most of the American Founding Fathers—that many people have in mind. For those in later ages who saw in Rome an oppressive tyranny, though, Virgil's lines attest to Rome's repugnant arrogance. Simone Weil, for example, believed that Hitler was partly to be excused "in so far as he simply reached out for the only form of greatness [i.e., Roman-style domination] he had been told about."[3] But that reaching back to Rome as an ideal image of a just and great global order has occurred many times in Western history, not always to evil effect, by any means. Charlemagne's failed reunification of Europe in the Middle Ages, the sporadic efforts of the Holy Roman Emperors down to the nineteenth century, the symbols of the American Revolution, the republican visions of the French Revolution, and perhaps even today's European Union and the United Nations reflect a recurrent Western dream of recovered unity, both sacred and just.

Yet far from being a totalitarian unity or a Eurocentric bias, the Roman model transmitted to the West a persistent and peculiar need to look outside itself for its multiple cultural roots. Ancient Rome, as Virgil remarked, saw Greece as the superior culture. When Christianity became the dominant religion within the empire, Jerusalem was added to Athens as one of the outside origins of the cultural whole. After the fall of the empire, Rome itself became for the West a distant standard to be recreated. One perpetual source of Western dynamism has been that Rome, Athens, and Jerusalem all lie partly outside the West proper and inspire a seeking and striving for lost origins, which prevent resting in contentment with what we are. The French philosopher Rémi Brague has argued in his book *Eccentric Culture*[4] that these various absent models—particularly as they first were embodied in Roman society—prevented a monolithic culture from forming in the West. Western culture is fundamentally ec-centric because it finds its center in multiple sources that transcend simple identity. In this sense, the West has always been multicultural and open to new influences, first from its own past and later that of others. One asset of the West, when it is in good order, is that it can simultaneously maintain identity and openness, and this perhaps is also one of the secrets of its growing strength and longevity.

Realistic Prophecies

It is quite odd that long before this "Roman" model of cultural complexity and stability was much understood, Virgil allowed his Zeus to promise "imperium without end" to Rome. There were many differing schools of thought in the ancient world, but one thing almost all agreed upon, on the basis of repeated human experience, was the impermanence of all things earthly. In a thinker like Plato, for example, the Ideas—the permanent forms that were perceptible to the human mind—might endure. Believers in the old anthropomorphic gods might think they were immortal, too. And an odd philosopher like Parmenides might come up with the belief that the world is actually unchanging and permanent, and that all we see is merely an illusion. But otherwise—and this otherwise took in a wide variety of views—the world seemed to be, almost by definition, impermanent. Much of Greek religion, as we saw in the previous chapter, was devoted to teaching human beings their modest and fleeting place in the cosmos.

In political affairs, the one exception seemed to be the notion that human life shows a tendency to move in cycles, what the historian Polybius and later writers would call *anakuklosis*. It is clear from human history, they all thought, that young, vigorous peoples with multiple virtues achieve success as a result. Success leads to wealth, ease, and a decline in the hardier virtues that made success possible. Decadence ensues, and with it public disorder and new hardships, to such a degree that the cycle begins all over again. People develop virtue once more in order to deal with their difficult conditions, and they begin their rise towards success again, eventually producing the very conditions that will lead to another round of decadence. There seemed no way out of this continuous cycle any more than there is any deliverance from the cycles of the seasons or the perpetual motions of the fixed stars in the sky.

The seemingly inescapable problem of the virtue-vice-virtue cycle exercised many intelligent minds for centuries after Virgil, mostly within the civic-republican tradition of the Renaissance, including Machiavelli. But it was a worry for the sober and practical men who founded the United States as well. They clearly looked for the many benefits to be had from the institution of a commercial republic, but even after the new nation had been created and seemed to be functioning basically well, the most astute among the early leaders recalled the sad histories of antiquity. For example, in 1791, John Adams wrote in a letter to Thomas Jefferson: "Will you tell me how to prevent riches from becoming the effects of temperance and industry? Will you tell me how to prevent riches from producing luxury? Will you tell me how to prevent luxury from producing effeminacy, intoxication, extravagance, vice, and folly?"[5] Jefferson's well-known aversion to cities and excessive confidence in the virtues of the countryside probably owed no small amount to these and similar considerations on virtue in the ancient world.

A Supernatural Claim

So Virgil was making an audacious, indeed, almost an unnatural or supernatural claim for the Augustan refounding. Once he put down the civil wars that followed Caesar's assassination and became emperor, Augustus had carefully revived ancient religious practices and festivals. He built temples to the gods and sought to reconnect public worship with the ancient Roman virtues of hardiness and dedication. But could all this, however well intentioned and executed, really put an end to the cycle of virtue and vice? There are some signs that Virgil, in his eclectic way, did not believe that this was the end of the story. Yet Virgil had some kind of undeniable intuition in his vision of Roman history as breaking with the older cyclical view and beginning a linear progress with a providential religious direction. It would only be with the coming of Christianity—based on the Jewish notion of history as a story with a beginning, a middle, and an end—that the passage of time would take on a cosmic meaning for much of the world. Virgil anticipated some of this, however, and it is one of the many mysteries about him and his work that it provided a bridge, much admired by later figures, to a very different concept of the world than had existed in ancient times.

To say all this does not mean that Virgil and, by implication, the Romans in general thought of Roman power as an unmixed political, moral, and spiritual good. Critics of the poet and of the regime often assert that Augustus simply needed a heroic poem to justify the Roman Empire and Virgil wrote one for him. In fact, Virgil and the Romans were quite aware of the tragic quality of even the best political arrangements. Virgil even coined a phrase, *lacrimae rerum* ("the tears of things"), that brilliantly formulates the paradoxical nature of human affairs. Some modern scholars, reflecting contemporary sensibilities, have detected ambiguities in the poem and raised the question of whether Virgil in his heart of hearts was a true believer in empire. He was, but only in a rather idealized and spiritualized—to say nothing of a somewhat melancholy—version of Rome, and later readers were not entirely wrong in seeing a strong sense of imperfection in Virgil and describing him as an *anima naturaliter christiana* ("a naturally Christian soul").

There is a deep religious vision in Virgil, and by implication in Roman culture, that of course is not identical with later Christian concerns, but which raises some serious questions about the larger spiritual purposes of political order.[6] Our modern view of the Romans as a practical rather than a speculative people compared with the Greeks, while true, has obscured this point; though to many people during the Middle Ages, the Renaissance, and the Enlightenment, it seemed obvious that Rome was, even in its practical and political activities, a moral and spiritual enterprise. The Founding Fathers of the United States also looked back to Rome for inspiration and, like Virgil, did not draw as sharp a distinction between politics and the larger questions of human life as might be natural to do today. In

The Federalist Papers, for example, James Madison argued: "what is government itself but the greatest of all reflections on human nature? If men were angels, no government would be necessary. If angels were to govern, neither external nor internal controls on government would be necessary."[7]

Of course, everything depends on the quality of that reflection and the nature of its embodiment in public life. Imperial Rome presents positive and negative aspects. On the one hand, it established peace and order, the Pax Romana, throughout the Mediterranean world for centuries. As Edward Gibbon wrote in his *Decline and Fall of the Roman Empire,* "If a man were called to fix the period in the history of the world during which the condition of the human race was most happy and prosperous, he would, without hesitation, name that which elapsed from the death of Domitian to the accession of Commodus,"[8] that is, from the period just after the turmoil of the first century A.D. to the end of Marcus Aurelius' rule near the end of the second century. That later achievement had its roots in the Rome of Virgil and Augustus' day, but they, in turn, looked back to a larger tradition.

In the balance against that, we might place the gladiator shows in the Colosseum, the brutal and massive crucifixions of insurgents (six thousand slaves were crucified along the entire distance between Capua and Rome after Spartacus' slave revolt alone), the merciless crushing of any people who resisted the Roman "peace" (for example, in ancient Palestine), and the slow withering of the traditional Roman virtues with the accumulation of wealth and power. Saint Augustine, who knew the empire from the inside, denounced Rome's virtues as "splendid vices" because they served the will to dominate. Simone Weil put the case somewhat unjustly, arguing that Roman religion was mostly brutality and that the Romans were the only unspiritual people of the ancient world. The kernel of truth in this exaggeration is that among the Romans we do not find the obvious religious uplift of Plato or even the vigorous polytheism of Homer and other Greek writers. But Rome came into its own at a time when the great age of Greece was centuries past, the imperial habits of Hellenistic civilization were widespread, and the spiritual and religious needs of people were shaped by a very different social world than that of the small Greek city-states, which had failed both as moral and as political entities.

Historical Decline

Large philosophical and religious developments lay behind Rome in Virgil's time. Virgil knew that the rise of Rome had been paid for with much suffering by both the innocent and the not so innocent, and it was not even clear that this achievement was likely to survive very long, let alone "without end," as Zeus promises in the *Aeneid.* Several of his recent predecessors and contemporaries had said as much. Indeed, it was one of the commonplaces of Roman thought in the first century B.C. that Romans were fallen from the energetic virtues and courage of their early ancestors because of the corruptions of wealth and power, which even showed themselves in the decay of public manners.

The Romans, Virgil prominent among them, had gone to school among the Greek philosophers and had absorbed various religious currents within the new empire. Beginning with the Greek historian Polybius (second century B.C.), it became clear to people of fair views that Rome had surpassed Greek achievements in war and government. Polybius had been a notable statesman in Greece, but he was captured after 168 B.C., sent to Rome, and kept in a kind of house arrest by the Roman statesman Scipio Aemilianus. He is sometimes disparaged as having become a toady to his new masters. But anyone who reads Polybius carefully has to concede that he noticed some things that no one else until his time had perceived to quite the same extent. For example, like all Greeks he cherished the memories of Thermopylae, Marathon, and other battles that displayed the virtues of free Greek warriors. Yet he believed that the actual results had been given an exaggerated grandeur by the talented writers in the golden age of Greece. Compared with the similar heroics that Romans displayed generation after generation and their ability to make sure that gains were not reversed by self-destructive internal quarrels, the Greek high points looked significantly less impressive.

Polybius could identify the various episodes in Roman history that confirmed this view, as well as the Roman virtues and dynamism that made them possible. He made a special point of mentioning something quite different from the Greek attitudes, at least in his own time:

> the most important difference for the better which the Roman com-
> monwealth appears to me to display is in their religious beliefs. For I
> conceive that what in other nations is looked on as a reproach, I mean
> the scrupulous fear of the gods, is the very thing which keeps the Ro-
> man commonwealth together.[9]

This claim carries real weight because Polybius did not personally have much use for religion per se, except insofar as it helped restrain the fickleness and vices that are inevitably found among the masses in any society. But the practical consequences of Roman religion were striking to him: "This is the reason why, apart from anything else, Greek statesmen, if entrusted with a single talent, though protected by ten checking-clerks, as many seals, and twice as many witnesses, yet cannot be induced to keep faith; where-as among the Romans, in their magistracies and embassies, men have the handling of a great amount of money, and yet from pure respect to their oath keep their faith intact." Rome would soon have its own dishonest officials in abundance, but it says something that 150 years before the *Aeneid* such a claim of religion-induced virtue could be made.

In the following century, the Roman historian Sallust (86–35 B.C.), a contemporary of Virgil's whose work, like the poet's, quickly became a school text and therefore was vastly influential on general attitudes in Rome for centuries to come, set himself "to describe the conduct of our ancestors in peace and war; how they managed the state, and how powerful they left it; and how, by gradual alteration, it became, from being the most virtuous, the most vicious and depraved."[10] In the beginning, the Romans—in the myth of Aeneas and the poor peoples who were to join his efforts—had little or nothing in the way of worldly wealth or land, and therefore had to rely on their own efforts and the favor of the gods. Their skills and determination were of such a high quality that they did what no other ancient people had done: created a system that ruled over vast regions and endured for centuries. This was something that neither the empires in the Middle East nor the

Greek empire of Alexander the Great and his heirs had been able to do. Empires seemed regularly to fall apart or replace one another. But Sallust, who did not know that the coming reforms of Augustus would allow Rome to continue in its domination over the Mediterranean for another half millennium, could only see in the turmoil preceding that conservative revolution the end of what had made Rome illustrious and the usual intervention of Fortune to bring down the mighty:

> when by perseverance and integrity, the public had increased its power; when mighty princes had been vanquished in war; when barbarous tribes and populous states had been reduced to subjection: when Carthage, the rival of Rome's dominion, had been utterly destroyed, and sea and land lay everywhere open to her sway, Fortune then began to exercise her tyranny, and to introduce universal innovation. To those who had easily endured toils, dangers, and doubtful and difficult circumstances, ease and wealth, the objects of desire to others, became a burden and a trouble.[11]

In Sallust's view, the early zeal for distinction declined into avarice. The Roman people got used to luxuries, intemperance, and softness. Successive gains only exacerbated the decline. Moral dissolution was reflected in the relative retreat of Roman religion: "It furnishes much matter for reflection, after viewing our modern mansions and villas extended to the size of cities, to contemplate the temples which our ancestors, a most devout race of men, erected to the Gods."[12]

Philosophical Religion

It would be impossible for Virgil not to have known all this, and probably equally impossible to imagine that, in the circumstances, he decided to write a merely fawning poem to Augustus and a whitewash of the Roman Empire. Something more complex was at work in his efforts, though it is not easy to spell out precisely what that was. In fact, Virgil died leaving the *Aeneid* unfinished while on a trip to Greece for three years of further philosophical study and polishing of the poem. As we saw in the previous chapter, we have to be careful about introducing too stark a separation between religion and philosophy in the ancient world. Naturally, we can say that in the West, philosophy leans more on reason and religion relies on narrative and image. But in the ancient world both were united in an integral pursuit of knowing the nature of the world and how human beings should act within it. As a contemporary philosopher has rightly argued:

> What is true of Plato and Socrates is just as true of Aristotle. It is true also of all the philosophic schools of the Greek and Roman world—Stoics, Epicureans, Neoplatonists—in whom indeed the most obvious feature is their religious and salvific character. The philosophers, we might say, were *more* serious about religion than most of their fellows, since they insisted on using their reason for this purpose instead of relying blindly on their hopes and fears.[13]

All of these Greek philosophic currents, along with non-Roman religious beliefs such as Judaism, Mithraism, and, a little later, Christianity, made their way to the imperial capital. And when we look at the most significant figures from Cicero to Seneca to Marcus Aurelius, it is clear that in Roman circumstances all of these influences took on a practical dimension, not unrelated to political affairs, but one that all the same had a "salvific" quality.

The Romans were initially wary of the clever Greek teachers who began arriving in ever larger numbers after an increasingly imperialistic Rome conquered, finally, both Carthage and Greece in 144 B.C. To the older Roman leaders, the simple peasant virtues that had made Rome strong appeared to be threatened by the sophisticated and not always salubrious philosophical thought that, like all things Greek, was valued by the Romans. In its way, this was similar to the instinctive American popular reaction to French or continental theories like existentialism or deconstructionism that, though intellectually formidable, seemed likely only to sap public and private virtues. The Romans had grown great worshiping their traditional gods and emphasizing practical virtues like courage and patriotism.

Some philosophies could easily be accommodated among traditional values, especially certain parts of Plato and the whole Platonic school that had developed in Greece and the Mediterranean in the previous four centuries. Plutarch says in his *Lives*, for example, that when the Roman general

Cato the Younger heard of Caesar's victory and, therefore, the end of Roman republican liberty, he nobly committed suicide rather than be slave to a tyrant. Significantly, he did so after a night spent reading Plato's arguments in the *Phaedo* about the immortality of the soul. This act resonated for centuries after. Dante, the preeminent Catholic poet of the Middle Ages, allows Cato to become the gatekeeper of Purgatory, despite what might seem the grave sin of suicide, and even has Virgil, a character in his *Divine Comedy*, plead with Cato to allow Dante to enter, because "He seeks freedom—and how dear that is, / he who refused his life for it knows well."[14] As late as the eighteenth century, Cato was the subject of a highly popular play by Joseph Addison and a central point of reference for the American Founders.

Greek Stoicism, too, was a natural fit with Roman sternness. Like many of the Hellenistic philosophy/religions, Stoicism responded to one of the central questions of life in the sprawling and chaotic empires around the Mediterranean: How to live a happy and noble life in conditions that constantly threatened tranquility and even survival? Broadly speaking, Stoicism combined strict teachings about the need to subordinate, perhaps even to extirpate, the passions and to subject all personal behavior to the demands of private and public duty.[15] By developing an indifference to pain and suffering and pursuing only the good and the virtuous, the perfect Stoic might live a life worthy of a human being even under moral monsters like the more bloody and capricious Roman emperors. For example, the Stoic Seneca, a guiding star in Western moral reflection for centuries and far too little known today, was forced to commit suicide under his former pupil, the emperor Nero. But like a golden thread through the age of the Pax Romana, Stoicism, though developed in fourth-century Greece, had strong affinities with some of the central Roman values. And it is no accident that one of the greatest Roman emperors, Marcus Aurelius, was also one of the greatest Stoic philosophers.

The Threat of the Epicureans

Where, then, lay the threat to Rome in philosophy? Primarily in the combination of indifference to the gods and softness of manners exemplified most fully in the philosophy known as Epicureanism. In its ancient form, Epicureanism was not a philosophy of hedonism in the modern sense. The Epicureans valued above all else what they called *ataraxia,* an untroubled spirit. In this, they made common cause in part with the Stoics. But where the Stoics emphasized indifference to pain and the embrace of public duties, the Epicureans focused on moderate pleasures and withdrawal from the turmoil of the world. Epicureans were not necessarily atheists. They took an indifferent attitude towards the divinities: Since the gods are unconcerned about us, we should be unconcerned about the gods. In their view, public activity cannot lead to a lasting happiness any more than can religion; so the simple pleasures of life among small groups of philosophical friends are the most that can be hoped for in this world. This philosophy had little in common with the Romans over the centuries during Rome's rise to power, but significantly, it attracted no small number of followers from among the imperial elite around the time of Virgil.

Indeed, we have reliable evidence that Virgil himself, as a young man and perhaps even later, was an Epicurean. He was also a devoted student of Lucretius, a poetic predecessor in Latin who brilliantly expounded the Epicurean system in his poem *De rerum natura* ("On the Nature of Things"). Virgil had a much more easygoing temperament than the fiery Lucretius, but in his quiet way the author of the *Aeneid* was philosophically acute and ambitious as well. In fact, it is a common opinion among scholars that Virgil's ambition was nothing less than to rival Homer and bring Lucretius' project to a more universal—and quite different—completion. In this view, the first half of the *Aeneid* is Virgil's *Odyssey,* recounting Aeneas's wanderings after the fall of Troy and eventually to Italy, where his later descendants will found Rome. The second half of the *Aeneid* is Virgil's *Iliad,* recounting the battles of the Trojans in Italy and connecting Roman history with the heroic age of the Trojan War. Homer lays out heroic deeds in the *Iliad* in a fashion common to all epics about warriors from the Bhagavad Gita to *Lord of the Rings.* His second poem, the *Odyssey,* is about a man's return to his proper home. The *Aeneid* reverses this order and gives us a hero forced to leave home and carry out a monumental task—even though he would often rather not—out of a sense of *pietas*, not merely piety in the modern sense but more like duty to his people and his gods.

Lurking behind this heroic portrait are Lucretian themes quite different from obvious Roman subjects, which put some serious questions to any understanding of the role of religion in an empire of the kind Augustus had founded. The most cynical way of formulating the problem came from the pen of Edward Gibbon: "The various modes of worship, which prevailed in the Roman world, were all considered by the people, as equally true; by the philosopher, as equally false; and by the magistrate, as equally useful."[16] This witticism is demonstrably false in each particular. Average people, especially those in a multinational empire, may be inclined to tolerance. But it is doubtful, given the wide and sometimes bizarre religious expression of which the human race is capable, that anyone exposed to them will not think some better and some worse, as the Romans did. Then, there were all sorts of philosophers who denied traditional religious truths, but for hundreds of years, in fact down to the fall of the Western Empire and beyond, there were Platonists, Neoplatonists, Gnostics, Jews, Christians, and many others skilled in philosophy who did not think all religions equally false. And as we know from the history of persecution of Christians and occasional anti-Semitism among the Greeks and Romans (including some quite urbane figures like Horace and Cicero),[17] the magistrates decidedly did not consider all religion equally useful. Indeed, quite the contrary.

The ancient Romans, like the modern, were pervasively religious without being too discriminating or exact in beliefs. Popular religion on that scale inevitably involves a considerable amount of superstition and credulity. We know that similar problems already existed in the classical Greek world. Outright disbelief in gods, however, was very rare throughout the world until modern times, so most philosophy was directed, as we have seen earlier, towards applying reason to religious categories and purifying belief.

The major exception to all this was Epicureanism. There is some dispute whether Epicurus believed that no gods exist, or that they exist but have nothing to do with us for good or ill. In any event, by the beliefs and behaviors we already described, he sought to relieve the human race of fears of hell or of simple dissolution after death. One of the central contentions of Epicurus' philosophy is the practical nature of true inquiry about the human condition: "Empty is that philosopher's argument by which no human suffering is therapeutically treated. For just as there is no use in a medical art that does not cast out the sickness of bodies, so too there is no use in philosophy if it does not throw out suffering from the soul."[18] This is a clear indication of the difference between the quite serious nature of ancient Epicurean inquiry in comparison with the Playboy-style philosophy of shallow appeal to pleasure that most people associate with an "Epicurean" philosophy in modern times. Epicurus' appeal to moderate pleasure and detachment may still strike us as a truncated form of human existence. But there is no question that he was trying to grapple in practical terms with what human life ought to be if we come to the conclusion that there is no help for us in traditional views of the gods and the afterlife.

For Epicurus understood that many of the vices we see—lust, greed, ambition, snobbery, violence—are ultimately the product of the fear of death. It is not an entirely strained comparison to say that in these dimensions Epicurus somewhat resembles the Buddha. Neither believed in a God or gods who are of much help to the human race. Both recognized that the various subterfuges that human beings individually and collectively use to distract themselves from the ultimate dissolution of death are the deep origin of the vices we see. Indeed, the two of them shared a belief that the hopes and fears induced by most forms of religion are merely another variation on the theme of the profound fear of death. So while Epicurus was, by his own open admission and by external observation, an implacable enemy of many forms of religion, in his aims he was not a vulgar advocate of bodily pleasures, but someone who sought to offer the kind of peace and contentment usually associated with religion in conditions that made the traditional approaches to these goals impossible.

Indeed, in a certain sense the ancient Epicureans, far from being unbridled libertines, exercised serious self-restraint. They distinguished, as sharply as any Christian monk, natural from unnecessary desires, and encouraged their students to see that false beliefs about goods led to the passions and ambitions that bring so much evil on the person and the race. This dimension of his thought appears quite striking in comparison with Aristotle, who took normal human behavior as a baseline and sought to purify it of its inner contradictions and elaborate the fullness of the virtues implicit within it. Epicurus was a much more radical thinker than that. For him, the human collectivity indoctrinates us in a number of things that we believe will make us happy, but which, in fact, are the very causes of our discontent and disturbance. That is one of the reasons why Epicureans typically ceased participating in society and withdrew to their own almost monastic enclaves, where the practice of their virtues would not be disturbed by the passions and follies of mankind in general. Epicurus even advised against marriage and family; as he often said, the ideal was to "live unknown."

All of this is, simultaneously, a structure of both skepticism and dogma. The Epicurean was skeptical of all previous systems, but was encouraged to take the master's teaching as unquestionable truth. Most students were taught and memorized the *Kuriai Doxai,* the principle beliefs that constituted Epicurean orthodoxy. From what we can discern in the fragments that have come down to us, members of the community were supposed to "confess" specific details of their past and were led through a rational analysis of their specific beliefs and emotions by one of the more advanced members of the community. As an astute scholar of ancient philosophy has described this situation:

> The Aristotelian pupil becomes a better Aristotelian by becoming better at taking charge of her own reasoning; the same . . . is true of the Stoic. The Epicurean pupil is not encouraged to bring objections of her own against the system, or to argue dialectically; and as she becomes more dependent on the text and doctrines of the master, she may be less adept at reasoning for herself.[19]

In antiquity, it was noticed that people who fell into this system spent a long time at it, much like modern people in psychoanalysis (with which Epicureanism has more than a few points of similarity); and though movement from one philosophical system to another was common in the ancient world, those who entered Epicureanism rarely exited. Their minds and their wills seem to have become permanently circumscribed by the worldview. As one ancient commentator graphically put it, this was "Because men can become eunuchs, but eunuchs never become men."[20]

A Roman Reaction

The Romans were particularly sensitive to this dimension of Epicureanism, perhaps no one more so than the eminent Roman writer Cicero. He was not an original philosopher, but he had a deep sense of Roman values in much the same way that Edmund Burke, in the eighteenth century, understood English values or Abraham Lincoln did American values. Cicero understood himself and what was best in the Roman tradition to descend from a people who began as virtuous farmers and, by those very virtues, conquered the world. Nothing could be further from the practical atheism and skepticism of Epicurus and Lucretius. Cicero himself was technically a philosophical Skeptic, that is, he did not believe we could have indisputable knowledge about the foundations of the world. But he did believe that we could reason to a high degree of probability about central truths. By contrast, the skepticism of the Epicureans threatened everything he valued about the Roman order: "Against these we must struggle 'with foot and horse' as the saying is, if our intention is to guard and maintain morality."[21] Believers in the necessity of virtue for public happiness have often agreed with Cicero, as did Montesquieu, the eighteenth-century author of *The Spirit of the Laws*, who wrote: "I believe that the sect of Epicurus, which was introduced at Rome towards the end of the Republic, contributed a great deal to corrupting the heart and spirit of the Romans."[22]

The Romans typically transmitted values by telling stories about virtuous ancestors rather than by abstract philosophizing. Cicero invokes one such story towards the end of his *De officiis* ("On Duties"), which until the second half of the twentieth century was a virtual guidebook for Western statesmen. Cicero writes of Marcus Attilius Regulus, who had been a Roman consul and was later taken prisoner at the battle of Tunes in Carthage. The Carthaginians wanted to send Regulus back to Rome to plead for the release of some of their own prisoners of war. But they first made him swear to return if his mission was unsuccessful. Regulus was by then an old man and could easily have justified breaking his vow. But he did not even give his opinion on the matter to the Roman Senate, since he might appear to be acting out of self-interest: "the prisoners were retained and he himself returned to Carthage; affection for his country and his family failed to hold him back. And even then he was not ignorant of the fact that he was going to a most cruel enemy and to exquisite torture; still, he thought his oath must be sacredly kept. And so even then, when he was being slowly put to death by enforced wakefulness, he enjoyed a happier lot than if he had remained at home an aged prisoner of war, a man of consular rank forsworn."[23] Cicero examines the various arguments—even the displeasure of Jupiter—that might have forced Regulus to keep his oath, but says none are valid except the belief that it was simply wrong to commit perjury. Indeed, he says, at the time no one would have believed an honorable man could do anything else: "That merit, therefore, belongs to the age, not to the man."

Cicero closes his book with the observation that stories like these explode the claims of the Epicureans, whom he sees as the foremost threat to the old ways that made Rome strong. Epicureans speak of the courageous endurance of pain, says Cicero, but it is difficult to imagine them undertaking the responsibilities of a Regulus or behaving as he did. Virtue by its very nature, in Cicero's view, must follow what is right, whether it is pleasurable or painful, expedient or not. Epicureans merely endure pain when it cannot be avoided. They have little interest in the right and their preaching only weakens the old beliefs as well as the old ways of acting.

All of this matters to understanding Virgil and the ideal Rome he envisioned and transmitted to subsequent history because he seems to be deliberately making a case against Epicureanism in the *Aeneid.* Aeneas often laments that he cannot pursue his private desires, but remains faithful to his God-given duty. In the tension between these two impulses, Virgil appears to be demonstrating a fatal flaw in the Epicurean system. While it may be true that the radically rational philosopher is freed from fear of both the gods and death, and will pursue his own modest pleasures privately, such philosophers are so rare as to be of almost no social effect. Almost all ancient thought in both Greece and Rome held that philosophy of any sort was only for the very few. And most ancient philosophies reinforced popular religious and moral traditions. Philosophies that diminished support for those props of civilization, whatever their intentions, by their very nature could only unleash *furor*, primarily anger and lust, both of which disturb the public order and, paradoxically, make the retired life of the Epicurean philosopher precarious. Virgil, like Cicero, may not be wholly certain in a strict philosophical sense about the ultimate nature of reality, but the shortcomings of Epicureanism convince him that force and religion are needed to remedy tendencies towards *furor* in human nature. And that is why Roman order, which will keep the peace within Italy and around the Mediterranean, has great moral and even religious value.

Virgil's powerful mind actually leads him to recast almost all the usual elements of this debate and in particular what it means to be a hero. For example, the war that his Aeneas will undertake is not conducted merely according to the old heroic ethos of Homer. There is not much emphasis on the honor and fame to be won through courage during battle in the *Aeneid.* Courage and disdain for death are much praised, but in Virgil warfare is at the service of something larger than the individual's status. It is part of *pietas.* Every bit of fighting, from the departure of the Trojans from their home city down to the founding of the new city, Rome, is part of the design of fate that will lead to a universal empire, and Aeneas must serve that cosmic destiny, which is not merely the interest of one people or his own family. Though some readers historically saw this goal as akin to totalitarianism— and the real historical behavior of Rome at times gives some support to this view—at least in Virgil's ideal conception the aim of bringing all peoples under universal rule is to eliminate war, whether the war arises among people outside Rome or among Roman citizens, as happened in the final, chaotic days of the republic.

So new and radical was this shift in the ancient world that it raised the question of whether Virgil's crucial notion, *pietas*—a mixture of duty, religiosity, and loyalty—is compatible with manliness, as the ancients understood that term. Epicureans could claim a kind of virtue in rejecting the consolations of religion, even if they lived relatively unstrenuous lives. But if you also demote the Homeric and very Roman notions of martial valor and domestic loyalty, what is left? Virgil's Aeneas braves death in battle and seeks a new homeland, but his main virtue, piety, is something without precedent in the stories of Achilles and Odysseus. Obedience to duty, which involves responsibilities to Rome and the gods, becomes the overriding value. Thus Aeneas tells his son, Ascanius, before the final battle that will enable his descendants to go on to found Rome: "Learn fortitude and toil from me, my son, / Ache of true toil. Good fortune learn from others." (Book XII.435–436)

The Religion of Rome

The political point here contains a philosophical and religious vision. Saint Augustine, who clearly loved Virgil, often quoted him against the real behavior of the Romans. In his *City of God,* he accused the Romans of having made idols of themselves under the guise of religious submission. Nevertheless, Virgil had posed a question that would occupy Christian thinkers and rulers also in subsequent centuries: how much of any political system partakes in the sacred ordering of human life and how much is merely the necessary apparatus of earthly life in community? Virgil makes the sacred connection a strong one because he sees the alternative as unleashing passions and forgoing the best means to curb them. The passage about Romans excelling in political rule that begins the present chapter, for example, occurs in the sixth book of the *Aeneid,* which tells of Aeneas's descent to the underworld. The person who speaks those lines is Aeneas's own father, Anchises, who had died earlier. After an elaborate preparation that includes various symbolic episodes, Aeneas enters the underworld guided by the Cumaean Sybil, a prophetess of the god Apollo. They see the various tortures inflicted on evildoers—murderers, traitors, adulterers, sinners against the gods such as Sisyphus, those who abused parents, rapists, the incestuous—by the monsters of classical mythology, and though the description of all this is full enough, the Sibyl tells Aeneas:

> If I had
>
> A hundred tongues, a hundred mouths, a voice
>
> Of iron, I could not tell of all the shapes
>
> Their crimes had taken, or their punishments.
>
> (Book VI.625–627)

All of this is a fairly straightforward reproduction of the punishments awaiting evildoers in the afterlife from traditional myths and key texts such as Plato's *Republic* (Book X) and his *Apology*. Significantly, the language Virgil uses here borrows a good deal from Lucretius, who described much of the same material, but for the opposite purpose of dismissing fears of such punishments as unfounded and as a bane to the human race.[24]

But all of this is only a prelude to a second strand in the classical tradition about the underworld, which Virgil rearranges for a particular purpose. Just as there are punishments for the wicked in the portion of the underworld known as Tartarus, so there are rewards for the virtuous in the region known as Elysium or the Elysian Fields:

> They came
>
> To place of delight, to green park land,
>
> Where souls take ease amid the Blessed Groves,
>
> Wider expanses of high air endow
>
> Each vista with a wealth of light. Souls here
>
> Possess their own familiar sun and stars.
>
> (Book VI.638–641)

Yet as pleasant as this may be, and a motive for good behavior in this world, it is clear that Virgil has set this traditional hell and paradise at the center of his poem for a further purpose—an argument about Rome's universal mission, in both the political and the cosmic sense.

For the conclusion of the excursion to the underworld echoes some of the teachings of Plato and the Stoics that are somewhat at odds with the traditional beliefs. First, Aeneas is instructed that the world, as in the cosmology of the Stoics, is the product of a divine fire which is the "soul of the world." This fire is the immortal part of each human being as well, even though our attachment to flesh and its desires obscures this truth for us. But that is not all. Anchises now tells Aeneas that good souls who come to Elysium somewhat weighed down by the earthy habits of their lives above are purified and reincarnated above. There were precedents for this view among the Platonists and Plato's teachers, the Orphics and the Pythagoreans. This enables Anchises to show Aeneas in a kind of future-perfect mode what will have happened in Rome to bring the city to the stature it will achieve by the time of Virgil and Augustus, precisely by the return of various great souls in the underworld to positions of distinction in the history of Rome. And all this will be guided by the Roman fate, the mission to rule justly, "to spare the conquered, battle down the proud."

But is all this a true vision? It may seem odd to raise the question after the elaborate tale told here and the historically accurate material towards the end of the story. And yet Virgil introduces a doubt. He closes with the statement that there are two gates from Hades to our world:

> One said to be
> Of horn, whereby the true shades pass with ease,
> The other all white with ivory agleam
> Without a flaw, and yet false dreams are sent
> Through this one by ghosts to the upper world.
> Anchises now, his last instructions given,
> Took son and Sibyl there and let them go
> By the Ivory Gate.

(Book VI.893–898)

So was the whole trip to the underworld nothing more than an elaborate illusion?

This is one of the most vexed questions in Virgil. Some readers think he could not make up his mind and left us with an incoherent vision that he may—or may not—have been able to resolve in the three years he planned to spend revising and polishing, which never occurred because of his death.[25] No entirely satisfactory solution to this problem exists, but the whole weight of the *Aeneid* and of Roman ideals supports the truth of the vision, and the sacred nature of political rule in Virgil seems beyond question despite theoretical uncertainties and the *lacrimae rerum*.

What is the lesson for us in this reading of Roman history? At the very least it encourages us to think more deeply about the contribution of Rome to the shape of the West. Most standard histories continue to repeat the truism that the Roman Empire provided models of law and administration to subsequent ages. And this is true, so far as it goes—but it does not go very far at all. The Pax Romana, the long period of peace in the Mediterranean, was an achievement not reproduced after the fall of Rome until the decades after World War II, when Western Europe united by necessity against the threat of Communism in Eastern Europe, and the nuclear "mutual assured destruction" between the United States and the Soviet Union froze national boundaries and the balance of forces where they were at the conclusion of the war. This, too, was no little blessing, but we have yet to take the measure of the benefits—admittedly paid for by many sufferings among the people conquered by Rome—of the practical and theoretical aspirations of the empire.

Curiously, it was the Christians of the Middle Ages, the heirs of the early Christians who had been persecuted and brutally martyred under the Roman system, who for a long time appreciated the old Roman standards and often tried to reproduce them with a Christian coloration. If we look solely at Rome's vigorous application of force to opponents, we will miss the ways in which roads were extended, communications improved, bands of robbers eliminated, pirates hunted down and killed throughout the Mediterranean, and life for millions made more secure, prosperous, and fulfilling. In these respects as well, the West would not match Rome's standards until the nineteenth century and Rome would persist as a dream of lost unity and justice.

Finally, there is the question of Rome's aspiration to universality in its rule. We do not need to think—as was certainly not the case—that the magistrates and soldiers who carried out the daily business of the empire had lofty philosophical or religious goals, though they were not for the most part the corrupt sybarites they were often portrayed as being by some of the Christians either. It is enough that Virgil and some of the other shapers of the Roman ethos were able to discern an ideal for such a massive undertaking to pursue. Nothing of the sort arose among any of the city-states of ancient Greece. And even the conquest of Alexander the Great, which spread Hellenistic culture to much of the known world, never generated a historical vision the way that Rome did. At least in this respect, Aeneas setting out from Troy on his fateful voyage to found a new city has parallels with the story of Abraham setting out from Ur of the Chaldees to inhabit the Holy Land. Unlike the *Odyssey*, these stories speak of historical currents guided by the gods or God, initiated by a single man but intended in their ultimate expression to affect the entire human race. Not a small vision for a people who allegedly were simple and unphilosophical magistrates, jurists, engineers, and soldiers.

This history of the vision of Rome is significant not only for what it tells us about a step in the development of the West, but for what it says about our time as well. It is no accident that the Epicureans in our own society who repudiate religion in favor of science and ease tend to be overly optimistic about human nature, and to dispute the need for war or other forms of coercion to restrain vice. Or that those with a religious vision similar to Virgil's own are more likely to see the need of piety both for the good order of their own nations and for the restraint of evil in the world. In that sense, we all still inhabit a world partly discovered and transmitted to us by Virgil in the *Aeneid*.

CHAPTER 3

The Bible and Its Worlds

> Now the Lord said to Abram, "Go from your coun-
> try and your kindred and your father's house to
> the land that I will show you. I will make of you a
> great nation, and I will bless you, and make your
> name great, so that you will be a blessing. I will
> bless those who bless you, and the one who curses
> you I will curse; and in you all the families of the
> earth shall be blessed."
>
> Genesis 12:1–3

MOST people in the modern West assume that they know what the Bible says about the world and human society. God made the world; he gave human beings various commandments; and, depending on whether you follow those commandments or not, you wind up in heaven or in hell after you die. Jews usually recognize that the Bible also claims that God made a special covenant with the Jewish people. Christians typically have some sense that it was necessary for God to become man in Jesus for salvation to become possible. None of these beliefs about Old and New Testaments are wrong, and even in the vastly diminished knowledge of the Bible among Jews and Christians alike, they get a good deal right. What most people fail to appreciate about all this, however, is how unusual the large claims about sacred history were in their time and how pervasive their influence remains for "all the families of the earth," so much so that it might be better for many of us to approach the Bible as if it were not the central and familiar spiritual influence in our civilization, but a text by a strange and foreign group of tribes.

For that is what, in a way, it is, starting from the very first words of the biblical story. The whole notion of Creation, as the Bible understands it, is quite unusual and will receive some careful attention below. But it may be useful to begin with a more immediate and perhaps even more surprising contention: that God, the Creator of the whole cosmos, chose an unknown man in a backwater of Mesopotamia, for no reason we can fathom, to carry forward his purposes for the world he had created.

Other ancient peoples, including Greeks and Romans, scoffed at this absurd assertion. And during the Enlightenment, the charge arose again, led by Voltaire, along with a modern form of anti-Semitism that blamed the Jews for the historical claims of particularity among the revealed faiths, which seemed to the *philosophes* to contradict "universal reason." Who was this Abraham who would become the father of the "Abrahamic" faiths (i.e., Judaism, Christianity, and Islam)*? Even according to Genesis, Abraham is not someone of any great moment in the Middle East, no king or prominent military figure. Nor did the land he is instructed to migrate to, today's Israel, possess much to recommend it in comparison with the major agricultural civilizations of Egypt and the Fertile Crescent. Yet Abraham's God starts him on a fateful journey that has still not come to an end in its effects. He promises this obscure man: "I have made you the ancestor of a multitude of nations. I will make you exceedingly fruitful; and I will make nations of you, and kings shall come from you. I will establish my covenant between you and your offspring after you throughout their generations for an everlasting covenant . . . ." (Genesis 17:5-7)

Scripture scholars argue over both the precise historical truth about Abraham and the exact date when these words were put into their final form. At the very least, such passages convey some archaic memory, even if they were not written down in this way, as seems likely, until the Babylonian Captivity of the Israelites during the sixth century B.C. But even if we allow that they were a "late" composition intended to shore up fading Jewish identity among a surviving remnant after the destruction of Jerusalem, the story is an odd one—if we look at it afresh. The Jewish people at that time

---

*"Abrahamic" is a common term to refer to the three main religions that claim descent from Abraham. But a qualification is in order: Judaism and Christianity agree on the same history, even most of the same texts that tell this story. Islam regards the Old and New Testaments alike as partly falsified accounts.

had no reason to believe that God's promises to Abraham were in the least likely to be fulfilled. And it was an unexpected genealogy to point to: a relatively unknown nomad who, at that point, nearly 1,500 years or so since he was supposed to have lived, had certainly given rise to nothing resembling a great nation, let alone multiple kingdoms. Yet the claims were made boldly, and not without plausibility in retrospect. The three major faiths who trace their origins back to Abraham have spread over the entire globe and are known even where they are not practiced. Now, more than 4,000 years after Abraham lived and died, they number about 3.5 billion (2.1 billion Christians, 1.3 billion Muslims, 14 million Jews, plus other biblical offshoots), or about 55 percent of the world's population and still growing, with no sign of letting up.*

But beyond sheer numbers, the biblical story of Abraham has an even greater significance. The claims about the singularity of Abraham and his offspring perform an important function for those of us in the modern West, by stopping us from thinking that all history is merely a question of abstract, classifiable types. Abraham is a particular person, his progeny a specific group of peoples, and in the biblical vision truth passes by way of particular persons. When we speak of the value of the individual, of the unrepeatable uniqueness of each of our lives in this world, of the larger meaning of history, we are—whether we know it or not—invoking something like the Bible's special sense of particularity in human life and the deep significance of time, which found expression nowhere to the same degree in the classical world or the ancient Near East.

We saw how Virgil made similarly strange claims for Rome, but also that he, at least, could point to several centuries of continuous growth in Roman power and influence. Some scholars have argued that, owing to his

---

*The American novelist Walker Percy captures the strangeness of this singularity in the form of a question and an answer:

Where are the Hittites?

Why does no one find it remarkable that in most world cities today there are Jews but not one single Hittite, even though the Hittites had a great flourishing civilization while the Jews nearby were a weak and obscure people?

When one meets a Jew in New York or New Orleans or Paris or Melbourne, it is remarkable that no one considers the event remarkable. What are they doing here? But it is even more remarkable to wonder, if there are Jews here, why are there not Hittites here?

Where are the Hittites? Show me one Hittite in New York City.

curiosity about religions and his poetic intuitions about the possibility of a true meaning and direction in history, Virgil may have read the Old Testament in the Greek Septuagint translation made at Alexandria in the centuries before he lived. There were numbers of Jews in ancient Rome and some such cross-fertilization of cultures could have taken place at that point. We know, for example, that a certain "Longinus," who seems to be writing in the context of Virgil's Augustan Rome, refers to Moses and Genesis as examples of literary sublimity:

> the lawgiver of the Jews, no ordinary man, having formed a worthy conception of divine power, gave expression to it at the very threshold of his *Laws* [i.e., the five books of the Pentateuch] where he says: "God said"—what? "'Let there be light,' and there was light. 'Let there be earth,' and there was earth."[1]

It is difficult to believe that a relatively obscure writer would know of the Bible and the greatest of the Roman poets would not. It would be equally difficult otherwise to account for Virgil's almost biblical sense of a salvation history present in the world, specifically in Rome's ascendance. But however the confluence may have come about—through literary influence or the subsequent rise of Christianity to dominance within the empire—two millennia of familiarity with these ideas in the West have made them so common that we need to appreciate how truly revolutionary they were and their particular contributions to subsequent Western developments. It is worth looking a little more closely at what those contributions were.

Jewish Ideas of Creation

A prominent scholar of Genesis has argued that "the Old Testament Jews were probably among the least speculative people known to history."[2] This is true if we understand its proper meaning. Clearly, philosophy of the kind that emerged in ancient Greece and that has persisted in the West ever since, with various ups and downs, did not exist among the ancient Hebrews. "Jewish earthiness," we are often reminded, shapes even their religious notions. For some people in the ancient world and even today, this means that the Creation accounts in Genesis are to be classified with the cosmological myths of the Babylonians or similar creation stories in other cultures around the world. Some elements in the Bible's Creation account may indeed have that "mythological" character. But an unprejudiced reader—and there were many such readers even among the ancient Greeks and Romans—might also be struck with the way that the sweeping account of Creation in the Bible reaches in one leap the point (and perhaps further) that philosophical geniuses like Plato and Aristotle were able to discover only after considerable labors.

During the early years of modern science, it seemed more and more that the Genesis account could not be true. Indeed, one of the constant bones of contention from the seventeenth to the twentieth century took the form of debates over the size, evolution, nature, and age of the world (4,000+ years in a literal interpretation of Genesis; around 15 billion years since the Big Bang according to scientific observations). Rightly understood, there is no insurmountable conflict here. Genesis was not intended as a scientific account of Creation in six 24-hour days, and even describes, after its own nonscientific fashion, an evolution from primordial light to the creation of humankind. A modern scientist looking at the physics of the early universe and the late appearance of man in cosmic development might allow for a rough correspondence, despite the fact that Genesis was written with nonscientific purposes in mind.

What were those purposes? To begin with, Genesis sets out deliberately to deny the mythological creation stories we associate with Babylon and ancient Egypt. In those common accounts, the gods themselves, as is the case with the gods of classical Greek and Roman mythology, are powerful and immortal persons, but they are part of the world—superhuman in the sense that they are stronger and not subject to death, yet almost human in their motivations and conflicts. The world already exists prior to any action by them. They may give order or shape to that world—typically, they are identified with some part of it like the sea or sky—but they are not "creators" in the Bible's sense of that term. Genesis simply bypasses these stories and posits a very different kind of being at the beginning of all things. God willed to create the world, and it came into existence. It is good, because he is good and can only do good.

What he made is wonderful, but is not, as among many ancient peoples, to be worshiped or held as sacred except insofar as it was his work. Those striking celestial lights the sun and moon, for example, were almost universally represented as important gods in all mythological systems. The planets, even in the more elaborate philosophical speculations, were often represented as gods themselves.* This is why our solar system is populated by spheres with the names Mercury, Venus, Mars, Jupiter, Saturn, Neptune, and Pluto. The Babylonians, whom the Israelites knew intimately, also regarded the seven planets as seven main gods. All these gods were thought of as having mighty influences on the earth and were the subject of devotional cults. Unless we keep this in mind, we will not appreciate the passage in Genesis, so familiar to us, that in a few words sweeps away what the ancients regarded as religion: "God made the two great lights, the greater light to rule the day and the smaller one to rule the night, and he made the stars. / God set them in the firmament of the heavens to shed light upon the earth, / to rule the day and the night and to separate the light from the darkness. God saw that it was good. / And there was evening and morning on the fourth day." (Genesis 1:16-19)

For the ancient Middle East, this way of referring to "the two great lights" in the heavens, almost as if they were merely torches or lamps, must have been shocking. Even the names "sun" and "moon" are absent, perhaps because they would have implied some sort of divinity. The Sun would remain an Egyptian god for centuries, and Helios was worshiped as a Greek divinity along with Gaia (Earth) and Oceanus. Not only did the Hebrew Creation story deny all this, it undercut many other superstitions as well. Astrology, at least in the sense of the influence of celestial gods on the earth, found no basis in God's Creation and the very notion of time was transformed: "All ancient Oriental (not Old Testament!) thinking with regard to time was determined by the cyclical course of the stars."[3] The biblical notion of the coming into being of the world gives time a direction and a special status

*"Planet" is derived from a Greek word meaning "wanderer," because the ancients could see that the planets did not move in lockstep with the "fixed" stars.

that was absent in Greece and Mesopotamia: the Hebrew verb *bārā* is used only of this initial creation, including the creation of living things, especially man.

This hints at a more direct relationship between God and humans than may be found in the surrounding cultures as well. Indeed, the description of man as created in God's "image and likeness" is unique in the Bible. Nowhere in the Bible is anything else described as the image and likeness of anything else.[4] What this image and likeness means is left unexplained, but at the very least it means "that man is entirely apart from the rest of visible creation." Man does not resemble God bodily here, as some have claimed, since God is not represented in bodily form in the Old Testament. Man himself had been mythologized in the Middle Eastern systems, with sex between man and woman represented as a cosmic marriage, *hieros gamos* in Greek. The way God creates male and female in Genesis both demythologizes and tames sex, but also exalts it in what we now think of as a more human way.[5] The implication in Genesis is that the "divine" resemblance consists in the special status and dignity of human beings—something that was starkly different from the position of men in Greek mythologies—which involves the human capacity to know the difference between good and evil and to act freely in ways that matter. Finally, the created world in Genesis is not a fall from some metaphysical fullness, but "completely perfect" as is. This would become an important bulwark against the various philosophies and religious systems that would claim from ancient times down to the present that life in this world is intrinsically imperfect if not outright evil. In the biblical vision, we are meant to live in this world, not to escape or despise it, though things went quite wrong quite fast in human history.

As a modern biblical scholar has characterized the Creation account in Genesis: "To write out these thirty-five verses, Israel's faith required centuries of carefully collected reflection. . . . The final form of the material as we have it may date from the exile, but its roots and beginnings certainly lie hidden in the bosom of the oldest Yahweh community." The upshot of this story is simply that there are no other gods, nor does chaos, mythologized or in a naturalistic sense, have any power of its own (Chaos and Night were basic forces in many ancient cosmologies). The world is the orderly, nondivine creation of a good God. Human beings, as will later become clear, may investigate this nature because it is not a sacred realm beyond human understanding. Human beings depend upon this creation and care for it, almost like gardeners. But at the same time, because they are made in the image and likeness of the Creator, they transcend nature and differ from it: "The simplest consequence of this statement is that man, therefore, cannot seek his direct relation to God in the world, in the realm of nature." Nature, for all its God-given importance, just does not partake of the same dignity and complexity as does human nature.[6]

This solves a problem that Plato would raise later in *The Laws:* the "materialism" of the Ionian physicists may be accurate as a description of how matter behaves, but matter—to use a term that would have been too abstract for the ancient Hebrews—is the work of and in some sense remains permeated by the wisdom of the Creator. It is worth mentioning here that a claim often made by environmentalists about Judaism and Christianity—that in desacralizing the world and exalting man they led to environmental destruction—is largely false. To begin with, even cultures that believed nature was sacred unwittingly harmed it. The biblical view is that the world is not sacred in the sense that the ancients and many of our contemporaries would give that word. It is a creation and deserves our respect, care, and love because it comes from the Creator. Many truths and powers are built into it, which the human race can discover and use for its own good purposes. The view of the Creation as mere matter and energy to be shaped however human beings will is the result of a modern project that changed desacralized Creation into a rough analogy with the dead nature that Plato feared.[7]

The Hebrew Creation, though it posited a nondivine realm created by the one God, did away with the multiple gods without entirely eliminating goodness, beauty, and truth in the process—because at the same time, it asserted a universal sovereignty of the one God over everything he had made at a time when that kind of divine providence remained confused, even in Greek thinking. It was a bold move and not without potentially significant drawbacks, for as anyone with any intelligence knows, the world as we experience it is hardly "good" in any simple sense. Accidents kill us, epidemics decimate entire continents, natural disasters wipe out whole civilizations, children die young and innocent. It may be, as has been argued throughout history, that the Creator wills these things because of evils we have committed. Greek and Hebrew thought sometimes converged on that explanation. But it is a hard saying because so much seems to escape us in this "explanation." The book of Job rejects any pretense of explaining anything directly, only showing that Job, despite the comments by his friends, was a blameless man who was tried for reasons obscure to us. And the only wisdom in such circumstances is Job's: "The Lord giveth and the Lord taketh away. Blessed be the name of the Lord."

Ancient Greece and Nature

The contrast between Jewish views of the world and those of others becomes even more striking when we turn to one of the other primary sources for Western culture: the ancient Greeks. Nature was variously explained among Greek thinkers. But this very term "nature," *phusis*, a kind of growth (plants are *phytes* in Greek), begins to show us the difference. The Hebrews had no word for nature. When the writer of Genesis wants to refer to the creation of everything that is, he says that God made "heaven and earth." The difference may, at first, seem small, but it reflects two kinds of genius: the Greeks with their stunning ability for abstract conceptualization; the Jews with their capacity to express the most breathtaking notions in concrete terms.

Genesis was given final form at around the same time, during the Babylonian Captivity (586–538 B.C.), when Thales (624–545) and Anaximenes (585–525) were trying out various scientific hypotheses about the origins of the world in Greek Ionia. These hypotheses were destined to fail, because, as Dietrich Bonhoeffer says in his own commentary on Genesis, "No one can speak of the beginning but the one who was in the beginning."[8] The ancient Hebrews made the daring claim that the one who was present at the beginning had told them what he did. And what he did in the beginning had ongoing consequences. Indeed, when Job and his friends famously tried to understand the nature of his suffering, they found that they came up against an inescapable human limit: "Where were you when I laid the foundations of the world?" (Job 38:4) Whatever stance we may choose to take towards the claims being made about Creation at the very beginning of the Bible—and it is good to remind ourselves constantly that they are not scientific claims—there is no question that this account of origins has changed the face not only of the West but of the world: "The Bible has itself created worlds. Wherever you stand on the spectrum from devout to atheist, you must acknowledge that the Bible has been a creative force without parallel in history."[9] It not only created the vast worlds of Judaism, Christianity, and Islam, it transformed our sense of the whole universe.

Take even something that seems to us wholly natural: time. For us in the West, time is linear and history is an unfolding event. This way of looking at the world is so ingrained in us that it is difficult to realize that for most of the human race for most of its existence, this view ran counter to common sense or, even worse, threatened the presumed order of the world. Most modern Westerners who have some sense of this difference know that, say, in the East, Hinduism and Buddhism have ideas that time or human existence are cyclical, participating in the Great Wheel of Life. Buddhism seems more concerned with the cyclical birth-death-rebirth of the reincarnated soul, whose task is to practice detachment and ultimate freedom from rebirth. In Hinduism, the universe itself goes through a long cycle of ages in which it comes to be, is destroyed, and is reborn again. Before the voyages of Columbus, there were similar beliefs among the Maya and Aztecs in what we today call Central America and Mexico.

Premodern human beings who were in touch with the rhythms of the world and other natural phenomena naturally gravitated towards these or similar views. The birth-death-rebirth of plants during the year provided a model that was taken up in many ancient religions in Egypt, the ancient Near East, and among the Greeks and Romans, just to select the most familiar examples. It is difficult to try to reconstruct the psychology of those peoples (it is not always easy even to see our own large assumptions), but it probably is not too much of a stretch to say that the pattern they discerned—and held to—was a comfort against what otherwise seemed like chaos on earth. The night sky with its "army of unalterable law," as a poet in the nineteenth century could still put it, was another natural image of something beautiful and pure that rose above the threats and changes of earthly existence. For many people even today, gazing on the night sky gives a sense of a transcendent and divine order vastly greater than ourselves, which is nowhere else to be found. The regular movements of heavenly bodies, the wanderings of the planets notwithstanding, also suggested a cyclical motion in nature that could be observed, admired—and imitated. Human life and human societies were deliberately patterned on the unchanging cycles of the cosmos.

One thing we see in the whole story of Israel is that for the biblical God, who made the heavens and the earth, cycles and the stability they brought to pagan religion are not the most important thing. The whole history—a significant term in this context—of the Jewish people showed that the process of history itself from Adam and Eve to Abraham through the Patriarchs to Moses and the Twelve Tribes had a meaning that cut across times and seasons. Jews, of course, like all other ancient (and not a few modern) peoples, had their harvest festivals and celebrations at recurring and specific times of the year. But the mere repetition of a pattern, however familiar and soothing, was not the point of their particular story. Time in this perspective was one of the dimensions that revealed something beyond all times and seasons.

This establishes a difference with other cultures. The Greek writer Herodotus, for example, is often called the "father of history" because he set down the first account that we possess of some of the main events that occurred among the Greek peoples. But the very word he used to describe his own work, *Historia*, denotes something like "investigations." What this means is that "history" in the classical world was typically not what we understand by the term. Herodotus himself is full of anecdotes; other classical histories are more like chronicles or illustrations of cyclical theories. History proper, as we think of it—i.e., the progressive unfolding of human realities over time—was a dangerous departure from the patterned world for most ancient peoples. Within the pattern, things could be understood and predicted as they went through their appointed cycles. Outside the pattern was primeval chaos, a fearful and anxious realm to be avoided at all cost. So even when we see things that we might describe as incipient histories in the annals of the ancient world, they are not real history—history as time having a meaning in its directionality and irreversibility—as it would come to be understood in cultures permeated by the Hebrew and, later, Christian views of the world.[10]

It took a long time for the consequences of the biblical view to make themselves fully felt. In fact, we have to say candidly that it was the most recent discoveries of modern science itself that confirmed the religious intuitions about linear time that first arose with Abraham and his journey from Ur of the Chaldees. In many ways, the slow emergence of the consequences of such truths was to be expected. Christians and Jews still lived a life that largely followed the pattern of the seasons, even if both of them expected God to lead them through history towards a fulfillment in the end times. One of the reasons that notions of progress and science and technology may have emerged in the West is precisely because this unique religious underpinning allowed for a different view of the significance of time and did not see the unfolding of new things as a threat to some pre-established order. It is much easier to accept novelty and change, indeed to pursue them consciously, if you also believe that the Creator goes with you on every path, as readers of the Bible in all ages believed. Indeed, such unprecedented developments are called for by the biblical idea of sacred history. God himself says so openly: "I will lead the blind by a path they do not know, By paths they have not known I will guide them. . . . I will not forsake them." (Isaiah 42:16) Closely connected with this concept of linear time that has a special, indeed cosmic, significance are several classical Jewish notions: covenant and exodus, chosen people and promised land. These ideas, which seem for many people to be merely sectarian religious categories, would also have immense effects in the West and in the history of the entire world.

Each of these, of course, is clear enough in the immediate biblical context. God is, from the beginning, steadfast in his love for the human race, which he created in his own image and likeness. Adam and Eve are expelled from the Garden of Eden for their disobedience, but hope is held out to them for the distant future, when God will heal the rift between the human race and himself. Even when growing and spreading sin leads God to destroy much of the human race in the Flood, he remains in solidarity with Noah and the surviving remnant in an early and personal form of covenant (Genesis 6:18–22). Later, at a crucial point (Genesis 17:10–14), circumcision becomes the sign of the covenant not only between God and Abraham (here called "the father of nations"), but between God and Abraham's descendants, with the further stipulation that they will be his chosen people in the Promised Land of Canaan, their permanent possession. In a sense, the entirety of the Old Testament, its many books of differing literary forms, can be reduced to the subsequent history of Israel as it breaks the covenant with God, is led back, breaks it again, only to be forgiven and reunited once more under God's love, all on the way to an ultimate culmination at the end of time.

This view of history injected dynamic elements into Western societies. Breaking with God's covenant has consequences for the chosen people: they lose their own land and become slaves of others. One of the great Old Testament stories, of course, is the account of the Exodus of the Israelites from slavery in Egypt under the leadership of Moses. The Exodus became, in subsequent Western history, not merely a story from ancient times, but what biblical scholars call a *typos,* a template for future events. Thus, Jesus himself effects a kind of exodus in leading Christians out of sin to salvation. The early Christians saw themselves as enslaved by the whore of Babylon (i.e., Rome, Revelation 17) and sought escape to their heavenly home. Protestants later identified Catholic Rome with Babylon and sought their deliverance in a different kind of exodus. The Puritans who fled the king's persecution in seventeenth-century England arrived in America and consciously compared their freedom in the New World to the Promised Land. African slaves, for whom that same land bore more resemblance to Egypt under the pharaoh than the land of Canaan, sang Moses' own words, "Let

my people go." Mormons crossing the Great Salt Lake remembered the Israelites crossing the desert. And this is the merest beginning of a much
longer list of reformations, renaissances, liberations, renewals, restora-
tions—in the West and around the world—that take their form and meaning from an event in Jewish history. In the course of time, this played no
little role in the rise of modern democracy. When the Fundamental Orders
of Connecticut, the first modern democratic constitution, were written in
1638, they did not refer to Greece, Rome, John Locke's works (he was only
six years old at the time), the Enlightenment (a century in the future), or
any of the other commonly cited sources for the idea. They were inspired
by Thomas Hooker, a preacher, who pointed out to the Hartford general as-
sembly God's commandment in Deuteronomy that, having left Egypt and
now being about to enter the Promised Land, the Israelites choose their
own judges. It was an old idea that with new additions would flower in various ways. References to the Jewish Exodus as parallel to the American situation were frequent in the writings of the American Founders over the
next two centuries.

The God of Love

Amid these large-scale public events and the social dynamism they began
to impart, there is another new element introduced by the Bible into human life as well: love—of God for man and, in some ways more surprisingly,
of man for God. There are moments of sincere love of one god or another in
the classical world, especially in popular religion, but the old Homeric pantheon of gods with little love for men and only sporadic interest in their lives
colors the whole. Aristotle, or one of his close followers, writing in the *Magna moralia* gives his considered opinion that love between men and Zeus is
impossible: "Men fancy that friendship (*philia*) for God is possible. . . . But
they are mistaken. Friendship as we define it exists only where friendly affection is returned. But the so-called friendship for God (*philein ton Dia*) admits
of no such return, not even of affection on our part; since it were an absurdity for a man to profess a friend's affection for Zeus."[11] This may be merely
an expression of the correct perception that there is an immense distance

between God and mortals, and that the relationship cannot be treated casually, as we do with human friends.*

But that said, there is nothing in the classics like the passionate expressions of love for God in the Bible. There is a Greek Hymn to Zeus by the Stoic Cleanthes (331–223 B.C.), but anyone who comes to it from the Bible will feel it is rather cool flattery addressed to a powerful monarch. By contrast, if we dip into the Psalms almost at random, we find passages like these: "As the deer longs for streams of water, so my soul longs for you, O God." (Psalm 44) Or even this (Psalm 63):

> O God, you are my God, for you I long;
>
> for you my soul is thirsting.
>
> My body pines for you
>
> like a dry weary land without water.
>
> So I gaze on you in the sanctuary
>
> to see your strength and your glory.
>
> For your love is better than life,
>
> my lips will speak your praise.
>
> So I will bless you all my life,
>
> in your name I will lift up my hands.
>
> My soul shall be filled as a banquet,
>
> my mouth shall praise you with joy.
>
> On my bed I remember you.
>
> On you I muse through the night.
>
> For you have been my help;
>
> in the shadow of your wings I rejoice.
>
> My soul clings to you;
>
> your right hand holds me fast.

Compared with the Greeks and the Romans, the Jews passionately loved their God. And the love was returned.

The prophets vehemently denounce evils among the Israelites precisely

---

* But compare Jesus, too: "No one has greater love than this, to lay down one's life for one's friends. You are my friends if you do what I command you. I no longer call you slaves, because a slave does not know what his master is doing. I have called you friends, because I have told you everything I have heard from my Father." (John 15:13–16).

because the beloved is betrayed when we mistreat the people whom he loves. When the prophets turn around and describe what the reconciliation will be like, they use quite fervent terms (Isaiah 62:2–5):

> Nations shall behold your vindication, and all kings your glory; You shall be called by a new name pronounced by the mouth of the Lord. You shall be a glorious crown in the hand of the Lord, a royal diadem held by your God. No more shall men call you "Forsaken," or your land "Desolate," but you shall be called "My Delight," and your land "Espoused." For the Lord delights in you, and makes your land his spouse. As a young man marries a virgin, your Builder shall marry you; And as a bridegroom rejoices in his bride so shall your God rejoice in you.

Believers used to get uncomfortable over these frankly sexual comparisons, or when they were informed that the passionate Song of Songs was really a secular love poem that they were misreading as an allegory of God and the soul. But the compilers of the Bible were not any more naive than we are, and they included it precisely because it provided a kind of range-finding for the passion with which God and man should love. It was the early modern scholarly and debunking reading that was naive in this case.

Jew and Greek

Hebrew and Greek notions were eventually to flow into one another. To understand how this happened, we have to dip into some lesser-know pathways of history. The leading Jews in Israel were captured and sent into exile by the Babylonian king Nebuchadnezzar in 597 B.C. In 587, the Babylonian army destroyed Jerusalem and most of the remaining Hebrews followed their leaders into exile. But in the tumultuous politics of the Middle East at the time, this situation did not last long. In 539, the Persian king Cyrus invaded Babylon and allowed the Jews, who had retained their faith in captivity, to return to Jerusalem. This was no small consolation for a people whose identity was tightly bound to the belief that Abraham and Moses had been directed by God to bring his people into Israel. The Temple that Solomon had built almost a half millennium earlier had been destroyed. The people who returned from exile began to rebuild it.

Yet a majority of the Jews who had gone into exile did not return. Some stayed in Babylon, which became one of the important centers, religiously and intellectually, of the Jewish Diaspora. Another large wave of Diaspora Judaism began with the conquests of Alexander the Great in the Middle East. These conquests, as we have seen, were not long lasting, but Hellenistic Greek culture spread from the Mediterranean to India within fifteen years and permanently influenced much of that territory, including Israel, for centuries to come. A highly important Jewish community also arose in Alexandria, the city that Alexander founded and named after himself in Egypt. Alexandria became an intellectual center for Greco-Roman civilization because of the Mouseion, the research institute there, and the fabled library of Alexandria assembled for the sake of those who studied in the Mouseion.

These developments had substantial effects on Jewish culture as well. It was in Alexandria around the middle of the third century B.C. that the Pentateuch, the first five books of the Bible, was translated into Greek so that, in theory, it could be read by any person educated in the lingua franca of Hellenistic civilization. Translations of the Prophets and the Psalms appeared in the next century, and the Wisdom Books in the century after that. This translation is called the Septuagint because seventy translators, legend has it, were commissioned by the Greek king of Egypt, Ptolemy II. Translating the Bible from the Hebrew meant more than simply turning a text into another language. The vocabulary that the Greeks had developed in their philosophical speculations needed to be adapted to express very different concepts, some of which did not even exist in the Greco-Roman civilization. And the traffic was not all in one direction. Greek concepts, which were familiar to educated Jews simply by their living in a Hellenistic culture, inevitably began to influence Jewish thinking as well.

After Alexander's death in 323, his vast empire was carved up by his former generals and advisers. Two of the relatively stable dynasties that were to emerge from this process were the Seleucids, whose capital, Antioch, was located in what we call Syria today, and the Ptolemies in Egypt. While there were continuing wars against rivals and movements of resistance to their political control, there was little opposition to the

Hellenistic culture that both dynasties continued to promote among the various peoples of the East. For those peoples, as for the Romans later, the Greek tradition seemed almost synonymous with high culture itself, even if local conditions colored the expression of that culture in the various Greek-style cities that were set up everywhere.

Judaism could use many Greek elements for its own purposes. And in Alexandria under the Ptolemies during the third century B.C. and later, as we shall see below, that is largely what happened. The Ptolemies controlled Palestine in the third century, but the rival Seleucids replaced them in 198 B.C., and before long they shifted to an aggressive Hellenization policy. In the ancient homeland of the Jewish people, a struggle arose not only between Seleucid forces and Jews over the attempt to Hellenize Jewish customs and beliefs, but even between one group of Jews and another. This whole struggle is recorded from a Jewish perspective in texts called the Books of Maccabees, which are included in Catholic and Orthodox versions of the Old Testament (Jewish authorities later excluded these texts from the Hebrew scriptures and Reformation Protestants classified them as "deutero-canonical"). What is clear from the history, whether it is thought of as formally part of the Bible or not, is that Jews in Palestine were gripped by a struggle for identity and fidelity to their beliefs, especially over the question of whether they would preserve Jewishness as a distinct way of life amid the general advance of Hellenistic city culture in the Middle East.

Some of them, by no means a negligible or uninfluential segment, thought Greek ways could be integrated with Jewish ways. In the second century B.C., astonishingly, there are even high priests of the Temple in Jerusalem with obviously Greek names such as Jason, Menelaus, and Linus, and they seemed quite content to cooperate with the Seleucid effort to turn Jerusalem into a Greek city with the name Antiochia. Greek gymnasiums appeared, where young Jewish aristocrats exercised naked and learned to regard circumcision as a disfigurement. Athletic games were organized that were associated, as they had been since time immemorial in the Greek homeland, with pagan gods. All of these developments contributed to a general sense that the old Jewish beliefs and practices were primitive and crude, while the newly introduced Greek forms were very modern and chic.

Yet even these changes might have been tolerated by the Jewish people in Palestine, who had not been free for almost two centuries, if Antiochus IV—called Epiphanes because he wished to encourage a religious cult of his rule as a manifestation ("epiphany") of divinity—had not desecrated the Temple. His forces took possession of it, carried off many of its sacred objects, raised an altar to Zeus, and ordered Jewish priests to teach that Zeus was the same as the God of the Jews. The old beliefs were declared illegal, and continued practice of them would be prosecuted as treason. This meant the Sabbath could not be observed, circumcision was outlawed, and Jewish kosher rules were suspended. Seleucid troops brutally killed resisters, including babies and old people from rebel families. The Hellenized Jews who cooperated with the Seleucids—and under the circumstances, the temptation to do so must have been quite strong—were given positions of prominence and protected by the citadel that had been erected in Jerusalem.

From 169 to 164 B.C., the Seleucids controlled the Temple. But two forms of resistance emerged. The Hasidim ("devout ones") offered nonviolence, while the Maccabeans engaged in armed resistance. One of the Hasidim at the time wrote the book of Daniel, whose subject, on the surface, is persecution during the Babylonian Captivity four hundred years earlier. But the book of Daniel is clearly intended as a veiled commentary on current problems and the ultimate triumph and return of the God of Israel, who justly judges the whole world. Not only will Israel be restored, says the author, the dead will be raised again in triumph: "Many of those who sleep in the dust of the earth shall awake; some shall live forever, others shall be an everlasting horror and disgrace." (Daniel 12:2) Daniel's miraculous survival in the lions' den and with his companions in the fiery furnace is a symbolic expression of the indestructibility of faithful resistance. (After his conversion to Christianity, Saint Paul would use some of this material to suggest the mystery of God's providential plan unfolding in history.)

All this might be thought of as a prophetic, nonviolent resistance to the unity of city and religion that was typical of the classical world. The other form of Jewish resistance to forced paganization was straightforward warfare. The Seleucid persecution drove all faithful Jews out of Jerusalem. In the countryside, which had been less affected by Hellenization and had remained more traditional, rebel Jewish forces organized under the leadership of Judas Maccabeus, the son of Mattathias, a faithful priest. The Syrian armies were unable to defeat this indigenous force—indeed, they suffered heavy casualties, and Antiochus' advisers convinced him to abandon his policy of forced conversion. But the revolt could not be stopped by that point. Jewish forces retook Jerusalem, including the Temple, in December of 164 B.C. and ritually purified it. A new feast arose as a result, Hanukkah, which means "Dedication" (or "Feast of Lights" in another interpretation). Judas Maccabeus died as he pursued the Syrians in other battles, but his brothers Jonathan and Simon carried on the fight until the Jews were able to achieve a measure of independence under their own rulers, the Hasmoneans, who remained in power until the Roman general Pompey took control of the Middle East in 63 B.C. and included Jewish territories in the new Roman province of Syria.

Some of this history may have been idealized in the Bible to cover over what may also have been political motivations. In fact, it would be surprising if there were not several motives at play in this resistance to the Seleucids. But that should not detract from the fact that the Jews were doing something here that almost no ancient people ever did—deciding to die for theological principles in opposition to the gods of the city. This comes through very beautifully in the gentle story about Eleazar in 2 Maccabees:

> Eleazar, one of the foremost scribes, a man of advanced age and noble appearance, was being forced to open his mouth to eat pork. But preferring a glorious death to a life of defilement, he spat out the meat, and went forward of his own accord to the instrument of torture, as men ought to do who have the courage to reject the food which it is unlawful to taste even for love of life. Those in charge of that unlawful ritual meal took the man aside privately, because of their long acquaintance with him, and urged him to bring meat of his own providing, such as he could legitimately eat, and to pretend to be eating some of the meat

of the sacrifice prescribed by the king; in this way he would escape the death penalty, and be treated kindly because of their old friendship with him.

But he made up his mind in a noble manner, worthy of his years, the dignity of his advanced age, the merited distinction of his gray hair, and of the admirable life he had lived from childhood; and so he declared that above all he would be loyal to the holy laws given by God. He told them to send him at once to the abode of the dead, explaining: "At our age it would be unbecoming to make such a pretense; many young men would think the ninety-year-old Eleazar had gone over to an alien religion. Should I thus dissimulate for the sake of a brief moment of life, they would be led astray by me, while I would bring shame and dishonor on my old age. Even if, for the time being, I avoid the punishment of men, I shall never, whether alive or dead, escape the hands of the Almighty. Therefore, by manfully giving up my life now, I will prove myself worthy of my old age, and I will leave to the young a noble example of how to die willingly and generously for the revered and holy laws." He spoke thus, and went immediately to the instrument of torture. . . . When he was about to die under the blows, he groaned and said: "The Lord in his holy knowledge knows full well that, although I could have escaped death, I am not only enduring terrible pain in my body from this scourging, but also suffering it with joy in my soul because of my devotion to him."

Some people at the time and since have thought of this kind of fidelity as fanaticism. (The same charge was made against the Christians killed in the Colosseum for essentially similar reasons.) But we see here a principled conviction, based in the Bible, that religious truths are important in a way that they were not thought to be in the relatively low-key and nontheological devotions to the Greek Olympians or the Roman household gods. Socrates may have been a martyr for truth, but he was not a martyr for religious faith.

Something new has entered the Western orbit here, capable of producing fanaticism but also capable of inspiring great deeds in the hearts and minds of millions in the face of all political pressures. As a distinguished historian of the period has written:

> In one crucial sense . . . the Jews were different from those other nation-
> al groups: they were not only unassimilated, they were unassimilable.
> . . . To live the life of the *polites* [citizen] meant to worship the gods of the
> *polis* [city], something the Jew was forbidden to do by a fundamental
> principle of his own *politeia* [system of government], the Mosaic Law.
> . . . Neither the Christian nor the Jewish intellectual had any difficul-
> ty making identification between his God and the gods of the Hellenes
> within the spacious confines of philosophy and in the approved Greek
> manner; but offer sacrifice he could not and would not do.[12]

Jews and Christians alike would come to share a history of persecution by paganism and, therefore, of critical distance from political power that echoes throughout Western history, even when the political forces had accepted biblical faith.

Philosophical Judaism

In the meantime, Jewish groups of various kinds made good use of Greek philosophical ideas such as body and soul, but for different ends than the philosophers had intended. The culmination of this difficult and dynamic balancing act came with the Jewish philosopher Philo of Alexandria (ca. 20 B.C.–50 A.D.). Philo was highly regarded in practical as well as philosophical questions: the Jews of Alexandria sent him to Rome at one point as their ambassador to the threatening emperor Caligula. In the sophisticated intellectual world of ancient Alexandria, the stories of the pagan gods were often treated as philosophical allegories anyway. Philo would use the same method to interpret certain biblical stories, but in keeping with the Jewish notion of history as not merely a meaningless passage of time with no intellectual importance, he also strove to preserve what today we call the literal sense of the text. He might find rough analogs to Plato or Aristotle in Genesis, but he, like other Jews, did not simply treat Jewish history as something that could be dispensed with once abstract truths were extracted from biblical narratives. Indeed, the philosophical concepts were, in Philo, submitted to the judgment of theological and moral principles with the final aim of reconciling philosophy with Jewish Law.

Philo went quite far in bringing the mixture of Platonism and Stoicism common to his age into close correspondence with Jewish thought. For him, Moses had received a revelation of the "pure being" of the Greek philosophers when God told him his name, "I AM" (Exodus 3:14). Philo believed that Pythagoras and other prominent Greek thinkers must have studied Moses, since the Jewish leader had lived and realized the truth centuries before them. The Neoplatonism of Philo's time had already been working in the direction of a transcendent God who was variously characterized as pure being or personal. Writing in one of the most sophisticated cities of the ancient world at a time when Neoplatonism was developing a system that acknowledged the One as the primary reality and regarded the traditional gods almost like angels or lesser servants of the One, Philo created a powerful synthesis of traditional Judaism and Platonism that would influence Jews, pagans, and Christians alike.[13]

He was not alone in this effort, though the destruction of Palestine and the Temple by the Romans shortly after Philo's death drove Jews within the Roman Empire into a defensive position. Vigorous dialogue with pagan thought passed to a new community built on Jewish foundations, the Christian Church. Contrary to modern prejudices that believers in revelation neglected reason, Justin Martyr, Clement of Alexandria, Origen, and especially Saint Augustine among the Christians participated in this same Platonist current, with different emphases.[14] But the Church as an institution that resisted assimilation into the Roman state, much as the Jewish people had, was to have an incalculable effect on the future of the West. Even when the empire became officially Christian, the parallel moral authority of the bishops and their collaborators introduced a new element that had existed neither in Greece nor in Rome—a structure of belief and moral reflection that could become independent, indeed opposed to the political structure. This would lead to a different social organization in Late Antiquity and subsequent ages in the West, with multiple distinct centers of power, which both corrected the purely political and opened up possibilities of liberty from it in an entirely new space.

CHAPTER 4

Christian Paradoxes

> Most people are unable to follow any demonstra-
> tive argument consecutively; hence they need
> parables, and benefit from them just as we now
> see the people called Christian drawing their
> faith from parables and miracles, and yet some-
> times acting in the same way as those who prac-
> tice philosophy. For their contempt of death and
> of its sequel is patent to us every day, and likewise
> their restraint in cohabitation. For they include
> not only men but also women who refrain from
> cohabiting through all their lives; and they also
> number individuals who, in self-discipline and
> self-control in matters of food and drink, and in
> their keen pursuit of justice, have attained a pitch
> not inferior to that of genuine philosophers.
>
> Galen the Physician[1]

> The impious Galileans support not only their
> poor, but ours as well, everyone can see that our
> people lack aid from us.
>
> Julian the Apostate, Emperor[2]

LIKE Judaism, Christianity is so familiar to us—or at least we think it
is—that in seeking to understand it, we might do better to treat it as
some strange cult that we have come on for the first time. (Some people in
the West are now born into families so distant from the biblical religions that
this is the very experience they have.) We might then come to appreciate the
sheer improbability of the rapid spread and wide influence of an initially
tiny offshoot of Judaism over the extensive areas controlled by the mighty
Roman Empire. All the religions of "the Book" seem to show similar
singularities. Judaism persisted, as we have seen in the previous chapter,

over millennia against all odds. In the seventh century, Islam spread from the Middle East across North Africa and into Spain within about seventy years of Mohammed's death. In merely human terms, such events were highly improbable and they mystified people who encountered them and thought about them. But in another way, they reveal something about human nature to which mere rational calculation is simply blind. As the old pagans used to say, *Veritas filia temporis.*

The two figures quoted at the beginning of the present chapter belonged to that group of mystified observers. Galen, the famous physician of the second century A.D., was a man of science and reason, and deeply suspicious of anything that smacked of faith or superstition as the ancients understood it. He had no use for Christianity or any of the other religions in Rome around the same time. But Galen was also a keen observer of phenomena, and as a believer in the old classical virtues and the life of the true philosopher, he clearly expressed surprise that the Christians seemed able to instill virtues in unexpected places. Philosophy and the life of reason had always been regarded in antiquity as the preserve of a very few. The vast majority of people in every age are unsuited by nature and situation in life to philosophical pursuits. That was one reason why elites in Greece and Rome had a low opinion of the common people. Christianity showed early on its potential for reaching a wide and not always well-educated audience. In fact, that was precisely Nietzsche's objection to it in the introduction to *Beyond Good and Evil:* it was "Platonism for the masses."[3]

But to formulate the issue in Nietzsche's way is to see Christianity's main appeal as a kind of popular intellectual movement. There is no question that ideals and images, if not reasoning in the strict sense of the word, have a certain attraction for larger numbers of people than do the relatively abstract formulas of philosophers and theologians. The early Christian movement, however, appears to have had popular appeal both as an idea and because it demonstrated a public *goodness* (something Nietzsche did not have much use for either) that affected individual lives and the whole structure of Roman society. The Roman emperor Julian (331–363 A.D.), also quoted above, called "the Apostate" because he had grown up as a Christian and then abandoned the faith for a rabid polytheism, crafted one of the strongest early critiques of Christian beliefs and made great efforts to stop Christianity's growth as a social force in the empire. Yet Julian conceded, in a realistic appraisal of what he had to overcome, that the Christian churches were carrying out relief efforts among the poor, pagan as well as Christian, that the pagans themselves were not.

Julian—and the whole classical world—suffered two disadvantages in competing with the new faith. First, there was no substantial set of principles within classical religion and philosophy to inspire such charitable works. The Stoics had come closest with their conception of the entire world as one city, the *cosmopolis.* But by Julian's day, Platonism was the only real pagan philosophy still standing and even the old Stoic principle was a far cry from the active and lively sense of the universal brotherhood and sisterhood within the Kingdom of God that the Christians called *caritas.* Had such ideas been influential in pagan societies, they would not have faced a second problem: the absence of the social structures needed to implement large-scale works of charity. The empire and its municipalities sometimes provided a public dole. But love and empowerment of the common people is something quite different from a state subsidy. No ancient city, let alone the whole empire, had ever even attempted that. In the world of Late Antiquity, Christianity introduced not only new beliefs and ideas, but new social practices that transformed ancient Mediterranean life.

Faith and Practice

Our attitudes about religion, which is to say primarily Christianity, in the West are largely determined by one of two story lines. In the first, which is dominant today among Western elites, Christianity is viewed as a series of problems or outright evils: the intolerance of the Christian emperors imposing a state religion; the spread of faith over reason and the loss of classical civilization in the "Dark Ages"; the subsequent superstition or—at the other extreme—painful rationalism of the High Middle Ages; and the Crusades, Inquisitions, religious wars, sectarian squabbles, witch hunts, theological hairsplitting, empty doctrinal disputes, and mutual anathemas that fill many of the pages of anti-Christian and pro-Christian histories alike. To see this as the central thread of Western religion is to see Christianity as a dangerous element to be contained within secular political forms, perhaps even as an antihuman cancer to be excised for the sake of human health. In several parts of the world over the past few centuries, this attitude animated various murderous anti-Christian and antireligious regimes, Communists and socialists prominent among them.

The second story line is less familiar to cultivated people and poorly argued, on the whole, by Christians and others aware of the religion's benefits to the West. Where the ideological anti-Christians see a long tale of horrors, their pro-Christian counterparts discern the slow and painful triumph of a force for good—the patient witness of the early martyrs, the providential Pax Romana that allowed the new faith and the new social practices to spread, the rise of locally elected Christian bishops as a counterforce to the state, and then, after the breakup of the empire, the emergence of a church that preserved what it could from the wreck of the classical order amid the chaos of the new barbarian kingdoms. In the new circumstances, religious orders played a crucial role in gradually rebuilding even as they conserved. Benedictines and other monks copied classical and Christian manuscripts and Bibles, practiced farming, developed early industries, brewed beers, fermented wines. In the later Middle Ages, Franciscans and Dominicans gave new impetus to charitable work and the intellectual life, created hospitals, and taught in universities. Many of them participated in the missions that accompanied the Age of Exploration, and thereby cared for the new peoples the Europeans encountered, tried to protect them from exploitation, and eventually had a strong hand in the ending of slavery worldwide. The inevitable problems that arose over time were, in this perspective, not the central element but sinful deviations from a remarkable historical achievement.

The Ancient Engagement

Decades of Hollywood B-movies and poor Christian literature in churches have inclined us to discount portrayals of the conflict between Christianity and paganism as the persecution of simple believers by corrupt and cynical Romans. But for all their simplemindedness and melodrama, such portrayals are not entirely wrong. The anti-Christian argument of the past few centuries that presents the Christians as the corrupting, superstitious element and the Roman emperors as representatives of rational inquiry and old Roman virtue has simply not stood up to historical scrutiny. For example, in the eighteenth century, Edward Gibbon, thinking primarily of the very good and pious emperors that Rome enjoyed in the second century A.D. (Trajan, Hadrian, Antoninus Pius, and Marcus Aurelius, among others), claimed that Christianity "debased and vitiated the faculties of the mind" and "extinguished the hostile light of philosophy and science."[4] Similarly, in the nineteenth century, the influential French writer Ernest Renan argued: "Christianity was a vampire which sucked the life-blood of ancient society and produced that state of general enervation against which patriotic emperors struggled in vain."[5] Millions of people have accepted such arguments.

But Gibbon, who certainly knew better, deliberately ignored the many Christian intellectuals who arose early in the history of the faith and downplayed the anti-intellectual decay within the Greco-Roman world itself. Renan, who had not read or chose to ignore the judgments of pagans such as Galen and Julian, does not seem to have grasped the basic realities of Roman history. Rome went into moral and intellectual decline, as Greece had done, prior to the advent of Christianity. Plutocracy and the social problems to which it gave rise led to civil war and political chaos. With Augustus' and Virgil's vision of an ideal Rome, the empire experienced a remarkable, but brief, rebound until the death of the second emperor, Tiberius, in 37 A.D. The rest of the first century is dominated by Caligula, Nero, and a series of emperors elected by the army—in other words, by corruption and tyranny. It took no blood-sucking Christian vampires for the pagan Romans to achieve this all on their own.

In the second century, another period of relative order began thanks to a fortunate series of good men beginning with Nerva (96–98) and ending with Marcus Aurelius in 180, after which Rome fell once again into the hands of despots who imposed crushing taxation and regulation on the subject peoples of the provinces. Christianity was growing quietly and swiftly during this period despite persecution. As yet, however, it was no great social or intellectual force, and the moral turpitude and disorder that existed depended solely on pagan principles and powers. It is no wonder that a relatively unprejudiced observer such as Galen (131–201 A.D.) thought the Christians, who showed remarkable qualities amid the general social chaos and threats to their very existence, seemed to be instilling virtues in large numbers of people that neither pagan religion nor philosophy were capable of producing. In fact, when Rome fell in the fifth century, the "barbarians" who invaded were Christians whose faith seemed not to have sapped their martial virtues.

In the ancient world, however, some Romans began making the case early that Christianity was a superstition (*superstitio*). In Latin, *super-stitio* means a "standing over" or "standing above," which in the context suggested that the Christians stood outside or held themselves above the religious beliefs and practices that kept the empire together. In several respects, Christians suffered at the hands of the Romans under the same charges that had been made by the Athenians against Socrates: they did not believe in the gods the city believed in and, as a result, allegedly corrupted the people. In this, at least, the pagans were partly right because Christianity was a direct challenge to the classical religion and, as events were to prove, to the kind of order it supported. The stern Roman historian Tacitus (56–117 A.D.), who deplored the corruption of the old Roman ways (*mos maiorum*) long before any substantial Christian influence in the city, called the new religion a "deadly superstition" whose followers were "notoriously depraved."* The historian Suetonius repeated the charge ("a class of men given to a new and

---

*Tacitus explained how Nero had unintentionally given a boost to the Christians after a devastating fire in Rome during his reign: "neither human resources, nor imperial generosity, nor appeasement of the gods, eliminated the sinister suspicion that the fire had been deliberately started. To stop the rumor, Nero made scapegoats—and punished with every refinement the notoriously depraved Christians (as they were popularly called). Their originator, Christ, had been executed in Tiberius' reign by the Procurator of Judaea, Pontius Pilatus [governor from 26 to 36 A.D.]. But in spite of this temporary setback, the deadly superstition had broken out again, not just in Judaea (where the mischief had started) but even in Rome. All degraded and shameful practices collect and flourish in the capital. First, Nero had the self-admitted Christians arrested. Then, on their information, large numbers of others were condemned—not so much for starting fires as because of their hatred for the human race. Their deaths were made amusing. Dressed in wild animals' skins,

mischievous superstition"),[6] as did the Roman official Pliny ("a depraved superstition carried to extravagant lengths").

Pliny actually had to deal with a legal charge against Christians in Asia Minor while he was serving as the personal legate of the emperor Trajan, famous for his virtue and compassion. Pliny was approached by some citizens in the province of Bithynia-Pontus near the Black Sea, who perhaps complained that the Christians were upsetting local customs by refusing to worship the gods and not purchasing meat slaughtered in sacrifice. Christianity was illegal, but both Pliny and the emperor believed in a "don't ask/don't tell" policy, just so long as Christians and other believers in nonclassical religions did not disturb public order. In fact, Pliny wrote to Trajan to be sure "whether it is the mere name of Christian which is punishable, even if innocent of crime, or rather the crimes associated with the name."[7] He had interrogated some Christian slave women and reported:

> They declared that the sum total of their guilt or error amounted to
> no more than this: they had met regularly before dawn on a fixed day
> to chant verses alternately among themselves in honor of Christ as to
> a god, and also to bind themselves by oath, not for any criminal pur-
> pose, but to abstain from theft, robbery, and adultery, and to commit no
> breach of trust and not to deny a deposit when called upon to restore it.
> After this ceremony it had been their custom to disperse and reassem-
> ble later to take food of an ordinary harmless kind.

Trajan replied with the kind of clemency (Virgil's *parcere subiectis*) and respect for law that were high Roman ideals:

> You have followed the right course of procedure, my dear Pliny. . . .
> These people must not be hunted out; if they are brought before you
> and the charge against them is proved, they must be punished, but in
> the case of anyone who denies that he is a Christian, and makes it clear
> that he is not by offering prayers to our gods, he is to be pardoned as a
> result of his repentance however suspect his past conduct may be. But

they were torn to pieces by dogs, or crucified, or made into torches to be set on fire after dark as illumination. . . . Despite their guilt as Christians, and the ruthless punishment it deserved, the victims were pitied. For it was felt that they were being sacrificed to one man's brutality rather than to the national interest." Cornelius Tacitus, The Histories, with English translation by Clifford H. Moore (London: Heinemann, 1925–1937), vol. 4 (Annals XV.44).

the pamphlets circulated anonymously must play no part in any ac-
cusation. They create the worst sort of precedent and are quite out of
keeping with the spirit of our age.[8]

In both men, there remained a dislike of foreign beliefs and potentially
harsh treatment for their adherents, along with a demand for conformity
by a public act of submission to the gods. But there is neither the persecut-
ing zeal often believed to have gripped the Romans, nor the mocking tone of
vice-ridden power holders. Pliny and Trajan were intelligent and pious pagans who considered sects like Christianity unfortunate, but to be tolerated
if they presented no threat to public order.

This last concern bulked large everywhere in the empire. We know that
the Romans were cautious about allowing private associations of any kind
because they had ample experience of their potential for civic disturbances. Pliny himself often wrote to the emperor to ask whether he wished to
concede a formal right to gather to one group or another. These two decent
men did not believe there was anything wrong per se about such groups.
And many were formally recognized that arose from men in similar trades
who wanted to socialize, or individuals with a special devotion to a particular god, or people who joined a "burial society," something like a primitive insurance system. Within the vast political structures of the empire at
its height, these provided more immediate face-to-face civil associations,
besides the family, in which citizens might feel a close sense of belonging:
"When the brotherhood, many of them of servile grade, met in full con-
clave in the temple of their patron deity, to pass a formal decree of thanks
to a benefactor, and regale themselves with a modest repast, or when they
passed through the streets and the forum with banners flying, and all the
emblems of their guild, the meanest member felt himself lifted for the moment above the dim, hopeless obscurity of plebeian life."[9]

But they always carried the risk of turning into political factions, and
for some time—especially given the Roman belief that there could be no
legitimate *superstitio* or standing outside the official cults—the Christians
and their churches appeared to be associations with a strong potential for

political upheaval. Suetonius notes in his life of the emperor Claudius, for example, that "Since the Jews constantly made disturbances at the instigation of Chrestus, [Claudius] expelled them from Rome."[10] We do not know if this Chrestus was a dim reflection of early Christian presence or some other figure, but it is significant that Suetonius specifies a Jewish connection here, since the Jews were often mocked, if tolerated, by the Romans for their claims to uniqueness and the sovereignty of the Lord (whom Romans thought of as the Jewish "tribal god") over all the earth. Either way, Suetonius is probably playing here on a widespread belief that odd religious views disrupt the god-given Roman order.

The Novelty of "Conversion"

To a modern person, it appears obvious that someone may "convert" from one religion to another. But in Greek and Roman antiquity, as shall become clearer below, it was assumed that any special religious beliefs should be simply incorporated into the capacious space of polytheism. We know of one emperor who erected a statue to Christ in his private chapel on the Palatine Hill and of many in the ancient world who thought that the God of the Jews, if he were to be retained at all, had to be identified with the supreme god in the pantheon. Jews who asserted that only one God existed and was supreme, and Christians who followed them with the Christian additions to that belief, were incomprehensible and, therefore, threatening to the whole scheme. So while the earliest reactions to the Christians scorned their beliefs but did not especially seek to stamp them out, as the Christian movement spread and started to rival the cults of the gods it was inevitable that pagan and Christian thinkers would begin to do battle.

The battle was both intellectual and social, because the Romans, like all ancient peoples including the Jews, believed in a corporate religiosity as well as a personal or familial religion. This may sound somewhat odd today, but we have vestiges of it in our beliefs that even modern democratic liberties and our political structures stand, to some extent, under God and his ethical orders for the human race. The Romans had a heightened sense of this dimension, which made certain positions that we would call theological into political issues as well. Cicero, who asserted with pride the religiosity of the Romans, also warned: "In all probability, disappearance of piety towards the gods will entail the disappearance of loyalty and social union among men as well, and of justice itself, the queen of all the virtues."[11] For the Greeks and the Romans, it has been argued, religion was not so much a question of believing as one of "having gods" of the city or the empire.[12] So the conflict with Christianity was joined not merely over theological principles—Greco-Roman religion, as we have seen, did not have such principles—but over a whole way of life.

In the latter part of the second century, the Christian apologist Tertullian (155–230 A.D.) replied directly to pagan charges in a way that anticipated what Galen, for all his dislike of "superstition," would remark in the following century:

> We are an association bound together by our religious profession, by the unity of our way of life and the bond of our common hope. . . . We meet together as an assembly and a society. . . . We pray for the emperors. . . . We gather together to read our sacred writing. . . . With the holy words we nourish our faith. . . . After the gathering is over the Christians go out as though they had come from a "school of virtue."

Tertullian also pointed out what the emperor Julian would exclaim over two centuries later: "It is our care of the helpless, our practice of loving kindness that brands us in the eyes of many of our opponents. 'Only look,' they say, 'look how they love one another!'"[13] But Tertullian, who had seen persecution in his native Africa, went on the offensive too about who was more of a "faction," the Christians or their pagan persecutors:

> On the contrary, they deserve the name of faction who conspire to bring odium on good men and virtuous, who cry out against innocent blood, offering as the justification of their enmity the baseless plea, that they think the Christians the cause of every public disaster, of every affliction with which the people are visited. If the Tiber rises as high as the city walls, if the Nile does not send its waters up over the fields, if the heavens give no rain, if there is an earthquake,

if there is famine or pestilence, straightway the cry is, "Away with the Christians to the lions!"

Intellectual Engagements

All of this political charge and countercharge was quite important, but we should not overlook the philosophical engagement that Christianity and paganism conducted, because the Christians began to absorb the lessons of Greek culture and to use them in the service of the new way of viewing the world. That element had already been present, of course, in the Jewish philosopher Philo of Alexandria, among others, and in the letters of Saint Paul, who as a highly literate Jew growing up in the Hellenistic culture of the East was familiar with Greek philosophical theories and could even cite Greek poets to make a point when he tried to evangelize. Paul did not, however, engage the broader metaphysical systems of the various Greek philosophical schools. That process began with the apostle John, who in the fourth Gospel identified Christ with the Logos of the Neoplatonic trinity, an even bolder move than Philo had made in his allegorizing and reconceptualizing of the Hebrew tradition. John, or his disciples, also wrote the book of Revelation towards the end of the first century A.D. when the emperor Domitian (81–96) was carrying out a rabid persecution of Christians. The Christians were already in a position to begin arguing with the philosophers if they could avoid being murdered.

That problem personally confronted the first full-blown Christian philosopher, Justin Martyr (ca. 100–167 A.D.). Justin had been born to a Greek-speaking Roman family in Flavia Neapolis, the modern-day Nablus in the Palestinian territories. He studied philosophy with teachers of several schools, but was most attracted by the Stoics and Platonists until a reading of the Old Testament Prophets and the Gospels led him to Christianity. So Justin understood Greco-Roman culture from the inside, owing to both birth and training. He wrote two "apologias," that is, explanations and justifications of his beliefs, both of which were addressed to the emperor Antoninus Pius, his adopted son Marcus Aurelius, and the Roman Senate—the most humane leaders of the empire at one of its most fortunate moments. There is no evidence that this hopeful and respectful effort had any influence or even reached the high officials it was aimed at. Justin's thought was still developing and the case is not entirely airtight. But he is an important witness—especially since he would die a martyr—to the growing confidence of the Christian movement even in the face of the most powerful Roman intellectual and social figures.

For Justin was not at all reticent to assert the superiority of his faith beginning from the antiquity of Judaism, especially the monotheism and moral precepts of Moses, which predated anything remotely similar among the Greeks by hundreds of years.* The prophets, in his reading, predicted Christ's coming, his mistreatment at the hands of evil men (crucifixion being a humiliation that the pagans could not believe a god would suffer, even assuming the highest god were somehow to come down to earth), and his drawing all nations to himself with a new, spiritual covenant. But even if the Roman leaders persisted in thinking Christians wildly mistaken, said Justin, they had no right to persecute and martyr them merely for their beliefs. Greek philosophy had produced movements that were openly atheist (a charge that Romans mistakenly applied to the Christians) or that authorized immoral behavior. Yet the Roman officials did not outlaw them or murder their adherents.

Justin was right, but like many people who were right throughout history—including Socrates, whom Justin explicitly mentioned as having been charged with infractions similar to those leveled at the Christians—he was caught and killed by the very forces he had refuted.

In a curious way, Justin's path resembled that of his near-contemporary Galen, in that both had been brought up in good pagan families in the Near East and had studied with teachers of several philosophical schools. Galen ended up in eclecticism and medical pursuits, while Justin was persecuted as a Christian. We saw at the outset that Galen was puzzled by the power of Christianity to promote virtuous behavior among the uneducated. He did not call it simple superstition, but could not tell what kind of philosophy it was. In this, too, he was like Justin, who when he first encountered Chris-

*Saint Augustine would call Plato the "Attic Moses."

tianity realized that its adherents could not be as corrupted as the critics maintained, since they faced death calmly, something the ancients believed only the most accomplished philosophers could do. By the latter half of the second century, therefore, Christianity had already impressed the Roman world, if not yet as a well-thought-out philosophy, then as a way of life.

In the same period, the Roman philosopher Celsus, something of a traditionalist in his beliefs, thought the new religious movement important enough to compose a full-scale rebuttal of its beliefs. For Celsus, Jesus' miracles were only magic, and his followers therefore adherents to a sect, but he took their principles seriously enough to assume that rational counterarguments were both necessary and potentially effective. Celsus pointed, in particular, to the absurdity of thinking that God came down to earth in Palestine during the reign of Augustus (what of distant places and prior ages?); that God can exercise choice like a person rather than having to act as an impersonal force; that Jesus rose from the dead, and, unlike the lesser gods and heroes of Greek mythology, should be worshiped as the God of Gods. In the following centuries, these remained the usual objections to the "scandal" of the whole Christian system. Celsus made a final point: that the Christians (for instance, Justin) boasted of their direct descent from the long line of inspired lawgivers and prophets that predated the Greeks, but had in many ways departed from the beliefs and practices of the Jews.

Yet the main thrust of Celsus' arguments—which set an agenda for pagan critics in the next century, such as the formidable mystic Porphyry, the pagan apologist Symmachus, and the emperor Julian—seems animated mostly by a sense that a new culture was arising parallel to and different from the ancient classical culture. As a scholar of the period has remarked:

> It was not a debate between paganism and Christianity, but a debate about a new concept of religion. Celsus sensed that Christians had severed the traditional bond between religion and a "nation" or people. The ancients took for granted that religion was indissolubly linked to a particular city or people. Indeed, there was no term for *religion* in the sense we now use it to refer to the beliefs and practices of a specific

group of people or of a voluntary association divorced from ethnic or national identity.[14]

Caesar and God were being put into an entirely new relationship with one another.

Philosophy and Christianity

A similar development was occurring in the relationship of Christianity and Greek philosophy. Greek and Roman thinkers had largely allowed for a modus vivendi with traditional religion. Outright atheists were, on the whole, few, but the place of God or the gods in various systems could vary widely. In popular religion, the gods could be quite present and active, and that belief found a place in several philosophical schools. The Epicureans were virtually unique in believing that perhaps the gods existed but did not concern themselves with human beings. Yet the overall drift in philosophy by the second and third centuries A.D. was to think of a supreme being as the fundamental principle of the universe and the gods as lesser immortals, sometimes supplemented by great men—a Hercules or one of the several "divine" Roman emperors—who were allowed to enter their ranks for the deeds they had performed on earth. This was the most common alternative to Christianity in the centuries before it became the dominant religion in the whole empire.

The most brilliant of the pagan thinkers to engage Christianity during this period was another figure with a serious Greek intellectual formation born in the Middle East (Tyre, ca. 233 A.D.), the philosopher Porphyry. He had the advantage of having both studied with pagan teachers of various schools and heard lectures in Caesarea by Origen, the most substantial Christian thinker of the first three Christian centuries. Origen was a slightly heterodox figure whose work was strongly marked by Plato and, as a result, was later partly condemned by Christian authorities, but he had lived and studied with Clement of Alexandria and the other Christian scholars of that studious city and could hold his own with anyone in intellectual debate. In addition, Origen had written a learned work, *Against Celsus*, that built a Christian intellectual case against the formidable pagan critic. Porphyry was impressed, but not converted; instead, he took over some of Origen's historical criticism of the Bible and his allegorizing efforts as a means of casting doubt on one of Christianity's central supports: the claim to historical reality.

Porphyry was a strongly religious man who seems not to have wanted to destroy the Christian movement entirely. To begin with, he appears to have recognized that by his day it had become too widespread and deeply rooted in the Roman world to be extirpated by methods like those tried by Celsus. Porphyry's strategy was a shrewd one: he would not destroy, he would co-opt. Christ had shown remarkable wisdom and virtue in his brief life. He was to be venerated, but not in the foolish way that common people thought of him as God or that the Christian intellectuals had tried to bolster their case with Greek philosophy. Jesus could be honored as a "hero," and therefore admitted into the pantheon of the lesser gods to whom sacrifices were offered (the supreme God had no need or desire for sacrifice). In other words, Jesus and his followers could be accepted, but only on Greek terms:

> The wise men of the Hebrews (and this Jesus was also one of them, as you have heard from the oracles of Apollo quoted above) warned religious men against the evil demons and lesser spirits, and forbade them to pay attention to them, telling their hearers rather to venerate the gods of heaven, but above all to worship God the Father. But this is what the gods also teach; and we have shown above how they advise us to turn our thoughts to God, and everywhere bid us worship him.[15]

This view may seem to us a moderate and almost modern philosophical judgment about Jesus and the Christians. But in the social struggle then being played out between Christians and pagans, it could be used to provide yet more fuel to the pagan persecutors who looked on the Christian movement as another threat to the traditional Roman order. Furthermore, arguments like Porphyry's within the Church itself forced the Christians into an internally contentious series of decisions about the exact nature of Jesus Christ. The various Church councils held in the East in the decades after Porphyry wrote tried to settle these questions, which for Christians led to the definition of Christ as truly God and truly man, quite different from Porphyry's

"Christ-as-hero" solution, which satisfied only pagans. In an empire about to reach a turning point in its official religiosity, Porphyry's challenge led the new faith into developing a philosophical sophistication it might never have achieved otherwise.

Christianity and History

Christianity in the empire, however, was a way of life as well as a teaching. The Christians were much criticized for their seemingly foolish beliefs, but—stubborn superstition aside—were generally admired for their capacity to instill virtue and inspire effective charity. That fact led to a different sort of attack by the emperor Julian in the late fourth century. By that time, the whole imperial household was Christian, a shift that had begun earlier in the century with the conversion of Constantine. In line with his Enlightenment prejudices, Edward Gibbon scorned Constantine's abandonment of his easygoing earlier faith in solar monotheism after he had a vision of Christ. It seems more accurate today to say that Constantine joined a movement that would soon have prevailed even without him. Theodosius I would declare Christianity the official religion of the empire in 380 A.D., less than two decades after Julian died. But in the meantime, Julian made one last effort to stem what seems to have been an inevitable tide not only at the highest levels of Roman society, but across the whole social world as well.

Julian, too, had been raised a Christian, but was a kind of "revert," one of the few prominent people to consciously return to the old pagan ways. In the nineteenth century, he was often portrayed as a sort of advocate for modern paganism, which was assumed to be, along with its ancient counterpart, both more "rational" and more joyful than the sect of the "pale Galilean." This is a fiction on both counts, however. Julian returned to paganism—partly because his father had been assassinated by Christian opponents in the imperial court—but it was a far from cheery paganism, being steeped in magic and theurgy rather than rationalism. Along with magical superstitions, Julian loved animal sacrifices, as did Celsus and Porphyry, as a tangible affirmation of the worship suited to the lesser gods in the classical pantheon. He also sought to wipe out educated Christianity by decreeing that teachers should be judged on their "character," meaning their adherence to pagan principles. Those who would not show such character could choose not to teach, that is, to form the next generation. The consequences for Christians who could not be educated in their faith or in the classical intellectual tradition would be the loss both of familiarity with the Christian thought that had emerged in competition with paganism, and of the opportunities that education makes possible in society. It was an indirect and relatively bloodless way to censor and marginalize Christian believers, which was imitated by totalitarians on many continents throughout history.

These were not measures casually adopted. Julian passionately meditated on ways to reverse Christian growth and even wrote a work titled *Against the Galileans.* In fact, he wanted nothing to do with compromise measures like those of Porphyry, which were intended to co-opt Jesus into the classical pantheon. He wanted to discredit the very notion of Christ as divine in any sense, and he hit upon a way to do so that only someone intimately acquainted with Christian beliefs from the inside would have noticed. Both Judaism and Christianity placed a strong emphasis on history as the story of salvation. Indeed, Christians often pointed to a prophecy in the book of Daniel as support for their claim that they had inherited a new covenant. Daniel 9:24 says, "There will be an abomination of desolation in the holy place until the end of time," a prediction, it was argued, of the destruction of the Temple by Hadrian after the Bar Kochba rebellion (133–135 A.D.), which Daniel had further prophesied would last "until the consummation of the world and the end." So Julian had available to him an easy way to refute such claims: he would rebuild the Temple.

He sent an architect named Alypius in 362 to Aelia Capitolina, the name the Romans had given to Jerusalem when they destroyed the Temple, expelled the Jews from Israel, and built a temple to Jupiter in the refounded city. It is not easy to reconstruct what happened at that point, but both pagan and Christian sources indicate some natural catastrophe—an earthquake or an explosion of natural gas near the site of the former Temple—that prevented the work from proceeding. By then, Julian had pressing matters on his hands, namely a military campaign against Persia, which diverted his attention from the anti-Christian scheme. During the campaign, Julian was killed, thus effectively ending any plans for rebuilding the Temple. His successors returned to the fostering of Christianity begun by Constantine.

Explosive Growth

Modern scholars have argued that they did so partly because of their own convictions, but partly as well because the growth of Christianity among the people made continuing in the old pagan ways impractical. How that growth occurred is one of the great mysteries of Western history. If we assume, as most scholars now do, that Christianity was the majority religion in the Roman Empire by 380 A.D., when it was also declared the official religion, the number of Christians would have had to grow from perhaps 120 at Jesus' death to 30 million roughly 350 years later. There are no sure data by which to understand this phenomenon, but we are not entirely without means to explain how it may have happened. One bold sociological analysis contends that all it would have taken was a yearly growth rate of about 4 percent, the same rate of expansion we see today in Mormonism. Compounded over 300 years, this rapid, though not impossible, conversion rate would produce more than 30 million believers in the late fourth century.[16]

But how could such conversion rates be sustained year after year for three centuries? Towards the beginning, there may have been some mass conversions, as the Bible and other sources claim. Similar phenomena would have been possible in the population centers of the empire in later times as well. Cities may have played a major role in this process, because, as in the modern world, they probably contained many people only weakly attached to the old religion and open to novel solutions to their religious needs.[17] Also as in the modern world, these converts would not be drawn primarily from the poor and marginalized, as was sometimes thought in the past. Sociological studies indicate that these groups generally tend to be more passive than active in social and religious movements. It is quite likely that most conversion happened in the middle to upper classes, among educated people in a network of friends that included Christians and pagans who were searching but did not find satisfaction in the old ways. That may be one

reason why intellectuals such as Celsus and Porphyry thought it worth-
while to launch an intellectual rebuttal of a set of beliefs that could not yet
have spread to many of Rome's 60 million people (maybe 70,000 in Celsus'
day and a million—still only a small percentage of the whole people—in
Porphyry's). Learned arguments are not addressed to the poor and uneducated, or against the uninfluential. By the early 300s, which is to say before Constantine's conversion and legalizing of Christianity with the Edict
of Milan (313 A.D.), the emperors Diocletian (303) and Gallienus (305)
launched the final wave of persecution against Christians. Clearly, if they
had been able to, they would have wiped out the new believers. That the
persecution, for all its bloodthirstiness, failed suggests that the numbers of
Christians had become too large even for a government-sponsored pogrom
to eliminate.[18]

If this analysis is true—and none other seems possible at the present
time—the old Marxist view of religion as the opiate of the people is false.
Marx and Engels wrote: "Christianity was originally a movement of oppressed people: it first appeared as the religion of slaves and emancipated
slaves, of poor people deprived of all rights, of people subjugated or dispersed by Rome."[19] As was often the case for supposedly scientific analysis of religion in the past two centuries, this view rested on neither fact
nor analysis, because the early Christians were more often what Marx and
Engels deplored, the bourgeoisie. The first Christians were Jews, a people
subject to Rome, but hardly for this reason susceptible to the kind of developments that the founders of Marxism imagined. When the apostles moved
out around the Mediterranean, they naturally gathered their first adherents from urban Jewish communities and the gentiles who were interested in the religiosity that Judaism offered. Many were middle-class artisans.
Their attraction to religion had less to do with the things that modern intellectuals believe important—class and status—than with what typically at-
tracts converts in all ages: the good behavior of believers and the sense of
meaning the belief brings to their lives.

Furthermore, among Diaspora Jews (who were present as a significant
minority in the major imperial cities including Rome), Christianity initial-

ly had the advantage of being a kind of reform Judaism that did not require meticulous observance of the Law—something difficult to do in the empire outside of narrow Jewish enclaves—but still offered a strong set of beliefs. The Jewish communities provided the social networks that conversion requires. It may be one sign of the continued social tie to Judaism that early Christianity resisted the attempts by figures like Marcion to declare the God of the New Testament a different God from the God of the Old. Intellectual and spiritual connections, of course, inescapably existed between the two, but social ties may also have contributed a great deal here.

Yet there were other natural factors that helped the budding Christian movement, one of them, oddly, disease. In the ancient world, epidemics periodically swept through the Mediterranean, carrying off large percentages of the population. One of the first ones reported, from the middle of the fifth century B.C., appears in Thucydides. We know of others that repeatedly struck the Roman world. The different behavior of pagans and Christians in these crises may have had serious demographic effects. To begin with, the pagans had no reason in belief or social custom to do anything for plague victims. The pagan physician Galen, whom we have seen praising Christians for their virtuous behavior, fled Rome when it was struck by disease in 161 A.D. And as one historian has characterized his behavior, "It was what any prudent person would have done, had they the means—unless, of course, they were 'Galileans.'"[20] By contrast, the Christians cared for their own, and to judge by the later laments of figures like Julian, for pagans as well. The consequences of this charity are not hard to imagine: in all likelihood, more Christians than pagans survived the epidemics, and the pagans who survived would have seen a model of virtue that surpassed anything, personal or institutional, typical of their culture.

Contrary to certain currents in modern feminism, Christianity also improved the status of women in the ancient world. Roman women were not as sequestered as Greek women had been, but they did not enjoy anything like the degree of respect they gained with the arrival of the new faith. To begin with, since boys were more valued in classical culture, as they are in many traditional cultures even today, female babies were often exposed, a common practice for unwanted children in general, but one that struck girls especially hard. We know that Athens suffered from a relative lack of females, partly because figures as eminent as Plato and Aristotle accepted exposure of infants as normal. Abortion in the conditions of antiquity also killed a certain percentage of adult women. Christianity, like Judaism, prohibited both practices (earning the hatred even of stern pagans like Tacitus for their "superstition")[21] and, therefore, not only gained the favor of women but made it possible for more females to survive, thereby increasing Christian demographic advantages again. In the second century A.D., the Christian Minucius Felix summed this all up by arguing that what we might call the "life issues" led to an increase in Christians from several directions: "we maintain our modesty not in appearance, but in our heart we gladly abide by the bond of a single marriage; in the desire of procreating, we know either one wife, or none at all. . . . And that day by day the number of us is increased, is not a ground for a charge of error, but is a testimony which claims praise; for, in a fair mode of life, our actual number both continues and abides undiminished, and strangers increase it."[22]

There was good reason, other than biological survival, for women to like this system. In Greek culture, women lived under rules similar to those in Muslim fundamentalism today. They were restricted to home, while their husbands were generally thought to be free to pursue sexual pleasures elsewhere, just as long as they cared for their families. Christianity put an end to that by preaching the evils of fornication and adultery for both women and men. Indeed, Saint Ambrose, the great archbishop of Milan and teacher of Saint Augustine, instructed Christian men in a treatise on the Creation that the dignity of women goes back to the very beginning: "You are not her master, but her husband; she was not given to you to be your slave, but your wife. . . . Reciprocate her attentiveness to you and be grateful to her for her love."[23] Women in classical society had difficulty exercising any influence. By contrast, we see even as early as the New Testament that women were numbered among the prominent followers of Jesus, and in the churches that Paul and the apostles founded around the Mediterranean, women, often well-born, exercised various responsibilities. Where the pagan population had a dearth of women, the Christians probably had more women than men, and many of those women probably served as evangelizers to non-Christian husbands.

The Beliefs behind the Practices

These social and ethical advantages depended, however, on the new Christian beliefs being in some way credible. Our distance from classical civilization and the distorting perspectives of Enlightenment critics of Christianity have led many people to misconstrue the whole situation. As we have seen in previous chapters, neither Greek nor Roman culture was rationalist in the way that many modern admirers want to present it as having been. Atheism, to repeat once again, was rare, and it is significant that the Christians were often accused by the pagans themselves of atheism. What they meant by this, of course, was that the Christians did not believe in the existence of the pagan gods, and this affront to the established beliefs also gave rise to rumors of Christian corruptions: cannibalism in their ritual eating of Christ's body and blood; "love feasts" thought to be sexual orgies; and depraved superstitions about the election of the Jews, to pagan minds an obscure and limited historical salvation rather than a philosophical one open to all. Finally, there was the miraculous death, resurrection, and ascension into heaven of Jesus.

Above and beyond misunderstanding and bias, there was a real bone of contention over whether the pagan or the Christian religious vision was the true one. But it was never, as Gibbon and other Enlightenment figures asserted with great force but equally great error, a question of reason and virtue being overcome by the triumph of "barbarism and religion." There are different forms of rationality, not least the form that recognizes the limits of human knowledge and the existence of realities beyond human capacities. Philosophical pagans and Christians both agreed about that. The premises from which "reason" begins may differ, but granted the premises, rationality may exist on one side as much as another. Christianity would spread the old Jewish notion of truth as grounded in history, events, persons, and witnesses far beyond the traditional Jewish horizons. And it could be argued that, as difficult as this starting point was initially for pagans to grasp, it actually revitalized classical civilization and virtue.

We see this most clearly in the way that Christianity harnessed classical learning for its own purposes. In the heyday of scientific rationalism and historical criticism, it was often asserted that Christianity was "Hellenized" in the centuries after its birth.[24] But that approach, too, was somewhat skewed in that it did not allow, as we have seen, for how much Greek culture had already influenced Jewish thought and life before Jesus was born. More importantly, it did not sufficiently appreciate that Christianity was not colonized by Hellenism as much as Hellenism was recast and re-presented in the service of fresh notions stemming from the Old and New Testaments. And this meant that Christian culture, in its relationship to Judaism, to Greek culture, and to Roman society, was, for all its own revolutionary characteristics, pluralist and multicultural in its very origins.

Yet while Christian writers subsequently would produce arguments and literary works for the sake of strengthening believers and defending their faith from pagan criticism, most Christians were quite happy to accept as true the salvation events they had been taught about, and to follow the ways of living that prevailed in Christian communities. Pagan and Christian views pointed in quite different directions. The Neoplatonists focused strongly on the otherworldly, transcendent intellectual principles outside of all earthly categories, a tendency that would later be attributed to Christians instead. The Christians focused on salvation through history in this world, which seemed absurd to the Greek point of view. Christians might ultimately believe in something like the transcendent One of Neoplatonism, but they also embraced the apparent absurdity that the transcendent could enter the world. Origen of Alexandria turned this argument against the pagans by admitting that Plato's views were noble and impressive: "But consider whether the Holy Scripture shows more compassion for humankind when it presents the divine Word (*logos*), who was in the beginning with God . . . as becoming flesh in order to reach everyone."[25]

Origen was martyred during the Decian persecution in 250 A.D, but he had earlier given intellectual formulation to the meaning of such personal witness by saying that the Gospel "has a proof that is proper to itself and is more divine than the dialectical arguments of the Greeks." For Origen, following Saint Paul, that proof was "of the Spirit and of power." And it could not be denied, as Galen and others noticed, that the Christians seemed capable of performing virtuous acts such as dying peacefully for their beliefs in the way that only the very rarest philosophers of antiquity had been able to do. Yet the behaviors were only an outward sign of the beliefs and the power they produced. Insofar as Christian figures were thinkers—and in Origen and especially Augustine they could be very gifted thinkers—they were quite familiar with arguments against them and offered arguments in return. Unlike many of the philosophical schools in Late Antiquity, Christianity seemed to believe in the possibility of truth, not in a skepticism that led to mere Stoic practice or ascetic mysticism.

In addition, it accorded high spiritual value to simple things before ideas. In line with earlier developments in Jewish thought, which saw the celebration of the Passover as making present again the historical event of the Exodus, the celebration of the Christian Eucharist and baptism tied believers to events in the life of Christ. Theories about these practices developed slowly, years later. It is important to understand the powerful reorientation this gave to the Greek intellectual tools employed in the process: "Before there were treatises on the Trinity, before there were learned disputes about the teaching on grace, or essays on the moral life, there was awe and adoration before the exalted Son of God alive and present in the Church's offering of the Eucharist. This truth preceded every effort to understand and nourished every attempt to express in words and concepts what Christians believed."[26] All Christians were equal in their communion with that reality. The ideas came after the life.

This recentering of Late Antiquity came from the power that the Bible and more specifically the life of Jesus exerted. Today, we take it as axiomatic that the Bible is one of the great books of the Western world and deserving of study alongside Homer, Plato, Thucydides, Virgil, Plutarch, and many other eminent writers in Greek and Latin. In the old classical perspective, it seemed an absurdity to claim that the truth about the world and the human race passed through an obscure Middle Eastern tribe and then, even more pointedly, through the life of a Jewish preacher who had been humiliated and crucified. Coupled with everything else described above, however, this was precisely what large numbers of people in the ancient world came to believe. And if they did not wholly abandon their previous cultural achievements as a result of the new center of attraction, they begin to use them for very different purposes.

We have been so shaped by their success at this project that it is hard to appraise the change in mentality it brought with it. To begin with, the new perspective immeasurably raised the real value of each and every human being beyond anything classical antiquity ever imagined. Christian salvation, unlike philosophical virtue, was aimed at everyone, not merely a few gifted minds. And that value was rooted in the nature of Creation as the Old Testament envisioned it, and in the restoration and redemption of a humanity that had fallen into darkness as the New Testament claimed. In this story, it did not matter that an individual Christian might not be of much worldly importance or interest. Some new spiritual power, a kind of "living water," seems to have touched many people in a way that could not have been anticipated. Clement of Alexandria, a highly cultivated literary figure of the second century, perceived in the literature of the Bible something new in the way the texts spoke of human beings made "in the image and likeness" of God. Saint Augustine, in his dramatic way, said that the words of scripture were so powerful that they had "pummeled" (*pulsatum*) his heart. Whatever judgments might later be made about the intellectual formulation of these experiences, it seems impossible to deny the energy they instilled across a wide social spectrum of the empire.

This is all the more curious in that the whole Judeo-Christian story depended on acceptance of a deep sense of sin, not merely the error that Plato posited as keeping us from seeing and doing the good. Error did exist and Christian thinkers also tried to correct it, often by relying on the Greek philosophers. But sin was a matter of a perverse will, a deliberate choice. How this could occur was a mystery. And how so many people who had lived in a society without such a sense of sin came to believe in it is more mysterious still. Most mysterious of all, Jesus of Nazareth, a man who had lived and died in Judea under the emperors Augustus and Tiberius, was believed to be the remedy for sin, the wisdom of God who existed before time began, and indeed God himself in a way difficult to grasp: Three-in-One Godhead, preserving both the threeness and the oneness despite the obvious objections of the simplest logic and mathematics, which were known, of course, to anyone then as much as now. The Christian Trinity had some parallels in the Neoplatonic trinity (the One, Mind, Soul) that had preceded it. Christ as Incarnate God might be compared with certain myths about Zeus visiting earth. But that this incarnation overcame sin and, more surprising still, death turned the whole of classical civilization in a new direction.

If Christian thought, as has so often been erroneously asserted, had turned away from reason and knowledge in the direction of blind faith, it probably would have remained a small sect within the empire. The new experience of freedom and spiritual power through the Christian story was primary and Christian thought was secondary. Yet it was inevitable that Christians would use pagan tools to describe, analyze, and defend their story. In fact, they began looking at philosophers as well as scientific figures such as Galen to borrow what might be useful for their own formulations about God and man. A Christian Greek thinker like Gregory of Nyssa, for instance, will cite Aristotle and Galen in discussion of body and soul. In many ways, these excursions result in a sense that the virtues aimed at by Plato, the Stoics, the Epicureans, and many others in the ancient world were proper virtues, but could not normally be attained even though they could be seen. For every Socrates, Epicurus, or Plotinus, countless tens of millions struggled to achieve the happiness and the peace of heart they sought, with little effect. Christianity, as Galen rightly noted, seemed to have put virtue within reach of many. Augustine summed up, in a way, much of the classical search with an expression of a new confidence: "You have made us for yourself and our hearts are restless til they rest in you."[27]

Thus the Enlightenment view, most powerfully expressed by Gibbon, that Christianity killed the classical aspirations to rationality and knowledge—

a view which has been widely disseminated and accepted over the past two centuries—was a false anachronism and simply has not withstood the test of greater knowledge about the ancient world. Origen, working within a tradition of Christian thought, echoes the famous line at the beginning of Aristotle's *Metaphysics* ("All men by nature desire to know") with a slight Christian twist to allow for the will of the Creator: "A desire to know the truth of things has been implanted in our souls and is natural to human beings." And he goes on to say that it must be possible to achieve knowledge of the truth of things, "For if the love of truth were never able to be satisfied, it would seem to have been implanted in our mind by the creator in vain."[28] This mode of knowledge consciously adopted a starting point different from the classical one. A line from the prophet Isaiah (7:9) as rendered into Latin turns up often in Christian thinkers: "If you believe, you will understand." Christianity relied on witnesses, not mere abstract reasoning, but it was not less "rational" for that choice, any more than a historian who tries to explain some contemporary situation on the basis of the testimony of past witnesses is being irrational. It all depends on whether the witnesses are judged believable and the past event's present consequences confirm the truth of their account.

Augustine, Bishop of Hippo

The preeminent Western figure in all these controversies, of course, was Saint Augustine, the bishop of Hippo in North Africa, who would have incalculable effects on the whole future of Western life and thought. It is impossible to summarize his vast and rich work in a few words. But in a sense, all of Augustine's thinking revolves around the Christian notion of love. Love plays a central role in Plato, too, and Augustine fruitfully marries Platonic and Christian ideas at many points, a linkage that would be transmitted to the entire Latin West. Unlike Plato, however, he speaks to everyone, a characteristic that he shares with almost all early Christian thinkers. He probably draws most of his power from Jesus' reply to the Pharisee's question about which was the greatest commandment: "You shall love the Lord, your God, with all your heart, with all your soul, and with all your mind. . . .

The second is like it: You shall love your neighbor as yourself." (Matthew 22:37) Scholars believe that Jesus may have been restating an old Jewish formula and that Christianity was, therefore, spreading the old Jewish passion of love for God that we have already met with. But in its charitable behavior towards all people throughout the empire, Christianity was doing something, out of love for God, largely unprecedented.

Augustine is much occupied with the various forms that love takes. For him, even evil cannot be the absolute contrary of good, but only a disordered love. The human will in Augustine is a faculty that loves one object or another. It is a good will if it puts God first and other things in their proper places, a bad will if it loses contact with the source of reality and makes a creature into a god. That was the error of paganism, in Augustine's view. The human person is defined by its loves. Augustine says of his own self: *Amor meus, pondus meum* ("My love is my weight"). He will even go so far as to redefine ancient concepts such as the cardinal virtues not as new intellectual categories but as kinds of love:

> *Temperance*—By love keeping oneself whole for that which is loved.
>
> *Fortitude*—Love easily bearing all things for the sake of what is loved.
>
> *Justice*—Love serving the beloved alone and on account of that ruling rightly.
>
> *Prudence*—Love wisely distinguishing those things by which it is helped from those that harm.[29]

A man who can turn even these pagan constructs into lessons on love is engaged in effecting a very unusual transvaluation of values, indeed.

Augustine stands at the head of two very powerful—and at first sight contradictory—developments in Western experience. On the one hand, he opens up some new areas in the interior life and individual personality. His *Confessions* have often been described as the first autobiography, and in some ways that is true. This work shows a preoccupation with interiority, deepened by the spiritual vistas of Christianity, that was simply unprecedented in the ancient world. Augustine recounts his early life, troubles, and eventual conversion in the *Confessions*, but not as self-revelation in the modern sense. Rather, he sees his story as a universal one, over and above the particulars that brought him to a new life. Though *Confessions* is more impersonal than a modern autobiography in that sense, it brought the particularities of the Christian story into the course of one life and in so doing pointed the way toward the Western concern for the individuality of persons and our inner lives. It is not surprising that the theorist of love shows how loves—disappointing as well as fulfilling loves—give a shape to human life.

Augustine focuses attention on the mind and the will because, he believes, the human mind reflects the divine and therefore deserves careful attention. In line with Genesis, the way man was created "in the image and likeness" of God refers primarily to the mind. The emphasis on inwardness in Luther, Calvin, Descartes, Pascal, Kant, Hegel, and other modern thinkers derives from Augustine by more or less direct descent. Augustine even anticipates the Cartesian *Cogito ergo sum* in several places,[30] but he does not give it much importance because he is not much concerned about radical skepticism. Instead, he uses the certainty achieved as a way to highlight the role of persons in knowing and the personal knowledge that opens each of us up to God. A modern philosopher has said of this: "It is a certainty of self-presence. Augustine was the inventor of the argument we know as the '*cogito,*' because Augustine was the first to make the first-person standpoint fundamental to our search for the truth."[31]

Augustine's emphasis on the interior life of the human person may display a certain tension with, even as it clarifies, the second large inheritance he left to the West, his social vision.

In Augustine's day, the social effects of Christianity took on renewed importance. Christians had always been accused by pagans of withdrawing from their civic duties—probably a true charge when Christians were a slender minority and liable to prejudice, persecution, or death. But the charge had special poignancy after 410 A.D., when the Goths succeeded in invading and sacking Rome. It was the first time the city had suffered invasion since the Celts in the fourth century B.C. Even Hannibal had never quite managed it. By 410, Christianity was the official religion of the Roman Empire, and pagans pointed to the shocking success of the Goths as evidence that Christianity had sapped the old Roman virtues and that the gods were no longer providing special protection for Rome.

Augustine's reply to this event and the subsequent charges was slow (it took sixteen years to be completed), but massive and brilliant. His *City of God* is beyond all dispute one of the greatest books ever written in the Latin language and one of the most influential texts in the development of the West. Two loves, he says, give rise to two kinds of cities, the City of God and the City of Man. Love of God and neighbor undergirds the City of God; love of self—in both individual and collective forms—inspires the City of Man. The perfectly harmonious City of God, properly speaking, will exist only at the end times when God will bring it into being. Man cannot create that perfect felicity; he can only accept it as a gift. By contrast, the City of Man, our world, cannot help, given its origin, but be riven by egoism, rivalries, jealousy, competition, and the violent clashes they generate. Augustine was a great lover of Virgil and could even credit the notion that God had given Rome "*imperium* without end" because of its virtues. But in "the terrestrial glory of that most excellent empire,"[32] it had already had its reward. Like Virgil, he felt ambivalence about the morally doubtful nature of all earthly regimes, even the best of them. In that sense, he leveled a radical critique against Plato's *Republic,* Aristotle's *Politics,* the *cosmopolis* of the Stoics, Virgil's idealized Rome, and even Cicero's more modest sketch of a practical republic. All these attempts to found the good society were destined to produce imperfection and, therefore, injustice. Christ had said that his kingdom was not of this world for that very reason. The Church, as a kind of perfect society alongside the imperfect secular society, gives us a foretaste of the world to come, the City of God, which will be governed in perfect justice and peace.*

What distinguishes the members of the City of God from the members of the City of Man is the quality of their loves. The former love the true God and his goodness, the latter love themselves and their false and private goods. For Augustine, this is not merely a matter of two equally valid orientations. Love of the true God is the only basis for real virtue. The Romans had, indeed, shown great courage, prudence, and other virtues in expanding the

---

*Augustine did not mean that the Church is the City of God or perfect in all its operations—two obvious falsehoods. Properly speaking, that city exists in its pure form only above and at the end of time. For now, its future members belong both to the Church, an institution that anticipates the future consummation, and to secular society.

empire, but because they worshiped false gods—mere creatures rather than the source of all good—they were worshiping their own fantasies and their virtues were in the service of a "lust for domination" (the Latin term for this, *libido dominandi*, shows up frequently in later Western discussions). By contrast, members of the Church who hoped someday for life in the eternal city of justice had an obligation to make justice and proper religion prevail as much as is possible in this life, both for its own sake and for its power of rightly ordering social virtues and society. For instance, Constantine, the first Christian emperor, had introduced laws intended to prevent the common pagan practice of exposure of infants by an increased state subsidy for orphans and the poor.[33] The "Augustinian" approach to politics as a way of prudently managing the public realm for the purposes of peace and justice insofar as that is humanly possible in a world riven by sin—and therefore incapable of achieving complete and lasting justice—became a standard way of understanding society in the West. Those who looked to politics for perfection or salvation in later centuries were not only utopians, they were invariably heretics.

Recognition of the need for prudent management did not have to sap the ability of the state to protect itself and its citizens, as some anti-Christian pagans, smarting from the barbarian invasion of Rome, claimed. Since sin was rampant in the world, military and police powers had an important role in restraining evil. That insight, as we have seen, had been Virgil's as well in the *Aeneid*. But in Augustine it receives a better grounding since the properly constituted state can make better distinctions between just and unjust wars, and can provide the necessary restraints on domestic vice. In practice, of course, Christian kingdoms over the following centuries would be susceptible to self-deception and injustice as much as any of their pagan predecessors. Augustine and other early Christian thinkers had no theory of the state, but it would not be an exaggeration to see in his mistrust of all sinful men one of the later hallmarks of Western political thought: the search for a way to keep power under control by wise institutional arrangements. No one is so virtuous as to be entrusted with absolute power; that is for God alone.

The West had to wait for institutions to arise that might implement

some of these insights; the institutions were usually more prepared to interpret Augustine to suit themselves. Charlemagne, for example, seems to
have believed that Augustine authorized him to pursue a new Christian
Roman Empire. Augustine was skeptical of all such attempts to make the
City of God one with the City of Man, whether it was an emperor seeking
power over the Church or vice versa. It is worth noting that the distinction between the two cities is also something quite different from the modern separation of church and state. That separation, unknown to Judaism
earlier or to Islam afterward, finds its roots in the New Testament. Later
theorists would cite Jesus' words "Render unto Caesar the things that are
Caesar's and to God the things that are God's." (Matthew 22:21) Though
this was not exactly a political theory, it gave Christians an authoritative
source for resisting the Roman emperor and his representatives when they
stepped beyond their prerogatives. Providentially in the West, emperor and
church (later, emperor and pope) divided powers and loyalties between
them. This de facto separation, despite its problems, would bring considerable benefits to Western societies, since neither party could rightly claim
absolute authority. Augustine's views would show their value precisely
at the point where the pagans and later thinkers like Rousseau would object to the "divided loyalties" of Christians. Division is bad where it is bad.
Where it is required by the nature of things, it is good. It would be one of
the advantages to life in the West that everyone, king and commoner alike,
was held to standards that existed outside of the ruling class, the society, or
the mass of individuals to whom they were addressed. The West would be
marked not by simple theocracies and state religions so much as by a continuing and salutary struggle between two human realms, each of which
is the better for its distinction from the other.

   The Christian revolution, then, not only changed the way people thought
about God and the individual soul; it had even further repercussions in the
ways it shifted political theorizing and social practice. Within fifty years of
Augustine's death, Rome would be invaded again, this time putting an end
to the Western Empire and plunging the West into cultural backwardness
for several centuries. Yet in those very Dark Ages, other currents would

emerge and join with the surviving Greco-Roman elements—not least Germanic notions of liberty and loyalty—and inaugurate what we think of today as the basic shape of the West. And when the Latin western part of the empire (the Greek eastern part survived until 1453) recovered population and rediscovered its cultural and social roots, the society that emerged during the High Middle Ages brought with it many institutions and attitudes that were to persist unbroken down into the modern world.

CHAPTER 5

Medieval Highs and Lows

> The Glory of Him who moves everything
> through the universe, penetrates and shines
> in one part more and in another less.
>
> Dante Alighieri, *Paradiso* I. 1–3

> To that conflict [between medieval kings and
> churchmen] of four hundred years we owe the rise
> of civil liberty. If the Church had continued to but-
> tress the thrones of the kings whom it anointed, or
> if the struggle had terminated speedily in undivid-
> ed victory, all Europe would have sunk down under
> a Byzantine or Muscovite despotism. . . . although
> liberty was not the end for which they strove, it was
> the means by which the temporal and the spiritual
> power called the nations to their aid.
>
> Lord Acton[1]

T HE Middle Ages exert a strange and deep allure over the modern imagination. This is especially surprising since in our everyday language to
call something medieval evokes images of almost everything we believe is
opposed to what is modern. "Medieval," used in a certain tone and context,
conveys a sense of the brutal, uncultivated, fearful, superstitious, ignorant,
authoritarian, repressive, dirty, backward, and many even more uncompli-
mentary qualities, all connected in some vague fashion to the allegedly pernicious influence of Christianity during the period. This sense of modern
secular superiority seems to have survived the less than edifying events of
human history since medieval times, though Auschwitz and the Gulag may
have changed the relative values slightly. Yet at the very same time that attitudes such as these persist, the West retains a powerful fascination with the

kind of world depicted in a work like *The Lord of the Rings*, which is clearly intended to echo medieval circumstances and to offer an idealized presentation of medieval Christian values.

The medieval world was materially and intellectually much less developed than ours and, coming after the collapse of classical culture and the fall of the Roman Empire, it operated at a much lower cultural level than ancient Rome. For many people from the Renaissance and Reformation to the Enlightenment, that alone was cause for scorn. The scorn was based, however, on almost total ignorance, since it was not until the nineteenth century that comprehensive study of the period began. For Renaissance humanists and Protestant reformers alike, it was enough that medieval civilization wrote bad Latin or did not know the pagan classics or refused to confine itself to the strict letter of the Bible to denounce it as plagued by obscurantism and superstition. For Enlightenment figures such as Voltaire and Kant, the very energetic uses of reason by medieval philosophers and theologians seemed absurdly unreasonable, bordering on the pathological. Today, we know that the Middle Ages were a crucial stage in the emergence of the West, indeed the first real appearance of all the necessary elements.

Even before more reliable information about the Middle Ages became available, many people had begun to turn away from an uncritical embrace of the kind of enlightenment and rationality that had marked the West after the Renaissance. The romantic movement of the nineteenth century saw in the Middle Ages, with some justice, a way of life that was not hemmed in— as it felt itself to be—by the shallow reason, dark factories, narrow materialism, and central political control that emerged in Europe after the French Revolution. Novels like Walter Scott's *Ivanhoe* (1815) and later cultural currents like the Pre-Raphaelite movement in England, as its very name suggests, envisioned the Middle Ages in ways akin to Tolkien's view. Tolkien was an Oxford professor of Old and Middle English and knew what he was about in ways the romantics did not. But their instincts were good. There really was something attractive in the period. And important, because, as one scholar puts it, the three centuries from 800 to 1100 A.D., a crucial portion of the Middle Ages, "set Western Europe on its phenomenal rise, which has never been fundamentally reversed or halted for a significant length of time and thereby distinguishes the West from all other civilizations among humankind."[2] The same scholar provides a reason why we detect something attractive in the age:

> The medievals had to work out the solution to the human condition for themselves. Until well into the Middle Ages, and then only fitfully and in certain places, they were not routinized into behavior patterns dictated by technologically powerful law and government that determined the behavioral relationship of the two spheres of human experience, the spiritual and the material. There is, therefore, a naive autonomy and a persistent choice-making about medieval people that we find fresh and exciting.[3]

In short, the Middle Ages attract us because they remind us of the fundamental drama of the sacred and the secular in human life.

Why the Middle Ages in particular? In that period the central values of our whole civilization come together for the first time with the freshness and energy of new life. There were, of course, lords and ladies, comrades-in-arms, lovers, troubadours, friends, and spiritual leaders in other ages. But we do not sense there being as much at stake in them as there was in the formative medieval period. To take just one example, had the joint efforts of churchmen and monarchs not created the beginnings of a common Christian culture among the barbarian kingdoms, would it have been possible to stop the advance of Islam? In their astonishing and rapid conquest of North Africa, Muslim armies crossed the Strait of Gibraltar and conquered Christian Visigothic Spain in 711. Charles Martel, the first of the leaders in Charlemagne's line, halted their advance at the Battle of Poitiers in 732 and was even able to push Islamic forces back for good from southern France. As Edward Gibbon put it, had the Muslim advance not been stopped, "Perhaps the interpretation of the Koran would now be taught in the schools of Oxford, and her pulpits might demonstrate to circumcised people the sanctity and truth of the revelation of Mohammed."[4] The West exists today only because of the secular and religious developments that made the victory at Poitiers possible.

A Spiritual Geography

We have seen how the notion of the Greeks as the first Westerners cannot be supported by the evidence. Indeed, the Greek themselves denied it. Most of the standard accounts, however, suggest that Herodotus and the Greeks after him thought of themselves and Europe as the West and Asia Minor as the East. When Herodotus and the later Greeks looked west from the Greek heartland, they did not see the European continent as the home of like-minded, freedom-loving peoples, but as the abode of barbarians.* The Romans later provided the intelligence, skill, political organization, and ruling ability in Europe—to say nothing of the unity in Europe and Greece that democracy in the Greek city-states could never achieve. But even that was not enough to define what we today think of as the West. For the Roman domination of the Mediterranean was, itself, unstable over time, whatever the hopes of Virgil and Augustus. Constantine's founding of an eastern capital on the Hellespont, which today we know as Istanbul in Turkey, and his division of the empire into an eastern and a western half was simply an acknowledgment of natural differences that reasserted themselves and could be better dealt with by separate administrations. The division between those who used the Latin alphabet (the West) and those who used the Greek or one of the forms of Greek alphabet later developed by the two missionary brothers Saints Cyril and Methodius (the East) persists today, and even largely coincides with western and eastern Europe.

But there was one more element of spiritual geography that came into play and gave rise to the West in the Middle Ages. Germanic tribes sacked Rome and North Africa, which remained a Latin Christian area, as did the regions the "barbarians" conquered in Europe such as Visigothic Spain.

---

*Aristotle, for example, lays out the full spiritual geography as the Greeks of the great period of Athens saw it: Those who live in a cold climate and in Europe are full of spirit, but wanting in intelligence and skill; and therefore they retain comparative freedom, but have no political organization, and are incapable of ruling over others. Whereas the natives of Asia are intelligent and inventive, but they are wanting in spirit, and therefore they are always in a state of subjection and slavery. But the Hellenic race, which is situated between them, is likewise intermediate in character, being high-spirited and also intelligent.(*Politics* VII.vii)

The invaders had superior energy and military forces, but they recognized the cultural superiority of Rome—which by the fifth century partly meant Christianity as well. Contrary to what many people believe, several barbarian tribes had long been Christianized. The Goths, for instance, had been the object of missionary efforts early in the fourth century, and by 340 A.D., Ulfila had even translated the Bible into their language. Other peoples, in fits and starts, eventually adopted Roman culture. The Visigoths who sacked Rome in 410 and the Vandals who landed in North Africa in 430 were Arian Christians. In some cases, as was true of Odoacer, the German military leader who deposed Romulus Augustulus, the last Western emperor, in 476 A.D.—the traditional date for the fall of Rome—the barbarians had already been soldiers in the Roman army. And their peoples typically had interacted with Roman culture, including Christianity, for significant periods. "Barbarians" had been allowed to settle in Roman provinces since the second century, and large numbers followed the same route over the next two hundred years. The Roman armies in the later years of the empire, from high-level officers to foot soldiers, were largely composed of these newly settled peoples. Theodoric the Great, who assassinated Odoacer and his sons in 493 and took control of Italy, hoping to unite the new barbarian kingdoms through dynastic marriages and political maneuvering, was a Christian Ostrogoth educated in the East and sent by the Christian Eastern emperor Zeno to take control.

As even these few facts suggest, while rulers did change and life was severely disrupted in Latin territories, the weaknesses of Roman culture itself led to the need for a slow and painful integration of the older Roman system with the newer peoples. Salvian, a priest in mid-fifth-century Marseille, claimed that many Romans in his region preferred the rough openness of Christian barbarian rule to the suffocating taxation and bureaucracy of the late empire. This is probably an exaggeration, but it also provides evidence that religion partly "broke the fall" of the empire. "Barbarian" warriors were found on both sides in this struggle. Theodoric established an Ostrogothic kingdom in Italy that encouraged coexistence between Gothic and Roman Christians.[5] Like later barbarian kings throughout the Middle

Ages, he maintained lively diplomatic contacts with both the Eastern emperor and the pope. His scheme to create a larger confederation did not immediately succeed; circumstances in the former Roman provinces were too unsettled for that. But there would arise a new German-Roman empire in the western Mediterranean in the eighth century, shortly after Muslim raiders swept into Europe, changing the whole dynamic in what the Romans had called *mare nostrum,* and shifting the focus of Western civilization from Rome and the Mediterranean to a truly western European center.

Religion and Empire

Religion played an integral role in defining this new empire, because the various barbarian tribes retained particular, if vague, identities that had to be integrated into some larger unity. The process started very early, though this important phase in Western history is little known and in the past was usually dismissed under the rubric "the Dark Ages." Clovis, king of the Franks, publicly converted to Christianity in 493, the same year as Theodoric took over in Rome, which is to say only sixteen years after the fall of Rome. Clovis might have converted even earlier if not for worries about whether his nobles would follow him. They did, three years later, along with the people. In the early part of the sixth century, this king of the Franks, who would become central players in the Western synthesis, received the title of honorary consul from the Eastern Roman emperor, founded a new capital (Paris), and presided over a church council.[6] The Merovingian dynasty to which he belonged was weak, but remained unbroken until the rise of the Carolingians. And both noble lines vigorously promoted conversion among the northern peoples.

The dynamism of this conversion is astonishing. Only a hundred years later, Pope Gregory the Great "looked out upon a world in which, by the 590s, all the barbarian successor-states had adopted Christianity excepting only the Anglo-Saxon kingdoms of England."[7] He organized a missionary effort that included sending a Benedictine monk called Augustine (later know as "Augustine of Canterbury" to distinguish him from Saint Augustine of Hippo) to England in 597 to restore the church that had existed in

Roman Britain but had been destroyed by the Anglo-Saxon invasion. This mission quickly bore fruit, including the conversion of King Ethelbert in Kent, who gave Augustine permission and means to create a church at Canterbury, the forerunner of the magnificent medieval structure that still exists today. Another member of Gregory's missionary team was a certain Paulinus, who traveled from Canterbury to Northumbria with Ethelburga, a noblewoman sent to seal a dynastic marriage with King Edwin. She was already a Christian and, along with the Roman priest, she helped convert the king and establish a strong Catholic presence in Northumbria, roughly modern Yorkshire, which included important monastic foundations at Lindisfarne and Jarrow. In turn, these missions in Anglo-Saxon lands, along with the Irish monasteries, were crucial to the evangelization of the Germanic tribes on the continent that had not already been drawn into the Christian orbit.

The barbarian kings not only became nominal Christians, some of them even weighed in on theological disputes. Around the same period, Sisebut, the king of Visigothic Spain, wrote to Adaloald, the king of the Lombards, a Germanic tribe that had occupied northern Italy. Like many of the Germanic peoples, the Lombards had become Arian Christians owing to earlier contacts with the Eastern Roman Empire. Sisebut urged Adaloald to embrace Catholicism instead. In the early sixth century, Clovis himself had undertaken a war against the Goths with the ostensible purpose of converting them from Arian to Catholic Christianity, and his military campaign was remarkably successful. This kind of success spoke volumes to barbarian kings, who often had only dim theological convictions when they converted, but understood a god of power. The Frankish kingdom cut a wide swath through western Europe and laid the foundation for the later expansion under Charlemagne.

But a deeper cultural and spiritual foundation also had to emerge. And for this the energies of Ireland and Britain, themselves only recently converted, were crucial. In a world where cities were rare and not very influential, the monastic movement in the islands provided a powerful alternative locale for teaching and administration. One of the great founders of this movement, Saint Patrick, was the son of a Christian Roman deacon, who was captured at sixteen and taken as a slave into Ireland. After regaining his freedom, he studied in Gaul, returned to his family in Britain, and there became convinced that he was called to evangelize the Irish, which he began to do in the 430s, just as Augustine was dying in North Africa. Since Ireland was relatively undeveloped, his monastic foundations served a function that bishops in formal dioceses did elsewhere. Before the fall of Rome, churchmen like Saint Ambrose of Milan, Augustine, and a host of others, along with scholars like Saint Jerome (the translator of the Bible into Latin and a Christian humanist), had served as a parallel social and intellectual power structure to the Roman state within the Latin West. After the fall of Rome, in the northern areas that had not been as fully developed, monasteries had to take on the tasks (somewhat foreign to their original purpose) of educating elites, providing medical care, sheltering travelers, promoting agriculture, developing industries, and—in their continent-wide interactions with one another—maintaining such civilizational achievements as could be preserved in the new circumstances.

Later prejudices against allegedly corrupt monks have obscured the central role that the Benedictine order in particular played in preserving and recovering culture. But testimonies to their contributions are a commonplace of modern scholarship.[8] Far from creating the Dark Ages, the monks prevented this era from being even darker than it actually was. The Benedictines civilized the barbarians who invaded Italy. Cassiodorus, a Christian nobleman of southern Italy, set up a center of humanist studies called the Vivarium in the mid-500s on the Benedictine model. The Benedictines who went to Canterbury and York taught both Christian and pagan classics, and their influence was so great that many scholars regard the history of English Benedictines as virtually identical with that of the early English church. As the monks moved out and evangelized Germany, Switzerland, Austria, Bavaria, and points further east, they not only set up monastic centers of learning, ran cathedrals, and established schools (twenty-seven under Charlemagne) from which several later universities such as Paris, Bologna, and Lyons would arise. They prepared critical editions of crucial pagan and Christian texts as they copied them for widespread use.

Perhaps even more surprising, Benedictine monasteries became centers of economic activity and technological innovation. A demographic collapse owing to plague and other factors at the end of Roman times had seriously hampered agriculture, for example, so that many formerly cultivated areas had gone wild. As the monks spread around the countryside and their enclaves became the functional equivalent of towns, a regular pattern was established. Fields were put back under cultivation, swamps drained, wine and beer production increased, and craft workshops opened. The local population benefited not only from the monastery, but from the visitors who brought goods and unusual techniques from elsewhere. As one history of economics points out, "the desire to free clerics from time-consuming earthly tasks led to the introduction and diffusion of power machinery."[9] Over time, the Benedictines developed ways of using water power to mill grain, propel looms, and even work metals. Far from turning away from the world, these monks became some of its most active practical benefactors at a time when there was no other social institution in a position to help.

Another monastic current that was to influence the West's future greatly came out of Ireland. Though the Irish did not "save civilization," as has recently been claimed,[10] the Irish monks copied Greek and Latin texts and taught one another how to read them during a period when the West mostly forgot the Greco-Roman culture and would otherwise have lost much of what was eventually recovered. The Irish, perhaps because they were mostly recruited from rural places, also had a strong feeling for nature and its beauties, something that has led to comparisons with the Franciscan movement of a half millennium later. All these features would be quite important both for the evangelization of Ireland itself and for the subsequent role of the Irish in the missions to the Germanic tribes on the continent.

The Irish currents and the Roman mission begun under Gregory the Great met and mingled in the area around the old Roman city of York in Northumbria. Irish monks from Iona helped establish the famous monastery at Lindisfarne after King Edwin was defeated in a battle there and the Christian presence was disrupted. Together with the Benedictines from Kent in the south, they agreed at the Synod of Whitby in 664 to regularize the Roman dating of Easter, thereby bringing all the Irish church into closer conformity with Rome. Of even greater importance, however, was the fact that this double movement created one of the major intellectual centers of the age. The Venerable Bede, for example, who resided a bit down the coast from Lindisfarne at the monastery of Jarrow, was a chronicler and one of the most accomplished scholars between the fall of Rome and the rise of Charlemagne. Alcuin, the leader of Charlemagne's efforts at intellectual development, came from the same background.

More important even than its intellectual leadership, Christianity in the offshore islands produced a characteristic Christian type of energetic and wide-ranging missionaries, among them notably Saint Columbanus (ca. 543–615). His story is in a way emblematic of many other developments. By his time, it was possible to get a solid Latin education in Ireland itself. When he and a dozen companions set sail for mission territories, they founded (after a brief stay in Britain) a whole series of monasteries in Burgundy. That part of France then resembled nothing so much as Tolkien's Middle Earth, with ruins of old Roman fortifications, rulers confused about their status, contested successions to the throne, and a largely rural population. Columbanus and his fellows, under the aegis of King Gontram, vigorously set up new foundations that affected both the religious and the secular conditions of the land. His monastery at Luxeuil attracted so many monks that he had to found another at Fontaines. In the following century, Luxeuil itself would be the source of many new missionaries who spread out all over Europe bringing civilization and Christian values with them. Never one to let the grass grow under his feet, Columbanus moved into the territories of the eastern Germanic tribes, which were much less ready for evangelization than the people he met in Burgundy. He journeyed to what is today Switzerland, leaving behind a follower named Gallus, after whom the famous monastery at St. Gall is named. He even worked among the Arian Lombards in northern Italy, where he founded a major monastery at Bobbio, which still exists today.

All this was a harbinger for what would take place in more northerly regions in the seventh and eighth centuries. These were crucial developments because without the evangelization of northern Europe, the Christian swath extending from Italy across today's southern France out to Spain and the British Isles would later have found itself narrowly hemmed in between Islam in the south and hostile barbarians to the north. As it was, this Christian world was under considerable pressure from several directions until after 1000. But had its base been narrower and more fragile, the whole history of Europe might have been quite different. The key figure in this evangelizing effort was Saint Boniface (Winfrid), a Benedictine from the south of England who undertook the mission to the Old Saxons of the continent. Boniface has been described as "a man who had a deeper influence on the history of Europe than any Englishman who has ever lived . . . who first realized the union of Teutonic initiative and Latin order which is the source of the whole medieval development of culture."[11]

Like Columbanus, Boniface visited Rome to confer with the pope on missionary activity. (It was there that he received the Roman name Boniface, which made clear his allegiances.) In 722, just ten years before the showdown with the Muslim marauders at Poitiers, the pope made him a bishop and sent him to the court of the Frankish king. By this point, the Merovingians had given up control of their lands to Charlemagne's grandfather and father. Under their protection, Boniface moved to evangelize central Germany, which was of mixed Christian and pagan belief. He had a double task: first, to reform the Christians, who had become lax and corrupt; but primarily to convert the Saxons, the old tribes from which the Christians in Britain had originally come and whose language the missionaries still spoke. In a famous episode, he cut down the sacred oak at Geismar, which seems to have been a major Germanic shrine, and somehow, instead of provoking the wrath of the population, he won them over. Boniface kept pressing outward until, on the North Sea coast at Dokkum in Frisia, beyond the territory protected by the royal powers, he and his followers were killed by a random band of seagoing raiders in 754.

Saint Boniface's efforts in cooperation with the Frankish kings were only a part of a much broader movement that had begun before his arrival and would continue, with some gaps, over the next two centuries. There is no question that the Merovingians and the Carolingians saw religious conversion as a useful tool for their political and military goals. But there was also mixed in with this earthly ambition a true commitment to the religious cause. As the historian Richard Fletcher sums it up, "The directing elites in the barbarian kingdoms were prepared to divert colossal, staggering resources into the service of the new spiritual ideals. These adjectives are not used loosely. The number of monasteries founded, and the extent of their aggregate endowments, in seventh-century Francia and elsewhere, strain credulity. But the facts are well attested."[12] These institutions would soon number over seven hundred and would make a total collapse of Latin learning virtually impossible; even if scores of monasteries disappeared at the hands of invaders, so many would remain that the ground could be reseeded quite easily.

The Large Presence of Charlemagne

Charlemagne was six feet five according to his comrade and biographer, the humanist Einhard, with abundant energy and ambitions (the statue of him and his companions near Notre Dame in Paris captures something of that outsized presence). His predecessors had also sought to conquer territory in today's Germany by mounting military campaigns from their stronghold in West Francia. But Charlemagne aimed at a goal much larger than the usual territorial expansion or ethnic hegemony: he consciously sought to create an *imperium christianum*. He was in touch with the Byzantine emperors, who were considerably more cultured than any Western leader. And it is likely that he got the idea from their example of re-establishing a Western Christian empire. But it is also significant that the word he uses for empire here is the very thing, *imperium*, that Virgil had said Zeus granted to the Romans "without end."[13] The old Roman idea had combined a regime of earthly justice with divine approval. Charlemagne sought to recreate something quite similar, but with the Christian God in place of Zeus. The Holy Roman Empire that began with him never attained stable jurisdiction over western Europe. In several ways, that was providential because otherwise the West might have settled into a static sacred order of the Oriental or Byzantine type. Instead, the very instability and division of the West forced both church and state into constant and dynamic negotiations.

Part of that legacy is troubling and a recurring problem for both politics and religion. In early Christianity, there were occasional eruptions of religious imperialism, especially as the balance shifted in the Roman Empire towards a Christian majority. Monks in the East destroyed pagan statues of the gods and even temples, and manuscripts of pagan writers might be burned with the approval of Christian emperors. In a sense, the Christians were only doing what they had already seen the pagans do when positions were reversed—understandable, perhaps, if not very edifying. But this was never very extensive and, given the considerable number of pagans that existed down to the fall of the Western Empire, could not become a universal policy. Charlemagne, however, was the first Christian leader to use Christianity for purposes of conquest and control. His military campaigns could be quite brutal. Yet at the same time, he was counseled, if not exactly constrained, by the groups of learned Christians he had brought together to help further his twofold purpose of conquest and conversion.

The most prominent figure in that group was the English monk Alcuin, who had distinguished himself in the city of York and become the director of the cathedral school there. He and Charlemagne met at Parma in 781 as the monk was returning from a visit to Rome. The future emperor persuaded him to take on the responsibility of running the cathedral school in his capital of Aachen, which under Alcuin's dynamic leadership began to draw students from all over Europe. Charlemagne and his queen, Liutgard, as well as his sister Gisela, were among those students—women in the early Middle Ages having greater equality than they would possess after the return of Roman law.*

*Charlemagne and his schoolmaster were not content with merely one intellectual center or influence on a single class. Alcuin trained many people for positions of leadership in church and state (Alcuin himself coined the phrase *imperium christianum*). One, Rabanus Maurus, became a significant intellectual figure in his own right at the German monastery in Fulda, and other monasteries developed educational facilities and levels of learning unseen since the days of Rome. John Scotus Erigena, an Irish monk who occupied Alcuin's post as the head of the palace school around 850, was a skilled Greek translator and original theologian.

The new interest in learning led to the widespread copying of manuscripts, both Christian and classical, many of which still survive, and the development of a new and more legible script, Carolingian minuscule, which influenced Western letters well into the period of the early printing press. Alcuin also helped Charlemagne craft legislation requiring literacy among all the clergy. In an even more ambitious vein, Charlemagne called a church council that ordered the establishment of a primary school in every town and village. Priests were expected to teach the people free of charge. Alcuin's motto was *Disce ut doceas*, "Learn so that you can teach." Standardized versions of the Latin Bible and liturgical texts were also produced so that the true faith could be properly presented everywhere. Though implementation of all this was uneven, it led to multiple pockets of learning in northwestern Europe that would spring into fuller life as conditions improved several centuries later. The monasteries flourished to such an extent that even when the Carolingian system collapsed from internal and external strains, they remained as centers of learning, agriculture, manufacture, trade, coinage, and even credit—no small matter for the eventual recovery of the Western economy.

These humane initiatives ran parallel, however, with much sheer butchery. The very year (782) Alcuin took over at Aachen, Charlemagne was in the middle of his bloody Saxon campaign. In just one battle, he slaughtered 4,500 of the enemy and enslaved or deported others. His victories carried him farther than any of his predecessors, all the way to the Elbe River. While the pope declared three days of celebration at this military success and the forced conversions that followed, it all came at a high and not very Christian price. The death penalty was imposed on people who refused baptism, continued the barbarian practice of cremation, engaged in the old rites, and a host of other offenses.[14] The clear intention was the systematic destruction of the old pagan culture. To his credit, Alcuin and other learned people saw such procedures as wrong in themselves and likely to frustrate the very goal—true conversion—they were intended to achieve. The pagans were being preyed on rather than preached to, he warned.

Charlemagne was crowned Holy Roman Emperor in Rome by Pope Leo III on Christmas Day, 800 A.D. The round red marble stone on which he knelt can still be seen just inside the door of St. Peter's Basilica. Like the stone, his empire has had lasting effects in the West. The coronation formally linked him back to the old Western Empire, a first for the barbarian kings. In addition to his military successes in Germany, he freed Italy from the Lombards and thereby permitted the papacy, for good and for bad, to control a good portion of the peninsula until Italian unification in 1870. The protection of the Carolingians also allowed the Western Church to turn away from Byzantium, with which it had doctrinal conflicts. Further east, he pushed back barbarian domination of the Avars and enabled a return of Christianity along the Danube. And he reversed some Islamic conquests in Spain as well. By the time he died in 814, Charlemagne's empire covered much of what we think of as western and central Europe: from the Atlantic coast to today's Slovakia and the Balkans; and from the North Sea down across the Pyrenees in Spain and halfway down the Italian boot.

But lurking behind these successes was a serious dispute. Charlemagne thought of himself as both the temporal and the spiritual leader of Christianity, the bearer of "the two swords."* During his lifetime this presented a few tensions, but it is perhaps in the nature of things that the exact relationship between a religion like Christianity and the state cannot be settled. During the investiture controversy in the eleventh and early twelfth centuries, a dispute over who had the authority to appoint bishops and other church leaders, a fortunate set of circumstances arose, namely a weak empire and a strong papacy. Gregory VII, a reformer from Tuscany, was able to thwart ecclesiastical appointments by the secular power. Most histories, looking back from a modern perspective, see the emergence of secular power from religious control as the key to Western freedoms. This was an important development. But it was equally important that the church not be subordinate to the state or a mere organ of it. That would have tamed the reforming power of independent religious establishments

---

*Pope Gelasius I had written a famous letter to the emperor Anastasius in 494 that spoke of "two swords," the sacred and secular authority; the first was supreme in spiritual matters, the second normally controlled worldly things, though Gelasius deftly tried to define secular power as derivative. Though often cited as a significant stage in church/state separation, this treatise hardly settled the medieval struggles between popes and bishops on the one hand and kings and princes on the other.

and the sometimes prophetic role they need to play against earthly authority. The immediate conflict between popes and emperors was settled to a
tolerable degree with the 1122 Concordat of Worms, which allowed emperors indirect influence over church appointments, but reserved primary
responsibility to the Church itself.

A Second Dark Age and Renaissance

After the death of Charlemagne, the West faced another crisis, one more
dangerous in several respects than the fall of Rome. The emperor's heirs
squabbled with one another over bits of his kingdom, perilously dividing up
its resources and using them against one another. To make matters worse,
the weakened empire found itself beset by three forces simultaneously: the
Vikings from the north, the Saracens from the south, and the Magyars from
the east. Though it was to survive these onslaughts and Christianize all
comers except the Muslims, the attackers cut short the social, spiritual, and
intellectual revival under way. The empire fragmented under various feudal lords who ran local political affairs and made appointments of religious
leaders. It was not until around the year 1000, when the most learned man
in Europe, Gerbert of Aurillac, was elected pope, that conditions were stable
enough for the Carolingian foundation to put out fresh shoots.

Most accounts of the eleventh century in the past tended to emphasize
the beginnings of the Crusades and what seemed to be the crude bellicos-
ity of Latin Christendom at the time. But this is far from being the whole or
even the central story. The Crusades were only a small part of a much wider
recovery in many areas simultaneously. Why this expansion occurred after 1000 is not easy to say. It may have been the product of several mutually
reinforcing factors. But we know that population doubled in Christian Europe from 1000 to about 1300. Today, some people regard rapid population
increases as a cause of poverty; in sparsely settled areas of western Europe
after 1000, it meant more hands to grow food and produce goods. Some
scientists believe that a warm, wet period, called the Medieval Optimum,
made agriculture more productive. That along with improved technologies
such as the heavy plow and padded horse collar may have helped prime the

pump. Clearly, the defeat or conversion of Scandinavians and Magyars contributed a great deal to the West's ability to turn its attention in other directions. Growing confidence even allowed medieval Latins to challenge the far more advanced culture of Islam. Muslims had occupied much of Sicily in 827, for example, and had massacred the entire population of Syracuse in 878. Arab pirates had sacked Rome in 846. Now the tide began to turn slowly. Sicily was retaken in 965, Toledo in 1085, and the First Crusade resulted in a Kingdom of Jerusalem from 1099 to 1187, with a continuing Latin presence in the region for another sixty years.* Baghdad was overrun by the Mongols in 1258, which is probably a sign that the Muslim world had earlier gone into some sort of decline of its own. But even this surprising turn in military and political fortunes pales in comparison with the intellectual renaissance.

Pope Sylvester and the New Learning

This early renaissance (there were others, notably in the twelfth and thirteenth centuries) occurred primarily in the regions central to Charlemagne's empire: modern France, Belgium, and northern Italy.[15] And the primary cause of this phenomenon was the network of scattered religious foundations that Charlemagne had helped found and support, though these had experienced gains and losses and uneven development. Yet even the Carolingian efforts at universal elementary education paid off in the new millennium. Gerbert of Aurillac, who became Pope Sylvester II, began his schooling as a boy at the monastery in his hometown. Because of his obvious talents he was sent to Spain, where he studied with several Arab teachers at Cordova and Seville. The future pope had a special talent for mathematics and science, in which the Arabs far surpassed the Latin West at the time. (He is said to have introduced Arabic numerals to Rome and invented the pendulum clock.) By all reports, he was a gifted teacher of scientific subjects and wrote a treatise on the abacus. To us an abacus is a simple computing device, but we have to real-

*Because of Western self-criticism, the Crusades are often thought of as having poisoned Latin-Muslim relations. In fact, they were not much noticed in the Islamic world until the nineteenth century, when the dominance of the West made them loom large in Muslim eyes. See Bernard Lewis, *The Crisis of Islam: Holy War and Unholy Terror* (New York: Modern Library, 2003), p. 51.

ize that in the context, it was as if a modern pope had written a book on computer programming. And Gerbert was far from being the only scientist to occupy high church office.

Perhaps the most common charge against the Middle Ages is that it ignored or even suppressed science for religious reasons. Since we identify Western culture so strongly with science and technology, the charge is virtually a statement that the medievals were not really Westerners. It is always possible to find some passage from a cranky church figure that lends credence to this view. But it would be far fairer to say that Christian thinkers welcomed and pursued learning as well as they could under contemporary circumstances, and for good theological reasons. Many of them believed and said frequently that, as Aquinas put it, "Mistakes about creatures lead to mistaken knowledge about God."[16] Christians in the western half of the Roman Empire, however, started at a double disadvantage. As we saw in an earlier chapter, even the poet Virgil conceded that the Romans were not skilled in the purer sciences such as astronomy. And during the half millennium after Rome fell, the Latins lost even the few opportunities they might have had for direct study of Greek science. That had to wait until the relatively stable period after 1000 and circumstances that allowed them to take advantage of the superior scientific learning of Muslims.

In terms of both science and philosophy, the Muslim world had a big impact on the Latin world at that point. The Arabs had had direct access to Greek in the East, and during the late 700s and early 800s there were many Arabic translations of Greek mathematical, medical, and astronomical texts by teams of Christian, Jewish, and Muslim scholars. Like Christianity and Judaism, Muslim monotheism and belief in a good and transcendent Creator reinforced notions of an independent and stable natural order that could—and should—be investigated by reason. When Latin Christianity found the tranquility to absorb this material, translation from the Arabic into Latin began, first in the monasteries of northern Spain just before the year 1000. Since Christian forces were retaking Toledo, Cordoba, and Seville from 1085 to 1248, there was opportunity for translation on a larger scale. Similar activity took place in Sicily and even the Middle East. Curiously, much of the early translating focused on mathematical and scientific texts rather than philosophy, perhaps because Western intellectuals were not yet aware of the philosophical and theological speculation in Greek that would in a short time so deeply mark the medieval universities.

Even before the universities, however, these and many other intellectual developments were aided by the emergence of various centers of learning in the more settled circumstances after 1000. The most important among these were the cathedral schools that arose in many places along with the groups of intellectuals gathered at royal and imperial courts—in particular, the school at Chartres, which was founded by one of Gerbert of Aurillac's science students who came to be known as Fulbert of Chartres. (As bishop, Fulbert also built the cathedral at Chartres after an earlier one burned down.)

Chartres was a physical as well as an intellectual crossroads. Manuscripts arrived from various places throughout Europe where its scholars had studied or where they had friends. Over the next centuries, until the emergence of true universities, Chartres was a hub of study including the sciences. Two of its main figures in the twelfth century, Thierry of Chartres and William of Conches, engaged in some fundamental speculation about astronomy and cosmology. To this day, Chartres bears the marks of its commitment to learning: the north portal of the facade shows the Virgin Mary as the Seat of Wisdom, but around her are arrayed figures representing the seven liberal arts (at the time, four of them were what we would call sciences: mathematics, geometry, music, and astronomy) as well as distinguished practitioners of them such as Aristotle and Pythagoras.

As towns and cities began to grow, they too played a role in educational expansion. A few cities—Salerno (medicine), Bologna (law), and Paris (theology and the liberal arts)—and cathedral schools were to give rise to the first universities. The grand cathedrals themselves arose during this period, along with new artistic styles. It was a Benedictine monk, Guido of Arezzo, who created the world's first true musical notation system around 1050. Some monasteries also served as way stations for pilgrims and visitors on the way to Rome (as travel increased in the more stable conditions).

In those places, ideas and perspectives could be exchanged and disseminated far and wide. But the most important development was the universities, and with them a cohort of men who thought with greater rigor and intellectual ambitiousness than had been seen in the West since the time of Aristotle, who was rediscovered around the same time and widely used in philosophical and theological disputes. And while they all operated in a basic Catholic framework, they engendered various schools of thought that sometimes clashed.

Berengar of Tours, for example, a product of the cathedral school of Chartres, invoked Genesis in arguing: "It is the part of courage to have recourse to dialectic in all things, for recourse to dialectic is recourse to reason, and he who does not avail himself of reason abandons his chief honor, since by virtue of reason he was made in the image of God." In histories Berengar is often portrayed as opposed to another great thinker, Lanfranc, of the prominent monastery at Bec, who emphasized the supra-rational truths of revelation. But Lanfranc himself could say that "dialectic is no enemy to the mysteries of God, rather it confirms them, if rightly used, when the matter demands it."[17] What was really at issue in the dispute was something that medieval philosophers and theologians would gradually come to formulate with clarity: the distinction between truths available to natural reason alone and revealed truths towards which reason could move but not ultimately grasp.

The most powerful of the early thinkers who followed this initial dispute was the amiable Saint Anselm, who is credited with two sayings that still retain force: *Fides quaerens intellectum* ("Faith seeking understanding") and *Credo ut intelligam* ("I believe in order to understand"). Some modern philosophers, such as Kant, have disputed Anselm's Ontological Argument, which claims that God must exist because by definition he is the greatest thing that can be conceived, and this necessarily means that he exists in fact as well as in theory. This argument continues to attract analysis. Less noticed, however, is the fact that Anselm's argument makes Creation something that is not necessary to God since it can add nothing to him if he is the greatest thing that can be conceived; this in turn implies that reason is sufficient for understanding the normal relations within the material world, a step beyond even the Greek view of knowledge since the Greeks had included their gods within the world. The freeing of reason in some of its uses also ran certain risks. Not a few of the resulting rational speculations veered off into heterodox and even heretical notions—a feature of medieval thought and practice that has been obscured by the mistaken characterization of the Middle Ages as having subordinated reason to faith.[18]

The new developments in medieval thinking were cross-fertilized by contacts with the East during the First Crusade (1095), but they had begun earlier and were rooted in native Western practices going back centuries. After 1000, Western Christian culture, which had always been multicultural in the sense that it was the product of Greek, Latin, Jewish, and Germanic elements, was also stimulated in some new directions by increased Muslim and Jewish influences. Some of the lost texts of Aristotle first made their way into Western philosophical and theological debates by means of translations from the Arabic. Aristotle's logical works had been important during the early medieval period, and because they had been translated into Latin by Boethius, a Christian writer in the sixth century, they had always been available. But Aristotle's major works such as the *Ethics*, *Politics*, and *Metaphysics*, along with his *Physics* and other scientific works, had to wait. Ironically, Aristotle and other Greek works—mostly Neoplatonic texts treating ideas that Western Christians more typically encountered in Augustine—had been translated into Arabic largely by Syrian Christians at Baghdad between roughly 750 and 900, the heyday of early Arabic philosophy. A series of later Arab thinkers added to this classical inheritance. Among the many names that crop up repeatedly in medieval Latin texts are Alfarabi, Avicenna (Ibn Sina), and Averroës (Ibn Rushd), the last a Muslim born in Cordoba, Spain, and sometimes known simply as the Commentator for his careful explications of Aristotle. And in addition to these Muslim figures, two Jewish philosophers of the period also influenced Western Christian thought: Avicebron (Salomon Ibn Gebrirol—whom Christians mistakenly believed was a Muslim) and Moses Maimonides, both of them from the Jewish communities of Spain. Maimonides has close affinities with his Christian counterparts, especially in his *Guide for the Perplexed*, which tries to establish the proper relations between philosophy and revelation, and anticipates Aquinas.

In addition to the many good things of an intellectual nature already going on in this period, Western learning got a push from two new religious orders of a novel kind that were founded in the early thirteenth century—the Dominicans by the Spaniard Dominic Guzman (1170–1221) and the Franciscans by the Italian Francis of Assisi (1181–1226).

Dominic and his Order of Preachers found widespread ignorance and dualistic heresy in Spain. His Dominicans were created to teach the ignorant and convince the misguided. The Franciscans focused on missions to the poor and on living a pure apostolic life. Within a short time after Francis's death, however, they felt compelled to respond to the intellectual poverty of the West. Franciscans and Dominicans both served as distinguished professors at the University of Paris. For example, Saint Bonaventure, a Franciscan, was probably second only to Thomas Aquinas, a Dominican, in theological sophistication in the thirteenth century. Both orders also helped advance the sciences, primarily through the Franciscan Roger Bacon in England and the Dominican Albertus Magnus in Germany, but also through numerous lesser figures.

The greatest of all the high medieval thinkers, of course, was Thomas Aquinas. The son of a prominent noble family in southern Italy, he made an early choice to become a Dominican, studied at Naples and Rome, and then at Paris with Albertus Magnus, one of the outstanding science writers of the Middle Ages. He accompanied Albertus to Cologne and taught there, before returning to Paris and producing the massive output for which he is known. A famous anecdote about him, well attested in the sources, is that after a lifetime of producing truly enormous quantities of philosophical and scriptural commentaries, ambitious summaries of theology and philosophy, and various other texts, he had a vision shortly before he died and pronounced that everything he had written was *ut palea* ("like straw") compared with what he had seen. It would appear to be a rare case of a great thinker turning away from intellectual labor because of an intuition of something higher than the human mind.

Aquinas was beyond all doubt a remarkable intellect, the kind of man whom the human race may neglect for a while but can never abandon. Not only did he set himself the task of writing a *summa*—a form of synthesis that was common at the time—of theology, he did so with a calmness and completeness that no other person came close to matching. The calmness has often been noted; what has been less noticed is that it takes strong emotional investment to keep at such a task over years and thousands of pages. If anything, however, the completeness may be even more remarkable. Aquinas is famous for distinguishing and classifying the various kinds and degrees of realities in order to present them in a coherent unity. But there is more than intellectual curiosity behind this method. No one passage from Thomas's immense *oeuvre* explains the intellectual love of God that he everywhere shows, unless it might be the following:

> [T]he distinction and multitude of things come from the intention of the first agent, who is God. For He brought things into being in order that His goodness might be communicated to creatures, and be represented by them; and because His goodness could not be adequately represented by one creature alone, He produced many and diverse creatures, that what was wanting to one in the representation of the divine goodness might be supplied by another. For goodness, which in God is simple and uniform, in creatures is manifold and divided; and hence the whole universe together participates the divine goodness [*sic*] more perfectly, and represents it better than any single creature whatever.[19]

It is no surprise that the man who wrote these almost poetic words believed that reflecting the fullness and variety of reality in his thought was a way to draw near to the rich simplicity at which that thought was ultimately aimed.

All of these medieval developments, which are better known today than in the past, force us to reject the usual presentation of medieval Christian philosophy as both a slave to authority and dogmatism, and a fruitless waste of energy on pointless questions. Medieval philosophers were almost universally Christians, so their thinking moves within Christian horizons.

Ecclesiastical authorities occasionally reeled in those engaged in dangerous speculation—defined as denying the existence of God, his power, or human free will, denials that were seen as rendering human life inhuman. But within that horizon—and all ages have limits—opinions varied a great deal. Contrary to widespread opinion, medieval scientists, philosophers, and theologians alike viewed arguments based on authority as feeble and said so in a variety of places. Aquinas, for example, said that "The argument from authority is the weakest." The scientists in particular did not espouse a dumb creationism, but by and large—much like modern scientists—they thought God, once he had created the world, operated in it by way of secondary causes. They had different opinions about how these causes worked and they disputed them with one another. From a modern standpoint, they reasoned more and observed less than we would like, a reflection of the relatively primitive state of their technology. But we can see that by the twelfth century something different from what existed in other cultures was starting to emerge in the West.

Historians of philosophy today point to two basic features of medieval scholastic philosophy: the question (*quaestio*) and the disputation (*disputatio*). A question was the typical way philosophers addressed specific points. In his *Summa theologica*, for example, Aquinas proceeds in an orderly fashion through a series of questions. Typically, he lines up all the known positions on that question and then seeks to sort out the way in which the various truths contained in them may be reconciled and the errors eliminated. Though most medieval questions had to do with problems of theology, others began to analyze issues that had both scientific and existential importance. But even the questions that seem abstruse to us had a discernible importance within the medieval system. No known medieval theologian asked the question usually cited to show their irrelevance: How many angels can dance on the head of a pin? But if someone had asked this, it would have been to make something like a true mathematical observation: if you believe that angels are pure spirits who do not occupy space, then an infinite number of angels could be said to fit on the smallest pin head—a reflection that resembles infinitesimal calculus more than it does mere foolishness.

Similarly, the *disputatio* had profound effects on the ways the West looked at truths. Since medieval philosophers and theologians were not merely parroting the ideas of distinguished figures like Aristotle or the Arabs, they developed different interpretations and outright refutations of them on many points. One way that the truth was sorted out was by public disputation, which at a place like the University of Paris seems to have drawn large crowds who saw the clash of opinion as something of a sporting event. In a disputation, a carefully formulated question, as clear and distinct as even Descartes could have wished, would be debated. Twice a year, during Advent and Lent, there would be more freewheeling debate on what were called *quodlibetal* questions, meaning essentially anything one might propose. Whatever we may think about the substance of these debates, their form certainly trained Western intellectuals to question and distinguish carefully. Robert de Sorbon, who gave his name to the institution he helped found in Paris, said: "Nothing is known perfectly which has not been masticated by the teeth of disputation." Later scholasticism might sometimes wallow in truly sterile and fruitless matters, but the method prepared sharp intellectual habits that would be applied with great benefit during the Renaissance and the scientific revolution.

The Poetry of Medievalism

The Middle Ages were not entirely about philosophy, theology, and politics. Another element appears with the most illustrious of medieval poets, Dante Alighieri (1265–1321), who brings into focus several features of the late Middle Ages. Dante was born in Florence, one of the new commercial centers that had risen with the recovery of learning and trade. There was no university in the city yet, but Dante was able to go quite far in his studies with the Dominicans at Santa Maria Novella and the Franciscans of Santa Croce. (Because of Dante we know about this work by the mendicants of Florence in some detail, but we can assume that similar educational efforts were going on in scores of new cities.) Florence was in many ways a typical medieval city, if a wealthier center of trade than most. The commune, as it called itself, was close-knit and hierarchical, but it allowed participation by all classes and professions through the guilds and other organizations. A historian has rightly pointed out that the medieval city "was essentially a unity—a visible and tangible unity, sharply defined by the circle of its walls and towers and centered in the cathedral, the visible embodiment of the faith and spiritual purpose of the community."[20] At the same time, Florence was riven by violent political factions, local interests that were drawn into the larger European conflict over the relationship between pope and emperor.

Dante spent his early years as a poet perfecting a style of verse that had appeared in the south of France in the preceding century, probably influenced by Spanish-Arab sources, courtly love poetry. We are so used to love poetry that it is hard to realize that it only came into prominence in the West during the late Middle Ages. In Dante's hands, the love between a man and a woman is coupled with the long Western tradition of love as a cosmic force. Like the great theological *summae*, *The Divine Comedy* is a summation of all times and cultures known to his age, but presented through a series of vivid encounters with various individuals. Dante casts his story as a literal journey that covers the whole universe: from being lost in a dark wood on earth, down through the circles of Hell, back up the mountain of Purgatory to the Earthly Paradise, and after that through the heavens to the beatific vision of God. No other work of the Middle Ages or of classical antiquity comes close to Dante's in scope. A modern literary critic has called it the Summa of Human Life.[21] It is an interesting question whether our own sense of the universe and human life is not considerably poorer. Indeed, Dante's poem shows two concepts that rose into prominence in the Middle Ages and are in danger of being lost today.

First, in *The Divine Comedy* the human person emerges for the first time in three dimensions. Dante says in a letter to his patron, Can Grande della Scala, that the subject of the poem is "the state of souls after death." For many of us today, that would be a sure formula for a lifeless, abstract art. But in Dante the souls after death are *more* themselves than they were in earthly life and have not lost anything of what they ever were. The very Christian doctrine of the immortality of the soul requires them to be present in the afterlife in all their fullness, but purified, clearer, more forcefully the essence of themselves. Far from taking away from their humanity, their extension into eternity reveals to us more about them than we could have known in this life alone.

But Dante has a second purpose: "The subject is man as according to his merits or demerits in his exercise of his free will he is deserving of reward or punishment by justice." On this point, *The Divine Comedy* shows itself to be encyclopedic in another sense. It seeks to include in a literary way everything that the medieval tradition thought of as constituting the world: Heaven and Hell, philosophy and theology, war and peace, learning and holiness, politics and religion, emperor and pope. Dante classifies figures from the distant past down to his own day, some world-famous and others known only to himself personally, with an industry and fine discrimination worthy of Thomas Aquinas. As in the Bible, his characters come from high and low social strata. To cite just a few: Adam, Aquinas, Augustine, Bernard, Pope Boniface VIII, Hugh Capet, Julius Caesar, Cato, Charlemagne, Pope Celestine V, Constantine, Arnaut Daniel, King David, Dominic, Francis, Frederick II, Justinian, Lucan, Charles Martel, the Virgin Mary, Mohammed, Odysseus, Saint Peter, Semiramis, Socrates, Solomon, Trajan, Tristan, and many more. The good pagans are in Limbo: Homer, Virgil, Ovid, Horace, Plato, and Aristotle ("the master of those who know"). Dante respects them enough that he places them in a region that preserves the dignity they had in life, but denies them Christian joy and hope. Judas Iscariot, Brutus, and Cassius are at the very bottom of Hell being chewed on by Satan because they committed the ultimate betrayal, the first against God, the other two against their lawful ruler, Julius Caesar.

Dante has guides through the three otherworldly realms. The first is Virgil, who though living in Limbo has been sent by Heaven to lead Dante through Hell and Purgatory, the two areas for which natural human reason, which Virgil sometimes symbolizes, is sufficient. As he nears the beatific vision, the great contemplative Saint Bernard of Clairvaux will gently take him along. But in the middle areas, after Dante reaches the top of Purgatory and enters the Earthly Paradise located there, he meets the person who lies behind all his life's labors, Beatrice, a woman of Florence with whom Dante fell in love. Beatrice symbolizes several things, but she is also a real woman, and this daring move by Dante scandalized some of the narrower church-men of his time. It was his great intuition to see that it was possible for or-dinary love that awakens us as full human beings to be coordinated with Love as Plato, Virgil, the Bible, Augustine, and Aquinas had elaborated it—as "The Love that moves the sun and the other stars."

Dante's vision is by design, therefore, both highly personal and ambi-tiously universal. Many of his saints and sinners occupy places in the world that we might expect. But he also puts popes in Hell and pagans in Para-dise. And one of his underlying motivations is to get right the relationship between church and state, not least because—as a man who had once oc-cupied the highest political office in his native city—he suffered exile for the last twenty years of his life on account of what he believed to be a disordered relationship between them, and specifically because of the political machi-nations of Pope Boniface VIII.

How can his work be both otherworldly and worldly at the same time? It is easy to misunderstand the "otherworldliness" of Dante and of the cen-tral medieval tradition. To many modern people, it seems as if ancient and medieval Christians turned their backs on the world and denigrated its im-portance. But the relationship between the medieval world and the great pagans and moderns is more complex than it seems and breaks down into different categories. In both ancient and medieval thought, the world had a severely limited importance because of what it truly is for us: a brief inter-lude between two eternities in which all things are passing. This realization did not lead Dante any more than it did the major pagan thinkers to neglect very real worldly duties; it merely put them in a different perspective.

For example, one pagan writer describes how "earth itself seemed to me so small that I was scornful of our empire, which covers only a single point, as it were, upon its surface," from the outermost sphere of the universe in the old Greek Ptolemaic system, and he cries out:

> How long will your thoughts be fixed upon the lowly earth? Do you not
> see what lofty regions you have entered? These are the nine circles, or

rather spheres by which the whole is joined. One of them, the outermost, is that of heaven; it contains all the rest, and is itself the supreme
God, holding and embracing within itself all the other spheres; in it are
fixed the eternal revolving courses of the stars. Beneath it are seven
other spheres which revolve in the opposite direction to that heaven.
. . . But below the Moon there is nothing except what is mortal, save
only the souls given to the human race by the bounty of the gods, while
above the Moon all things are eternal. For the ninth and central sphere,
which is the earth, is immovable and the lowest of all, and toward it all
weighted bodies are drawn by their own tendency.

This passage is not drawn from some crabbed medieval theologian, but from
the genial old Roman Marcus Tullius Cicero, and in his treatise *On the Republic*, no less. Cicero here continues a long classical tradition of taking
responsibility for the world—indeed, of seeing that responsibility as a religious duty—but simultaneously accepting the wisdom of not being too focused on our brief sojourn here.

Dante, of course, has a more developed theology behind him than did the
pagans. But even the more rationalist philosophers like Aristotle made room
in their political philosophy for the fact that our human reality includes the
ethical and the political, but goes beyond to a contemplative dimension. As
Aristotle says in the *Ethics*, in a passage that drew much attention from the
medievals: "We ought not to obey those who enjoin that a man should have
man's thoughts and a mortal the thoughts of mortality, but we ought as
far as possible to achieve immortality, and do all that man may to live in ac-
cordance with the highest things in him; for though this be small in bulk, in
power and value it far surpasses all the rest."[22] This is only one of many passages that may make us wonder whether the "rational" Greeks were closer
to the medievals than to us.

Dante had another problem associated with the theological tradition,
however, because unlike the old Roman system, Christian teaching identified the Church as striving towards Augustine's City of God. In the two
centuries prior to Dante's birth, a furious debate had gone on concerning

the relative status of pope and emperor. As a serious and orthodox Catholic,[23] Dante had to allow for the spiritual and moral prerogatives of the successor of Saint Peter. But as an Italian politician with sad experience of the consequences of a pope's wielding temporal power—consequences both for the state and for the holiness of the Church—he felt a responsibility to analyze the problem in his treatise *De monarchia.* His views there are quite original, in keeping with the typical medieval handling of received texts: the classical authorities are accorded great respect, but contrary to the historical stereotypes that saw medieval thinkers as slaves to "authorities," the ancient texts are treated with additions, clarifications, and even corrections.

Ever since Jesus said to the followers of the Pharisees and the Herodians, "Render unto Caesar the things that are Caesar's and to God the things that are God's" (Matthew 22:12), Christianity had a special problem that might admit of several solutions. Under the pagan empire, of course, what was owed to Caesar was limited and specifiable, primarily taxes and obedience. The early Christians, following Saint Paul's advice in various places, could agree to that. But what if Caesar were a Christian emperor? In the ancient world, the opposition of pope and emperor was not as stark as it had become by the High Middle Ages. Nor had Christians had experience of what it might do to the position of the Church itself if a pope exercised temporal authority, with all the potential corruptions and injustices to which it might lead, as had actually happened in the century of Dante's birth. Pro-papal theorists formulated the question in a way that made the pope a spiritual sun and the secular power a moon shining with reflected light. Thomas Aquinas, securely in the papal camp, said that the pope "holds the supreme authority in either sphere."

Though Dante adopted much from Aquinas and was in many ways a man of the scholastic philosophers, he directly contradicted the theologian on this point. For Dante in *De monarchia* speaks of "the Sovereign Pontiff, vicar of Our Lord Jesus Christ and Peter's successor, to whom we owe what is the due, not of Christ, but of Peter." He further claims that the secular "moon" shines with its own kind of light, and that it derives its authority over its own proper sphere not through the mediation of the pope but directly from God. By the time he came to write the *Purgatorio*, he was ready to state this point more strongly:

> Rome, which formed the world for good,
>
> once held two suns, that lit the one road,
>
> and the other, the world's and that to God.[24]

Dante was a poet and not a philosopher, though he was an astute and relentless thinker. So the image here may not be intended to bear the full philosophical weight it might have carried in a prose treatise. But the image itself suggests he was arguing for something he believed important. Dante also made another unprecedented claim: human beings have "two beatitudes," happiness in this life and blessedness in the next. This led some to task him with Averroism, which, in a famous theological misunderstanding of the Islamic philosopher Ibn Rushd, argued that there were two truths: one of reason, the other of faith. Averroës' true position has since been clarified,[25] and it seems more likely that Dante, accepting the harmony of reason and faith that he found in Aquinas, believed that a similar harmony could prevail between church and empire if both understood properly their God-given roles.[26]

The one chance he discerned of achieving a new Roman order in his lifetime proved illusory. The Count of Luxemburg, later Emperor Henry VII, began his descent into Italy in 1309 to claim the imperial crown. Dante wrote a moving letter to the princes of Italy to welcome this new "strong lion of Judah," this Moses who would lead his people out of the oppression of the Egyptians, this new Caesar Augustus.[27] Henry's task seemed almost possible because he had the backing of Pope Clement V, who was in exile in Avignon, during a period often called the "Babylonian Captivity" of the papacy. Dante also wrote to Henry encouraging him to think of himself as the latest in a line of biblical and classical liberators, including Moses and even Aeneas. With expectations so high, it came as a shock when the pope betrayed the imperial cause and sided with forces in France, Naples, and—most painfully for the exiled poet—Dante's enemies in Florence. Clement died in 1313 and Henry in the following year, putting an end to the whole dream. (Beatrice says in *Paradiso*, which was written later, that the emperor has a place ready in heaven, and the pope in hell.)[28]

Dante had gotten hold of a serious point that runs backwards and forwards from him: the need for global order that had also occupied Virgil. He gave relatively little attention to the Augustinian sense of the fallen nature of human institutions. For Augustine, governments were not much to be trusted, nor was there much that could be hoped for from them. Dante had certainly seen the corruption and violent factionalism that his native Florence had produced, with disastrous effects for him personally, for the city, and for Italy and the world. But in his zeal to resolve all those partisan passions, he became blind to the way that the same evils might arise in the universal monarchy. He had a point against the factions. Augustine, however, had deeper insight into the consequences of the Fall for all human beings, the God-appointed emperor as much as the pope or the warring princes. The balance between universalism and the necessity of limited governments remained a problem that received various solutions, all of them, even the modern ones, imperfect.

The Allure of the Source

We have been right in the past two centuries to maintain a lively interest in the Middle Ages, a period once thought to be dark and of little consequence except, perhaps, as a cautionary tale. Many of the issues that medieval people tried to resolve as best they could with the resources available to them remain very much with us today. We owe our existence as Western civilization to the missionaries and the warriors who kept the weak barbarian kingdoms from becoming part of the Muslim empire. The ongoing and productive quarrel between religious and political authority is distinctive to the West; it is found in almost no other culture. And far from being a drawback, the basic division of Western civilization between a sacred and a secular power, shot through with the multiple cultural influences we have studied in earlier chapters, has been the source of much of our restless exploration and our discontent with mere inherited forms.

Medieval religion played a more dynamic role in the recovery and re-newed evolution of scientific, social, and political life than it has been giv-en credit for. Without the presence of energetic religious institutions and varied manifestations of religious devotion, the West would most certainly have become an unrecognizably different place.

CHAPTER 6

Renaissances and Reforms

> What a piece of work is man! How noble in rea-
> son! how infinite in faculties! in form and moving,
> how express and admirable! in action how like an
> angel! in apprehension, how like a god! the beau-
> ty of the world! the paragon of animals! And yet,
> to me, what is this quintessence of dust?
>
> *Hamlet* II.ii.115–117

AT the end of the long corridors of the Vatican Museums that lead to the Sistine Chapel, quite near the chapel itself, is the Stanza della Segnatura, the room in which the pope and his curia once made legal decisions, and where Raphael created on an entire wall one of the greatest paintings from one of the high points of Western culture: *The School of Athens*. Pope Julius II, a man known more for his desire to secure the Church through military exploits than for anything else, had commissioned Raphael to do several paintings (1508–1511) in the chamber because magnificent art, he believed, brought prestige and therefore more stability to the Holy See. Michelangelo was painting the Sistine Chapel ceiling at roughly the same time. Papal motives aside, the result of Raphael's commission was quite astonishing even among the many astonishments of the Italian Renaissance. In a classically balanced, singular work he placed figures from Greek antiquity[1] who symbolized everything that Christian Rome in the early sixteenth century felt was most valuable about the Greek inheritance—philosophy, theology, ethics, mathematics, science, astronomy, and political thought—all then still being rediscovered, often by artists and scholars in the pay of the Church.

The School of Athens is quite well known, but for many university-educated people who have seen or studied it, the painting seems never to have provoked an obvious question. One powerful strand in contemporary culture maintains that the Greeks represent reason and enlightenment (a position that, as we have seen, needs serious qualification), and that Christianity, especially in its Roman Catholic version, is irrational and superstitious (another position needing qualification). Christians were persecuted by the ancient Roman emperors precisely for that reason, the story runs, and the early Christians suppressed Greek thought and science when they got the upper hand in Rome, leading to the Closing of the Western Mind[2] (a gross historical error that got its start among anti-Christian propagandists during the Enlightenment in the eighteenth century). In this view, the Christian legacy in the West is a history of Dark Ages, Crusades, Inquisitions, opposition to science (e.g., Galileo), religious wars, and various other forms of intolerance. But then what is the meaning of Raphael's painting in the very heart of the only ChristianChurch in the West?

The answer deserves some careful consideration, because we have also inherited an opposite view—that this engagement with the Greeks existed within the Church but should be deplored on religious grounds, as Martin Luther did (in one of his periodic outbursts, Luther referred to Aristotle, one of the two central figures in *The School of Athens,* as "that buffoon who misled the Church"). Centuries of historical partisanship have accustomed those of us in the English-speaking world who are heirs to Protestantism to think, with the more automatic religious and ethical parts of our minds, that in spite of its attractions there was something deeply corrupt about the cultural flowering during the Renaissance. Without question, papal Rome was suffering under many obvious corruptions at the time, as Luther was able to observe personally during a pilgrimage to that city at exactly the same time as Raphael was at work in the Segnatura. And his vehemence in later denouncing that corruption prepared large swaths of Western opinion to believe that there was something particularly decadent in Christian Rome's involvement in the Renaissance and its renewed interest in the pagan Greeks.

But there were already quite different views of the recovery of learning and the new artistic techniques in the earliest days of the Protestant Reformation. To begin with, not all the major Protestant figures took as dim a view of pagan learning as Luther did, nor did they necessarily see a connection between classical culture and corruption. One of Luther's own closest collaborators, Philipp Melanchthon, was an accomplished humanist in the Renaissance sense of the term, which unlike modern humanism did not necessarily have anything to do with secularism. John Calvin, too, had been trained in the new learning. His first book was a commentary on the *De clementia* of Seneca, the Roman Stoic, and he admired what the Greeks and Romans had been able to achieve, even as he sharply distinguished those achievements from what he regarded as the wholly other dimension of authentic Christianity. The Catholic Church had been fostering the recovery of ancient knowledge all during the Middle Ages, but especially once western Europe settled down after the year 1000. Indeed, as we saw in the previous chapter, there were even medieval precedents for *The School of Athens:* the north portal of Chartres Cathedral, among other monuments, celebrated learning by prominently displaying the seven liberal arts and ancient figures who practiced them.

One of the most interesting developments in studies about the Middle Ages and the Renaissance during the twentieth century has been the discovery of the continuities between the two periods and an attempt to better formulate their true differences. To begin with, the usual notion that the Middle Ages were a period of faith while the Renaissance was an age of reason is simply wrong. Faith was strong in both, and if anything, the prominent thinkers of the Middle Ages were inclined to rely on strict logic and reasoning to a greater degree than most people can bear. That was one reason why Catholics of the Renaissance and early Protestant reformers alike turned towards more personal, less abstract forms of reason and faith in opposition to medieval intellectualism. The major writers of the Renaissance, particularly in the fourteenth and fifteenth centuries, felt a need to emphasize both the practical and the personal in their own work and in their efforts at educational reform in subjects such as grammar, rhetoric, history, poetry, and ethics. The Middle Ages, by contrast, put far more emphasis on logic, science, technical philosophy, and systematic theology. Anyone who studies the Renaissance will read much about the recovery of Greek, and this, of course, did occur. But what the Renaissance did with the Greeks is curious. In fact, it resembles nothing so much as what the ancient Romans did with those same sources: they used them for pragmatic and public, rather than speculative, purposes. In a curious way, medieval thinkers were closer to the Greeks in their brilliant dedication to purely philosophical pursuits, while Renaissance scholars were more like reincarnated Romans in their emphasis on virtue and responsibility in common life. In this respect, the characteristic beliefs and practices of the Reformation show many similarities with Renaissance philosophy, because the main reformers, too, tended to downplay pure theological speculation in favor of personal piety and good public order.

The Context of Early Humanism

The early Renaissance began in Italy, a nation that was not at the center of the notable scholastic developments of the medieval universities. That had taken place largely in France, the old center of the Carolingian king-dom, with offshoots in England and Germany. During the Middle Ages, Ita-ly had remained more urbanized than the rest of western Europe, with the exception of Flanders, another densely populated region. Three Italian cit-ies—Palermo, Venice, and Florence—had quite large populations for the time, over a hundred thousand each. Their needs were primarily practical. Italy could boast the distinguished law school at Bologna and the medical and scientific centers of Salerno and Padua. But scholastic philosophy and theology came to Italy only around Dante's time, roughly the same time as the Renaissance began there. In other words, the humanism with which we are familiar and the largely Aristotelian scholasticism that it is thought to have replaced actually grew together in Italy. They also clashed, as any two schools might, over institutional turf and ideas.

If we look at Raphael's early-sixteenth-century fresco, it confirms this history. His two central figures, Plato and Aristotle, were beyond all reasonable dispute the preeminent thinkers of antiquity. Raphael learned about them from the Christian humanist circles in Florence and Rome who were then studying them passionately. In his painterly manner, he gets the difference between the two of them pretty much right. Plato, the spiritual writer, points towards the heavens, which appear in the open classical dome above. Aristotle, who rose to the heights of speculation from observation and analysis of the earth, does not, as is often claimed, point towards the earth; he is looking at Plato as his teacher, as in fact he was, and raising his own hand into the same position a little behind the master. In this image, much of Western intellectual history is recapped. Plato had continued to be influential over the centuries, albeit indirectly, by way of the Neoplatonist mystics, Augustine, the medieval monks who studied Augustine (especially the Franciscans), and the Renaissance scholars who were finally able to read Plato in the original Greek. Aristotle had had a more uneven legacy. His logical works had been partly translated into Latin during the early Middle Ages, but his large, substantive works were rediscovered late, inspiring no deep tradition within the West, and touted only at the universities by the Dominicans and other scholastics. Yet the two strains they represented—the contemplative, otherworldly impulse on the one hand and the active, worldly service on the other hand—continued, with some tensions, into the Renaissance.

But it was not only the easy cases—Aristotle and Plato—who found their way into Raphael's fresco. Raphael portrayed and therefore rendered homage not only to philosophers who groped towards biblical truths, but also scientists like the geographer and cosmologist Ptolemy, mystical mathematicians like Pythagoras and the geometer Euclid, and even somewhat dangerous theorists such as the materialist philosopher Epicurus. Raphael had no problem including these on a wall intended for use by the pope himself because the Renaissance as a whole was still open to all truth, which, as Augustine famously said, by whomever spoken is from God.

There is yet another dimension to this conjunction of cultures: The Renaissance artists and intellectuals closely identified with the innovators and pious thinkers of antiquity. Raphael visually superimposed them. Thus,

Leonardo da Vinci seems to be the model for Plato, for example, while the architect Donato Bramante stands in for Euclid. The implication is clear. The greatest Renaissance artists were operating virtually in the skins of their illustrious forebears. So strong was this perception for Raphael that it even overcame the well-known rivalries among Renaissance artists. When Raphael first saw the stunning ceiling of the Sistine Chapel, he was so moved that he returned to his own work, chipped out one of the prominent figures in *The School of Athens,* and repainted the figure of the mystical philosopher Heraclitus, who appears in a central place just below Aristotle and Plato, with the features of Michelangelo. Raphael signs the work by including himself in the composition, in a much less conspicuous place.

It is worth pointing out that on the opposite wall to *The School of Athens*—which many continue to misread as a statement of the growing Renaissance departure from Christianity and embrace of the merely human and rational—is another celebrated work by Raphael: *The Dispute of the Most Holy Sacrament,* which in parallel fashion to the other fresco assembles, in addition to the Holy Trinity, famous persons from Christianity such as the Virgin Mary, John the Baptist, Saints Gregory and Jerome, Aquinas, Bonaventure, Dante, Pope Sixtus IV, Savonarola, Fra Angelico, and many more. Clearly, Raphael intended to show by this juxtaposition that good Christian as well as good pagan thought should be brought to bear on the kinds of decisions the Vatican had to make in the room. And he underscored this still further by a third fresco of the four cardinal virtues, and a ceiling representing poetry. Art historians continue to discuss the interpretation of the whole, but it is clear that Raphael had tried to offer a comprehensive, Christian humanist view of the good, the true, and the beautiful in the three frescoes.

Early Humanism

The term "humanist" suggests to our modern minds a stance opposed to the religious. We have to be careful not to introduce an anachronism into our interpretation of this Renaissance notion, however, because—as was the case for Raphael, Michelangelo, Botticelli, and as would be the case for humanists as different as Erasmus, Thomas More, Copernicus, Bacon,

Galileo, Calvin, Ignatius of Loyola, Cervantes, Donne, Pascal, Descartes, Milton, and even Montaigne—there was no necessary opposition between learning and belief in the Renaissance idea of a *humanista*. Humanism as a term for a certain type of nonreligious rationalism was invented in the nineteenth century with a very different meaning. In its main developments, the older concept of a humanist was another chapter in the long Christian effort to lay out the relative claims of faith and reason, and bring them into harmony at a new historical moment.

There were "humanistic" impulses in the so-called Carolingian Renaissance as well as at other times in the Middle Ages. As a noted Renaissance scholar has observed:

> it can be plausibly maintained that medieval culture at its height was generally "humanistic" in a deeper sense than that of the Renaissance. It was truly humanistic because perhaps to a greater degree than in any other period of European history, it valued and appreciated the natural values of man. . . . It put man at the center of a creation adapted to his intelligence, and it brought him closer to a benevolent and intelligible God.[3]

There were various continuities between the medieval and the Renaissance ideas of a humanist, but notable differences as well.[4] To begin with, since theology, law, medicine, and the sciences began to develop as professions and distinct university faculties, they did not exactly address the more general interests of the humanists. These fell into what had been called the *studia humanitatis* ("studies of humanity") in antiquity. Medieval universities had proposed a list of basic studies divided into the *trivium* (grammar, dialectic, rhetoric) and the *quadrivium* (arithmetic, geometry, astronomy, music), but the schools, libraries, and universities dedicated to Renaissance humanism proposed five areas of study: grammar, rhetoric, history, poetry, and moral philosophy. As this bare list indicates, humanism was less concerned with theoretical speculation than with practical and moral questions, but not to the exclusion of religious matters.

The main figures of the early Italian Renaissance clearly show as much, though there is naturally greater or lesser engagement with spiritual questions from one of them to another. What this means can be seen quite early, even in a precursor such as Francesco Petrarca (English: Petrarch, 1304–1374). Petrarch was religiously an Augustinian in the sense that—like the Franciscans, the Ockhamists, Luther, and others—he did not have much interest in the kind of theoretical theology, usually based in Aristotle, that was common in the Middle Ages. Petrarch is most famous for work that he himself regarded as of small value: the love sonnets and lyric poetry he composed in Italian. His more serious work, as he saw it, lay in the composition of moral treatises, letters, and even an epic poem, all in Latin, intended literally to resurrect ancient styles once mastered by Seneca, Cicero, and Virgil. As often happens in history, however, this effort at revival had the exact opposite of its intended effect. The rejection of the Latin then in use in favor of a classical model had the effect not of reviving the classical world, but of ensuring that Latin became a dead language, since the forms enthusiastically recovered and imitated from the ancient pagans did not correspond with Renaissance life.*

Petrarch and the other humanists emphasized the classical heritage as a tool for reforming the Christian tradition, but this aim led them into a divided consciousness that occasionally showed itself as outright bad conscience. In a letter, Petrarch wrote: "When it comes to thinking or speaking of religion, that is, of the highest truth, of true happiness and eternal salvation, I am certainly not a Ciceronian or a Platonist, but a Christian." The fact that he felt it necessary to defend himself in this way is telling. Yet at one point, Petrarch anticipated the kind of simple theological assertion that would be common to various other figures of the Renaissance, but today is often thought to have appeared only later, with Martin Luther: "[God] must be humbly beseeched that He should liberate us from the body of this death, whence the merit of man does not liberate but the grace of God alone (*gratia Dei solius*)."[5] In full harmony with his Renaissance contemporaries, Petrarch saw human thought and faith as needing one another: "In order to philosophize truly, we must above all love and worship Christ."[6] Still, a tension remained between the two traditions. In a Latin treatise he never

*Ernst Robert Curtius in *European Literature and the Latin Middle Ages* explains how the vernacular literatures thus came to the fore.

intended to publish entitled *Secretum* ("The Secret"), Petrarch wrestled with his own vanity and desire for human glory—glory being one of the new values that emerged strongly in the Renaissance. He tells us that one day he went climbing up Mont Ventoux in France, and at the top he randomly opened Augustine's *Confessions* to this passage: "Men go to admire the heights of mountains, the great floods of the sea, the shores of the ocean, and the orbits of the stars, and neglect themselves." And he continues: "I was angry at myself because I still admired earthly things, I who should have learned long ago from the pagan philosophers that nothing is admirable but the soul; to it when it is great nothing is great."[7]

Ambivalence like Petrarch's surfaced in other early humanists, though in them it took different forms. One of his followers, Coluccio Salutati (1331–1406), also embraced both sacred and secular learning, but in Salutati, as later in Calvin (both had been much impressed by the Roman Stoics), Christians had a responsibility for the public order, a responsibility that Petrarch, in his more retiring literary fashion, had not much recognized. Salutati was the first in a series of Florentine chancellors—including also Leonardo Bruni and Poggio Bracciolini—who took advantage of the freedom and prosperity of the city in the early fifteenth century to use humanistic learning in the service of both politics and religion. Florence had been threatened with conquest at the start of the century and these scholars developed what has since become known as "civic humanism,"[8] a useful term to denote the attention they brought to bear on public affairs, but misleading if we do not know that these civic humanists derived a good portion of their concern for public order from their religious beliefs.

This fact has been partly obscured because a later successor of theirs as Florentine chancellor, Niccolò Machiavelli, notoriously rejected both classical virtue and Christian ethics in favor of *virtù*, meaning power and shrewdness in the service of political goals. Christian princes had long done what they wanted to preserve power; Machiavelli was merely the first to advise them openly that this was fine. But Machiavellianism, at least in its classic form, did not become the dominant mode of conceiving politics in the West because the old pagan and Christian traditions continued on quite vigorously in other channels. In Machiavelli's own Florence, by the second half of the fifteenth century, the Medici offered patronage for Platonic studies and even set up a Platonic Academy in the Tuscan countryside under the leadership of a priest, Marsilio Ficino. This academy fostered the Christian humanist tradition not only in Italy but throughout Europe. Italian artists such as Michelangelo and Raphael came under its spell. Various foreigners also studied there, including the Englishmen John Colet, a Catholic preacher and educational reformer who founded St. Paul's School in London, and Thomas Linacre, a physician, who in turn exerted influence on Thomas More. Colet also had a famous follower in Erasmus, the Dutch humanist and Catholic reformer who turned to a more fervently evangelical Christian humanism after hearing Colet preach.

In the heyday of twentieth-century interpretations of the Renaissance as a secular and pagan humanism freeing itself from religious bonds, probably no text was more studied in college and university humanities programs than the *Oration on the Dignity of Man* by Giovanni Pico della Mirandola (1463–1494). Since most readers in the nineteenth and twentieth centuries had a low opinion of the Middle Ages, they failed to notice the connections between Pico's brilliant argument and its medieval predecessors. Medieval thinkers, as we saw in the last chapter, understood quite well the fallen nature of life in this world but, as in Dante and his own predecessors, could not deny the basic Christian truth that we have a high destiny because of our place in the Creation. Pico's modern admirers were further unaware that Pico himself had explicitly defended scholastic philosophy from the attacks on it by Petrarch and by Pico's own humanist friends who promoted style and rhetoric over substance and philosophy. Pico was a real thinker and came down squarely on the side of the philosophers, with much good to say of the scholastics. Indeed, far from being a precursor of modern secularism, Pico's central preoccupation in his brief life—he died at thirty-one—was to reconcile Neoplatonism with Christianity, using along the way the Aristotelian ideas he had absorbed as well as Chaldeanism, Arabic thought, and the mysticism of Jewish Cabbala. After troubles with the Church that were eventually resolved, he returned to Florence, where he, too, worked with Ficino at the Platonic Academy and continued his efforts at a Christian universalism that sought to unify all knowledge in ways that bear comparison with the universalism of Aquinas.[9]

The Voyages of Discovery

Attempts to unify the new learning and religious beliefs grew to worldwide dimensions in the series of voyages of discovery that began with the Portuguese exploration down the coast of Africa in the early fifteenth century. These voyages established African Christian missions virtually at the same time that the last pagan lands in Europe, on the Baltic Sea, were being evangelized. (The black king of the Congo was quite proud to be given the title *defensor fidei* around the same time as Henry VIII.)[10] Columbus's epoch-making trip to the New World occurred in 1492, the same year that Ferdinand and Isabella reconquered Spain from the Muslims and expelled all Muslims and Jews who did not convert. For several centuries afterwards, this European expansionism continued until every part of the world had finally been brought into concrete contact with every other part. Most people are taught today to think that these voyages were simply a matter of European imperialism, colonialism, and slave trading. Sadly, all those evils form an undeniable part of the story, but they are not the whole story by any means. The Christian missionaries who accompanied the explorers generally sought to restrain what might have become even worse atrocities, and they often carried out loud propaganda campaigns back home against abuses. Furthermore, the global expansion of Christianity to Africa, Asia, and the Americas, a momentous religious phenomenon, had quite significant effects of its own on Europe and the world, even down to the present day. A look at some of the religious dimensions of the Renaissance explorations reveals the ways in which they dealt with truly unprecedented situations.

In the preface to his *Libro de las profecías* ("Book of Prophecies"), an anthology of prophetic texts that he had been assembling since early adulthood, Christopher Columbus relates to Ferdinand and Isabella how, long before he ever approached them, he became convinced that the westward voyage was not merely a possibility but his own personal vocation:

> During this time, I searched out and studied all kinds of texts: geographies, histories, chronologies, philosophies, and other subjects. With a hand that could be felt, the Lord opened my mind to the fact that it would be possible to sail from here to the Indies, and He opened my will to desire to accomplish this project. This was the fire that burned within me when I came to visit your Highnesses.[11]

Columbus's mention of reading in itself suggests we are dealing with an unusual kind of sailor, one who, like the humanists of his day, has engaged in sifting and comparing ancient and modern knowledge for new purposes. There is some irony, then, in the fact that he claims that God intended to produce a *milagro ebidentísimo* ("highly visible miracle") in this enterprise by using an uneducated man: "For the execution of the journey to the Indies, I was not aided by intelligence, by mathematics, or by maps. It was simply the fulfillment of what Isaiah had prophesied."[12]

This is not, strictly speaking, true. The inspiration may have come from Isaiah, but for the execution, as he notes in the earlier passage, much more was involved. Columbus was a typical Renaissance person in the way he combined a fundamental religious inspiration with a practical use of the new knowledge and techniques discovered by the revival of classical antiquity and extended further by men eager to know God's world better. Before his famous appearance in front of a panel of skeptical experts assembled by the Spanish monarchs, for example, he had corresponded with the Florentine mathematician Paolo Toscanelli, whose work also helped Filippo Brunelleschi a bit later convince a panel of skeptical Florentines that it was possible to build the magnificent unsupported dome of the city's cathedral. In some older accounts, Columbus has been presented as a bold, rational, modern man and the church leaders who opposed him as superstitious conservatives. Every scholar of the period today knows that the religious experts were right about the science: if the then-unknown Americas had not been where they are, Columbus would have failed. The distance to the "Indies" was far greater than he claimed. Columbus probably knew this from his own studies, but played it down to gain the support of the king and queen for his faith-induced project.

In this, he resembled many other Renaissance men who were very religious and who also studied the world anew to understand how God had made it. Pascal, Descartes, and Newton were superb mathematicians and scientists, but all of them also had authentic religious interests. Newton, perhaps the most brilliant of all, spent a good part of his later life writing commentaries on the prophecies in the book of Daniel, and often spoke of his scientific labors as an effort to understand truly how God made the world. Even Galileo, whose case is usually thought of as a simple conflict between science and religion, was really engaged in a complex debate, made more complex by his own clumsy arrogance, over how to interpret new astronomical data. During his lifetime, there was still little good evidence that the earth moved, and church leaders, following Augustine's view that the truths of science had to inform interpretations of the Bible, were initially quite willing to listen to his theories. Gregory XIII founded the Vatican Observatory and Pope Urban VIII was a friend until Galileo's own prickly habits broke up the friendship. Another friend, Cardinal Baronio, was the one who gave Galileo the defense that the "Holy Spirit tells how to go to heaven, not how the heaven goes."

Columbus belonged very much to this Renaissance type. He not only searched the scriptures for direction in his life's work, he also made a careful study of ancient and modern knowledge of all kinds. Current experience was also carefully factored in. He had observed in his many Atlantic voyages prior to the expedition to the New World that winds in the Atlantic near the equator blow primarily towards the west, while those farther north blow east, back to Europe. That knowledge was crucial to his success, since both he and the panel that opposed him knew that he would have to sail a much longer distance than he was admitting. During his first voyage to the Americas, at one point he turned south to follow a flock of birds that he rightly assumed were headed towards land. Without this chance or providential fact, he probably would have come ashore somewhere between Virginia and Florida instead of the Caribbean, with doubtless immensely different effects on subsequent world history.

But this learning, as with other humanists, had a religious purpose.

Columbus's spiritual side appears to have been a product of a religious renaissance that occurred in fifteenth-century Europe. Long before Luther, the *devotio moderna,* beginning with Gerard Groote and the Brethren of the Common Life in Holland, spread among both religious and lay people all over Europe, calling for a return to a more personal religion modeled on the evangelical virtues of the early Church. Its best-known writer was Thomas à Kempis, whose *Imitation of Christ* (ca. 1427) has influenced numerous individuals and movements, Catholic and Protestant, over the centuries. As late as the middle of the sixteenth century, Ignatius of Loyola, for example, the founder of the Jesuits, chose it as the first book to read when he decided to begin a serious religious life. The *devotio moderna* shaped figures as diverse as Nicholas of Cusa and Erasmus of Rotterdam. In many ways, it paralleled the impulses behind the secular Renaissance in its living reappropriation of the religious past as the basis for a significantly new future.

Religion and Colonization

In recent years, critics have reversed the old secular admiration for Columbus and, with equal inaccuracy, have portrayed him and the culture he represented as responsible for the modern cultural dominance of Europe and every subsequent world evil: colonialism, slavery, cultural imperialism, environmental damage, and religious bigotry. There is a kernel of truth in these charges, but obviously to equate either a single individual or a complex entity like a culture with what are currently judged to be the negative dimensions of an interconnected human world is to do an injustice to both individuals and ideas. Europeans had a far from uniformly negative view towards the new peoples they encountered. The myth of the "noble savage" arose almost immediately in various Renaissance writers and had a rich career in the hands of Thomas More, Montaigne, Shakespeare, and—much later—Rousseau. (Indeed, it still flourishes in certain intellectual backwaters.) Actual contact with the new cultures introduced no little complexity into the initial situation, however, because the noble savages often displayed much savagery and little nobility.

Columbus himself had contradictory feelings about the peoples he had encountered at different times in his life. In one of his first communications with the Spanish monarchs after the discovery, he described the Taínos of the Caribbean in glowing terms:

> I see and know that these people have no religion whatever, nor are they idolaters, but rather they are very meek and know no evil. They do not kill or capture others and are without weapons. They are so timid that a hundred of them flee from one of us, even if we are teasing. They are very trusting; they believe there is a God in Heaven, and they firmly believe that we come from Heaven. They learn very quickly any prayer we tell them to say, and they make the sign of the cross. Therefore Your Highnesses must resolve to make them Christians.

As the self-contradictions of this passage suggest, Columbus was here under the spell of one current in Renaissance mythology that believed such "uncivilized" peoples to be somehow closer to the conditions of the Garden of Eden than those enmeshed in the conflicts of "civilization."

In fact, the Taínos themselves were enmeshed in tribal raiding, slavery, and cannibalism, all of which existed in the Caribbean long before any European arrived. Columbus was for a while on surprisingly good terms with his Taínos, who in turn used the Spaniards to their advantage against their enemies. But the distance between the cultures was great, and, with the arrival of less-than-ideal explorers in subsequent voyages, the situation took a bad turn. Towards the end of his third voyage, Columbus wrote to complain about criticism of his governorship over both natives and Spaniards: "At home they judge me as a governor sent to Sicily or to a city or two under settled government and where the laws can be fully maintained, without fear of all being lost. . . . I ought to be judged as a captain who went from Spain to the Indies to conquer a people, warlike and numerous, and with customs and beliefs very different from ours." Columbus had discovered that the Indians were real flesh-and-blood human beings, with the same mix of good and evil that everywhere constitutes the human condition.

Today, the usual way of characterizing the behavior of the Europeans at this early stage is to fault them for not having the same sensitivity to the "Other" that a modern anthropologist or ethnologist would bring to such situations. Overlooked in this condemnation is the fact that precursors of scientific disciplines such as anthropology, ethnology, and others arose in the West because the Franciscan, Dominican, and Jesuit missionaries knew they needed to understand native peoples to convert them and studied their languages, customs, and religion. The records of people such as the Franciscan friar Bernardino de Sahagún in Mexico and the Jesuit José de Acosta in Peru are our richest sources of information about native peoples. Columbus himself astutely noted differences between the various subgroupings of Taínos as well as their distinctness from other tribes. And even when he was driven to harsh action—against both Indians and Spaniards—it was not out of mere desire for power. The Dominican priest Bartolomé de Las Casas, the well-known "Defender of the Indians," noted the "sweetness and benignity" of the admiral's character and, even while condemning what actually occurred, he remarked, "Truly I would not dare blame the admiral's intentions, for I knew him well and I know his intentions were good." Las Casas attributes Columbus's shortcomings not to malign intent but to ignorance concerning how to handle an unprecedented situation.

The atrocities committed by Spain, England, Holland, and other European powers as they spread out over the globe in ensuing centuries are clear enough. No one today defends them. Less known, however, are the currents within European culture that have led to the very universal principles by which, in retrospect, we criticize that behavior today. For instance, not only Las Casas but a weighty array of other religious thinkers began trying to specify what European moral obligations were to the new peoples. Las Casas, who was the bishop of Chiapas, Mexico—where relations between native populations and the central government remain tense even today— bent over backwards to understand local practices. He once went so far as to describe Aztec human sacrifices as reflecting an authentic piety and said that "even if cruel [they] were meticulous, delicate, and exquisite," a view that some of his critics have remarked exhibits a certain coldness towards the thousands of victims that belief system produced yearly. The information coming from the New World inspired Francisco de Vitoria, a Dominican theologian at the University of Salamanca in Spain, to develop principles of natural law in new directions that, in standard histories, are rightly given credit as among the origins of modern international law. To read Vitoria on the Indians is to encounter an atmosphere closer to the UN Universal Declaration of Human Rights than to sinister Eurocentrism.

Las Casas and Vitoria influenced Pope Paul III to make a remarkable statement in his 1536 encyclical *Sublimis Deus:*

> Indians and all other people who may later be discovered by the Christians are by no means to be deprived of their liberty or the possession of their property, even though they be outside the faith of Jesus Christ. . . . Should the contrary happen it shall be null and of no effect. . . . By virtue of our apostolic authority we declare . . . that the said Indians and other peoples should be converted to the faith of Jesus Christ by preaching the word of God and by the example of good and holy living.

The Spanish Crown itself had moral qualms about the conquest. Besides passing various laws trying to eliminate abuses, it took a step unmatched before or since by any expanding empire: it called a halt to the process while moral theologians examined the question. In the middle of the sixteenth century, Charles V ordered a theological commission to debate the issue at the monastery of Valladolid. Las Casas defended the Indians. Juan Ginés de Sepúlveda, the greatest authority on Aristotle at the time, argued that Indians were "slaves by nature" (a notorious phrase in Aristotle's *Politics* that clashed with Christian views of human dignity) and thus could rightly be subjected to Spanish authorities. Though the commission never arrived at a final vote and the Spanish settlers were soon back to their old ways, Las Casas' views were clearly superior and eventually prevailed.

Conquest aside, the question of even peaceful evangelizing remains very much with us. Most people today, whether believers or not, do not think there was much need to evangelize—a view that usually rests on the assumption that native religions were all essentially valid in their own way. Given the anthropological evidence, however, it will not do to make facile assumptions that all spiritual practices are on an equal plane. The early explorers who encountered them did not think so, and neither should we. For example, the Mexican novelist Carlos Fuentes, no special friend of Christianity or the

Spanish conquest, in the very act of admiring the richness of Aztec culture characterizes the Aztec gods as "a whole pantheon of fear." Fuentes deplores the way that missionaries collaborated with unjust appropriation of native land, but on a theological level he notes the epochal shift in native cultures thanks to Christian influence: "One can only imagine the astonishment of the hundreds and thousands of Indians who asked for baptism as they came to realize that they were being asked to adore a god who sacrificed himself for men instead of asking men to sacrifice themselves to gods, as the Aztec religion demanded."[13] This Copernican Revolution in religious thought has changed religious practice around the world since it was first proclaimed in Palestine two millennia ago, yet is all but invisible to modern critics of evangelization.

The Protestant Reformation

As the first voyages of exploration were occurring, religious developments were opening up new worlds in Europe as well. The Reformation is a varied and, in several ways, self-contradictory phenomenon, like all major historical turning points. And it has been subjected to so many partisan interpretations for and against that it may be useful at the very outset to point out some of the things it was not, especially at a time when Westerners often say, without much reflection, that the Islamic world needs to undergo a Reformation:

- The Reformation was not a movement for religious tolerance. All major groups during the Reformation—Catholic, Lutheran, Calvinist, Anabaptist—believed they possessed the saving religious truth and sought to make that faith pervasive in society.
- Similarly, the Reformation was not, as Catholics charged, a license for "private interpretation" of the Bible, nor, as Protestants have sometimes claimed since, an assertion of individualism and conscience. All particular Christian denominations continued to believe in the Bible as the authoritative revelation of God.
- The Reformation did not promote religious or political liberty, or free markets. In fact, most of the currents dominant in the Reformation led

to greater control by kings and other secular leaders over religious, political, and economic affairs. The "divine right of kings" emerges in the Renaissance and Reformation as a greater assertion of secular authority than was the case in the Middle Ages.

- The Reformation did indirectly and unintentionally result in religious tolerance and contributed something to the emergence of individualism, but only after martyrdom, warfare, and massacres perpetrated by each group against the others—Catholic against Protestant, Protestant against Catholic, Catholic against Catholic, and Protestant against Protestant—convinced many people that for prudential reasons it was better to tolerate others to a greater or lesser extent, or to divide up into jurisdictions that would not go to war over religious questions or political interests hiding behind religious interests.

Since these points, and many of their corollaries, are not at all common in discussion of the Reformation, they bear closer scrutiny.

The Imperative of Faith Alone

Waves of reformations had been going on in the Western Church, as we have seen in previous chapters, at least since the Irish and English monks arrived on the continent, then later with the Carolingian, Cluniac, and Cistercian efforts to restore good order to the monasteries, and notably with the Franciscan and Dominican orders in the twelfth century, which sought reform of both church and society. In addition, contrary to popular Protestant views, a host of Catholic critics in the century prior to Martin Luther had made equally fervent cases against the corruptions of Rome and greed among the church leadership. One distinguished historian notes that prior to the Reformation, "A preacher who inveighed against the ecclesiastical state was sure of being applauded. As soon as a homilist broaches this subject, says Bernardino of Siena, his hearers forget all the rest; there is no more effective means of reviving attention when the congregation is dropping off to sleep, or suffering from heat or cold. Everybody instantly becomes attentive and cheerful."[14]

The motto *Ecclesia semper reformanda* ("A church always in need of reform") is an old Catholic notion, and some modern Protestants have learned to apply it beyond Rome in the formula *Ecclesia reformata semper reformanda* ("The reformed church always needs reforming"). This awareness of the dangers of any religious body believing itself to represent perfection or settling into success is a very good thing in any age, but no age in the West carried out a reformation with more far-reaching effects, for good and bad, than Luther's. Yet reformation of Catholic abuses, such as the famous selling of indulgences in Germany by Johann Tetzel, was not the central point in Lutheranism. Luther's famous Ninety-five Theses, which he nailed to the door of the church at Wittenberg (a common practice for inviting public debate at the time), contrary to popular impressions, are a relatively ordinary criticism of church abuses offered in the hope of achieving a truer and purer understanding of papal authority and Catholic faith.

But the Ninety-five Theses were only an early point in what became a real revolution. The truly explosive impulse in Luther's thought came from within, as he described it in a famous passage:

> Day and night I pondered until by God's mercy I discerned the connection in the wording, namely, "the justice of God is revealed in it [the Gospel], as it is written, the just man liveth by faith." I then began to understand "the justice of God" as one by which the just person lives by God's gift, that is, out of faith, and I realized that this was the meaning: by God the passive justice of God is revealed, by which the merciful God justifies us through faith, as it is written, "the just man liveth by faith."
> Now I truly felt quite new born and as though I had entered through open gates into Paradise itself.

Because Luther grew up in a household with an overbearing and irascible father, attempts have been made to link his spiritual experience to an overcoming of psychological impediments, a theory which at this historical distance can be neither proved nor disproved. He initially wanted to study law, the usual path to a career in his day, but when he thought he was about to die during a sudden thunderstorm, the young Martin made a vow to enter a monastery if he survived. He took monastic life seriously—so seriously that he felt grave anxiety over his own sinfulness. But the significance of all these psychological factors is uncertain. What is certain is the genuine sense of spiritual liberation and rebirth in the final sentence quoted above, and the explanation of that liberation as proceeding *sola fide*, by faith alone, a battle cry that inspired a host of new religious currents in the Reformation.

Another famous claim of Luther's also shaped many later developments. At the 1521 Diet of Worms, Luther stated openly the substance of his faith: "If I am not refuted by Scripture nor clear evidence of reason—for I believe neither pope nor councils, since it is evident that they have often erred—I am bound only by the passages of Scripture I have quoted, and by my conscience, which is bound by the Word of God.* I neither can nor will recant anything, for it is neither safe nor becoming to do anything contrary to conscience. I can do no other, here I stand. God help me. Amen." The contention that scripture alone, *sola scriptura*, was the rule of Christianity was far more radical than the claim about faith. Whatever their differences, Catholics could agree with Protestants that believers are saved by faith, not works. That was the whole point of Augustine's famous controversies with the Pelagians, who thought salvation was a mere matter of human adherence to rules. Catholics and Protestants furthermore agreed that good works should flow from faith, though they differed about the way they were theoretically connected to belief. But to claim that the individual could interpret the text of scripture without need for religious authority or a community of believers was, despite some anticipations in earlier reform movements, a radically novel idea as Luther presented it.

Nonetheless, Luther stood in a sense within a tradition. He was taught at the University of Erfurt and the Augustinian monastery in the same city by professors who followed the medieval nominalist William of Ockham in believing that rational attempts to understand revelation—even by brilliant thinkers like Aquinas—were wholly inadequate to the subject. At the same time, Luther had been influenced by the *devotio moderna* to look at the spiritual life as an immediate activity of the whole person much more than an intellectual endeavor. Like almost everyone else, he studied Thomas à Kempis's *Imitation of Christ*, which, while remaining well within the Catholic system, says in its first chapter:

*Note that the Word of God *binds* conscience even in this passionate outpouring.

> What avail is it to a man to reason about the high, secret mysteries of the Trinity, if he lack humility and so displeases the Holy Trinity. Truly, it avails nothing. Deeply inquisitive reasoning does not make a man holy or righteous, but a good life makes him beloved by God. I would rather feel compunction of heart for my sins, than merely know the definition of compunction. If you know all the books of the Bible merely by rote and all the sayings of the philosophers by heart, what will it profit you without grace and charity? [15]

In retrospect, it is easy to see how certain intuitions of this form of devotion could lead to Lutheran developments. And that tendency was further reinforced by the German pietists and the great Rhineland mystics whom Luther also valued, such as Meister Eckhart and, above all, Johann Tauler. These men seemed to have had a powerful and deep relationship with God in quite new ways.

But Luther also introduced several novelties that, in the way he presented them, were in some tension with the tradition in which he had been raised. One involved what he called the "bondage of the will" after the Fall. In this view, sin had so corrupted and enslaved the will that it was impossible for a human being to do anything purely good except by divine grace. As we have seen, this view had already been expressed by Petrarch in the fourteenth century and could be regarded as Catholic so long as it was not emphasized too exclusively to the detriment of other truths, because the scriptural basis for this teaching is complicated and fraught with difficulties. Driven in part by polemics against the Catholics, Luther had to infringe on his own notion of *sola scriptura* by declaring the Epistle of James to be "straw" because it asked:

> What good is it, my brothers, if someone says he has faith but does not have works? Can that faith save him? If a brother or sister has nothing to wear and has no food for the day, and one of you says to them, "Go in peace, keep warm, and eat well," but you do not give them the necessities of the body, what good is it? So also faith of itself, if it does not have works, is dead. . . . See how a person is justified by works and not by faith alone. (James 2:14–24)

The Epistle to the Romans, as Luther accurately quoted it in his profession of faith, had not said "faith *alone*," so he had added something in his polemics, and Catholic counter-polemicists were quick to point it out as well as invoke the Epistle of James.

But more problems lay ahead. Luther's collaborator Philipp Melanchthon, possessing a more systematic mind than Luther, later developed a notion of "synergism" to avoid this difficulty, by which the will somehow collaborated with grace. A later offshoot of Calvinism, the Arminians, were to try something similar. At the most practical level, reliance on faith alone seemed to mean that the human struggle to do right is impossible, and that only after an act of faith—itself, it would seem, impossible except through grace and therefore not the product of individual will or of preaching and reading of the scriptures—can we be justified by imputation from Christ's redeeming death. Luther was aware of some of the paradoxes in his position, but still seemed quite able to denounce those who, apparently through no fault of their own by his system, had not been given the grace to make a proper act of faith.

Luther's view of the scriptures came into similar difficulties, not least that the very popes and councils he repudiated had, historically, defined the canon of scripture, and that Christianity had existed for several decades before there was any New Testament to be based on. Of more immediate importance, however, was the fact that what seemed to be a return to the plain meaning of scripture was not as simple as it first appeared. Holy Communion, for example, became a bone of contention between Catholics and Lutherans, the former believing in transubstantiation or the total transformation of the bread and wine into the body and blood of Christ, the latter believing in consubstantiation or the continuing existence of the bread and wine along with the Catholic transformation.

But these differences proved trivial compared with the views that emerged soon among other Protestants equally intent on faithfulness to scripture. Both Huldrych Zwingli in Zurich and John Calvin in Geneva regarded Communion, which they began calling the Lord's Supper, as merely a memorial. When representatives of various Protestant factions met in

Marburg in 1529, Luther tried to refute his opponents by quoting the very words of Jesus that Catholics use for consecration: "This is my body." But this was to no avail and "the plain words of scripture" proved to be no easy rule to apply. Later in the sixteenth century, a book appeared entitled *Two Hundred Interpretations of the Words: This Is My Body*, which was a compilation of the positions that had arisen within the first decades of the Reformation alone.[16] This was not Luther's intention, to say the least, in proclaiming *sola scriptura*.

Similar problems arose over behavior. Though it was a traditional principle that no one should act against conscience, how was this conscience to be formed if not in conversation with those who had lived Christian lives, however they were to be defined? Lurking within Luther's statement was a powerful surge towards autonomous reason (though Luther would often mock reason as such, even when he was not decrying the influence of Aristotle in the Church) under the guise of loyalty to original revelation. It is important to keep in mind the unintended consequences of Luther's views because otherwise we mistakenly attribute to him and to the other Reformation leaders opinions that were not theirs. Unfortunately, it commonly appears even in quite good analyses that the Reformation exhibited an "emerging spirit of rebelliousness, self-determining individualism, and particularly the growing impulse for intellectual and spiritual independence."[17] In fact, it would be difficult to find a group of Western figures less rebellious (aside from their opposition to the Catholic Church), individualist, and independent than the major Protestant reformers. On the contrary, they passionately sought to submit themselves to scriptural revelation, to conform themselves to the example of Christ, and to realize their total dependency on God's mercy and love. They expected that their personal piety would lead to a revolutionary reform of the entire Church, which would remain one, as Christ had intended.

And yet there is some truth in the counterclaim. Luther's teaching inadvertently turned the locus of authority from scripture as publicly interpreted in the Church to scripture as interpreted by individuals who then proclaimed those interpretations as the one authoritative truth. He intended the "plain words" of scripture to provide a plain rule, but that was an illusion, as subsequent events proved. Differing interpretations of key points led to conflict even within the Protestant orbit. For the most part, the Protestant churches each sought their own hegemony by alliances with secular powers, just as the Catholics had done and continued to do. All the Protestant churches—except for sectarians like the Anabaptists—had to rely on sympathetic rulers for protection against Catholic forces like the Holy Roman Emperor, a particular threat in Germany. Those rulers often took advantage of religious controversies to dominate ecclesiastical as well as secular matters. But in the long run, confessional divisions could not help but contribute to the emergence of a secular realm that brought the benefit of tolerance, though at the price of religious potency.

Paradoxically, even Luther's rejection of reason in favor of faith unintentionally contributed to the secularizing process. Though reformers like Calvin and Zwingli were quite learned men with strong humanist credentials, they too accepted that reason was radically separated from faith, and this tended to divorce faith from other forms of knowledge, whether of a philosophic or a scientific kind. Catholic suppression of Galileo is a notorious mark against the Church, although orthodox Catholic theologians at the time defended him and knew his views could have been accommodated within Catholic theology. But Luther and Calvin had been equally uncomprehending of Copernicus; both cited the Old Testament against him as if that could settle the scientific issue.

Yet Luther's position and the movement to which it gave rise struck a chord with many people, primarily in Germany but also throughout the West, even when they had little appreciation of the theological stakes. For besides being a religious reformer, Luther was a great mover of men. He was fortunate that in his time the development of towns and the new social arrangements they generated—not least among them widespread literacy and the easy distribution of information owing to the printing press—provided him with many to move, among them traders, artisans, and peasants—social classes usually bypassed in historical events. But it was part of Luther's power, if also of his weakness, that he did not always think before speaking. In a notorious case, he allowed Philipp of Hesse to contract a big-amous marriage and counseled him if asked about it to "tell a good strong lie for the sake and good of the Christian church."[18] And he was not a dem-ocratic populist, as the modern Lutheran scholar Martin Marty has point-ed out: "more fearful of anarchy than of authoritarianism, despite his own rejection of authoritarianism. Luther saw anarchy in the uprising of peas-ants, who had thought Luther would take their side in the Peasants' War. He called on princes to smite and stab the peasants. The princes didn't need much encouragement. Later he asked for restraint and penitence from the murderous princes — but that was too little and too late. . . . Up to 100,000 lost their lives."[19]

Yet Luther was also a man of the people as few other Christian leaders of his time. He did not take a sentimental view that the people, uninstructed as they were, could spontaneously conceive a true theology or biblical inter-pretation. But his whole life was pointed in a direction that few European leaders before him had chosen to pursue. In an earlier chapter we saw how Dante deliberately wrote in the vernacular in order to be able to share "the bread of angels" even with women and children. Few others believed that writing in anything other than Latin would ensure them an audience or influence. Luther, however, was one of the first and most powerful among them. His efforts at writing hymns and above all his vigorous translation of the Bible into German helped bring Christianity close to ordinary people, as was clearly intended by its founder. These literary achievements also played no small role in the creation of German national identity and the simple bib-lical flavor Luther brought to it.

Some Protestant enthusiasts have had a tendency to find seeds of economic and political liberty in the Lutheran Reformation. In complex historical and social developments, of course, many factors are always at work, not least the fractured state of political jurisdictions in German-speaking lands, which tended to resist external domination whether by papal power or by the designs of the Holy Roman Emperor. In his explicit teachings, however, Luther was not as modern as many of his admirers have credited him with being. Towards the end of "An Open Letter to the

Christian Nobility," his first important tract, Luther identifies five "failings of the temporal estate" and asks good Christian leaders to take steps to remedy them. Two of these remedies are essentially sumptuary laws to restrict dress and food consumption, along with the vanity and other immodesties that accompany them. He singles out a third problem, prostitution, as especially in need of suppression by the temporal government. Beyond these social failings, Luther even decries commerce, employing a biblical argument: "I do not see that many good customs have ever come to a land through commerce, and in ancient times God made his people of Israel dwell away from the sea on this account, and did not let them engage much in commerce." And he denounces loans at interest, which in his day took the form of "annuities," saying that "The devil invented the practice, and the pope, by confirming it, has injured the whole world. . . . [W]e must put a bit into the mouth of the Fuggers [a prominent German banking family] and similar corporations."[20] Whatever Lutherans and other Protestants may later have made of commerce and investment, these practices did not have the endorsement of the first Protestant leader.

In the early twentieth century, the German sociologist Max Weber proposed the theory that Calvinism, with its strong belief in predestination, produced a psychology that led businessmen, unsure of their status, to work harder so as to convince themselves that they had God's favor in this world and perhaps the next as well. His book *The Protestant Ethic and the Spirit of Capitalism* (1904–1905) argued that a kind of "this-worldly asceticism" replaced the older monastic asceticism, and that this might be used to explain commercial development in countries like the Netherlands where Calvinism predominated. R. H. Tawney publicized the view further with his *Religion and the Rise of Capitalism*. Economic historians studied this intriguing theory very carefully and have generally agreed for several decades now that such attitudes may have helped capitalism in the areas touched by Calvinism after the Reformation, but that Weber had generalized too much and exaggerated one factor among many.[21] Today, we tend to think of the political structures that assure contracts and property rights, relatively free economic activity, and nonconfiscatory tax policies as contributing much more to economic development, since we can see that capitalist systems have flourished historically in societies with quite different religious or metaphysical presuppositions. And in fact, the Reformation contributed little to new business practices.

Concerning the persistence of the Calvinist pro-business myth, one Protestant historian has written in some frustration:

> Almost every feature of the sixteenth-century business world, including double-entry bookkeeping, had already existed in late medieval Europe. The Fuggers and most of the Augsburg bankers remained Catholic at the Reformation, while Europe's other chief centers of high finance—Antwerp, Lyons, Genoa, Venice—lay in Catholic countries.
> . . . [T]he ideal of hard-working and methodical life was preached by seventeenth-century Jesuits and Jansenists, as well as by their Puritan contemporaries. On the whole, Calvinism fought the practices of unfettered capitalism more consistently than did any other of the Christian churches. Calvin himself placed even the banker under demands of the Sermon on the Mount, and he regarded the charging of interest as a dubious activity for a Christian.[22]

As for the development of political freedom, it is worth noting that those more radical elements in the Reformation that did explicitly call for political and religious liberty elicited some unintended consequences. Groups like the Anabaptists and the Spiritualists who either refused to call on the secular arm for support or even withdrew into distinctive sectarian communities did break with the general pattern of Catholic and Protestant alliances with political forces. In a world that deeply feared the disruption of order and hierarchy, they reaped bloody persecutions by reformed Catholics and Protestants alike. The Peasants' Rebellion of 1525, which frightened both Luther and his Catholic enemies because of the ways in which ill-digested Protestant principles had led to anarchy and slaughter, was the first bad omen. But it was followed by even worse, from the Christian perspective. Seemingly boundless experiments such as the ill-fated radical regime of Münster, with innovations such as polygamy in the moral sphere and all sorts of theological speculations including anti-Trinitarianism, could not help but evoke repression—in the case of Münster, both Protestant and Catholic forces put down the anarchy. The more sober churches all had to contend with questions of how to prevent radical religious currents from leading to the total breakdown of Christian faith and morals as those had universally been understood in the West since the earliest days of Christianity.

One of the strong reactions to Protestant tendencies towards disorder, a reaction that anticipated a much wider movement of retrenchment in the later Renaissance and Reformation period, was the work of John Calvin. He had studied law and was a student at the Sorbonne during the same time as Ignatius of Loyola, the founder of the Jesuits. From his earliest days, Calvin displayed an orderly and consistent manner of thinking. Like the Jesuit movement, Calvinism highly valued education and a principled kind of prudence. In successive editions of his *Institutes of the Christian Religion,* Calvin provided a systematic and stabilizing vision of Protestant belief and practice. He pushed Luther's notion of dependency on the divine mercy to the extreme point of predestination, which Luther had both acknowledged and seemingly not wanted to look at too closely. But Calvin—perhaps owing to his strong sense of human depravity—was never in doubt, as Luther sometimes was, about the need for a strong church and a strong secular arm. Protestant preaching of the Bible did not lead to automatic conversion. For Calvin, faith is not opposed to law, nor the New Testament to the Old. Accordingly, when he ran Geneva, it took on many of the hard-line traits of his theology, including the execution of anti-Trinitarian heretics like Michael Servetus and the burning of alleged witches, practices hardly exceptional among any of the religious movements in his time. To many people, however, Geneva appeared on balance to be as well-run a city as was possible in a fallen world.

Calvinism had a wider influence in the world than did Lutheranism, partly because of its more orderly and, therefore, persuasive theology, partly because Lutheranism seems to have been more tied to specifically German circumstances. Calvinism was able to gain a footing in France, for example, something Luther's followers were mostly unsuccessful in doing. Of course, Calvinism also found a ready welcome in Holland, along with some areas in Poland and Hungary, but perhaps its greatest influence was exercised through the powerful figure of John Knox in Scotland. Scottish Calvinism played an important role in the development of Anglicanism, even though the English church, like the Lutheran, would continue to bear many affinities with Catholicism in structure and liturgy. And through English Puritanism, Calvin would transmit many religious and social ideas to the United States. As is clear in documents like *The Federalist Papers*, the Puritan heritage of New England usefully tempered the Enlightenment strains in America's founding to produce a system that was realistic about human nature while moderately optimistic about the way that good institutions might promote human happiness. All these achievements were quite important to Protestant survival as the Catholic Counter-Reformation regained territory in Europe and as missionaries in the New World, Africa, and the Far East expanded Catholicism to a global scope.

The Catholic Reformation (or Counter-Reformation)

In English-speaking countries, the Catholic Reformation or Counter-Reformation is little known, and what is known of it is often misconstrued. It is generally assumed that Catholicism retreated into a reactionary stance in response to the challenges of the Reformation and that Protestant countries, therefore, flourished while Catholic countries declined. In fact, there were already potent intellectual, spiritual, and reform movements in Catholic nations prior to the Protestant outbreak. In Spain, for example, a nation usually identified with backward or reactionary Catholicism among English speakers owing to long historical tensions between England and Spain, serious reform was under way in the early 1500s under the guidance of Cardinal Ximenes. The cardinal personally paid for the preparation and publication of the Complutensian Polyglot, a multilingual version of the Bible. (The standard Latin Vulgate appeared in the center of each page with the Hebrew on one side, the Septuagint Greek version on the other, and a Chaldean paraphrase at the bottom.) The project started in 1502 and its six volumes appeared between 1514 and 1517. Erasmus's Greek New Testament was published in 1516, Luther's German version in 1522.

In 1521, the very year of Luther's famous "Here I Stand" speech at the Diet of Worms, Ignatius of Loyola, future founder of the Jesuits, experienced a conversion comparable to Luther's or Calvin's as he read works of spirituality, including *The Imitation of Christ*, while convalescing from a wound received in battle. Towards the middle of the sixteenth century, Saint Teresa of Ávila and Saint John of the Cross reformed the Carmelite order in Spain and developed some of the most striking mystical writings in Europe since the Rhineland mystics—neither development much beholden to the confrontation with Protestantism. And they were only the most prominent figures in one country usually believed to be sterile in its Catholicism. Other renewals were under way elsewhere. By the second half of the sixteenth century, the European picture had changed from one in which the total triumph of Protestantism seemed inevitable to one in which Catholicism had reasserted itself almost everywhere.

The main obstacle in the meantime remained Rome. The papacy entered the sixteenth century in turmoil. The conciliar movement, an effort in the previous century to control papal power through church councils, coming on top of the "Babylonian Captivity" in France for most of the fourteenth century, had weakened and confused the role of Rome. As nation-states began to form and grow stronger, the old question—pope or emperor—turned even more complicated as several powerful new kingdoms, some of them ruled by Catholic kings, took up places among the forces arrayed against Rome. There had actually been several very good popes in the fifteenth century. Nicholas V and Pius II (the grandly named Aeneas Sylvius Piccolomini) were both humanists—Piccolomini was even a novelist prior to becoming pope—as well as pious men. But the sixteenth century began with the notorious Rodrigo Borgia as Alexander VI. Though there have been some recent scholarly attempts to rehabilitate the Borgia family, they all leave untouched the fact that if they were no worse than many high-placed Renaissance families, they were no better either.[23] And for a pope in Alexander's situation, that was not nearly enough. Alexander VI was followed (after the brief papacy of Pius III) by Julius II (Giuliano della Rovere) and Leo X (Giovanni de' Medici). Julius was a warrior pope trying to make the Papal States into a power to compete with other political formations. Leo X had learned as a member of the Medici family to put more emphasis on diplomacy and culture, but he spent—as the wags said—the surplus left him by his predecessor, his own revenues, and those of his successors to provide an image of papal magnificence.

Leo failed to take Luther's case seriously because it seemed to him merely a "quarrel of monks." But the scandal created by the crude selling of indulgences by the Dominican monk Johann Tetzel to finance the new St. Peter's Basilica put a match to a powder keg. Leo's nephew, Pope Clement VII, would pay the price for his misdeeds and those of other popes. Clement was by nature a holy but indecisive man and he had to face not only the growing Protestant movement but opposition from secular powers. All the sixteenth-century popes up to that point—with the exception of the Dutch reformer Adrian VI—had been guilty of playing European powers off against one another to enhance Rome's position in comparison with the other main Italian powers such as Venice, Milan, Florence, and Naples. Clement played the game badly, but even more he was hampered by the virtual bankruptcy in which the Vatican had been left by Leo.

One of the forces that he was particularly unable to control was Charles V, the Spanish king and Holy Roman Emperor, a serious Catholic who considered Clement a disaster for both the Church and the empire. Charles's troops entered northern Italy at first to fend off threats to imperial interests, but later began marching on Rome. At the time, even the emperor could not really afford to pay a large army in the field, so soldiers were led to believe that booty would be available along the way, especially in Italy, then the richest nation in Europe. In a move that shocked the civilized world, the hungry and ill-tempered imperial forces breached the wall around Rome on May 6, 1527. Some were Lutherans who thought of Rome as the home of the Antichrist and were determined to inflict punishment.

Ordinary human decency simply disappeared. All the patients of the Hospital of Santo Spirito were killed, as were the children of the Pietà orphanage. The same occurred at other places of healing and charity throughout the city. Diplomatic immunities were disregarded: embassies, usually sacrosanct, were ransacked as blithely as churches. Convents were invaded and nuns raped and then often sold into prostitution, as were many of the city's female nobility. Lutheran soldiers killed an old priest for refusing to give the Eucharist to a donkey. Five hundred men were killed at the main altar of St. Peter's, tombs were violated, relics desecrated, the basilica itself was turned into a stable, as was the Sistine Chapel. Probably no outrage committed in war up to that time failed to occur during the imperial sack of Rome. Contemporaries commented that even the Turks had never done such things.

The immediate destruction was terrible and it had long-term effects on the city. Within the year, the population was half of what it had been before the invasion. No one can say for certain how many Romans died, but ten to twenty thousand is a safe estimate. Some died immediately of violence, others slowly starved or succumbed to the plague that began as a result of bodies left to rot in piles in the streets. The accumulated wealth and art of the city had been mostly defaced or simply stolen. Whole libraries had disappeared. Fortunately, the Vatican Library had been spared because of strong intervention by the imperial commanders, but the papal archives suffered serious damage. The Holy See was able to buy back many lost items over the next two decades. Some, however, were never accounted for. Rome lost many of the scholars, artists, and humanists who had helped make it such a splendid prize when they fled to their places of origin or other centers of culture and feared to return to Rome.

If there was any good to come out of this unprecedented outrage, it was the immediate shock it delivered to the whole papal system. Paul III, Clement's successor was not a very distinguished man personally, but he set serious reform of the Roman curia in motion. He also opened up the Council of Trent, which from 1545 to 1563 carried out a sweeping reform of the whole Church including total reform of the clergy by assuring that a seminary for intellectual and spiritual formation of priests would be administered in every diocese. He and succeeding popes were assisted in all this by many good men and new movements, almost all of them equipped by humanist training for the task. In England, men like Reginald Pole, John Fisher, and Thomas More joined in, as did Erasmus and others in France and Poland.

New spiritual and charitable developments followed. The strict The-
atine order had already been founded in 1524, and the Barnabites and Ca-
puchins a little later. For women, the Ursulines appeared thanks to Angela
Merici, who had grown up in one of the many pious Catholic households
that had persisted in Italy even in the worst of papal times. Perhaps most important to the whole atmosphere at Rome, however, was the establishment
of the Oratorians under the jovial and energetic Saint Philip Neri, a Florentine who brought an attractive charm to everything he did. His prayer meetings and missions in Rome appealed directly to ordinary people, and also
introduced organized musical performances. Neri drew the Italian com-
poser Palestrina into his orbit, and it was from Palestrina's innovative poly-
phonic compositions for Neri's Oratorian prayer meetings that the musical
genre known as the oratorio came into existence. The Oratorians not only
set a new tone in Rome; their influence later spread to France, owing to the
creation of an Oratory there in 1611 by Pierre de Bérulle. The French Oratorians were at the center of the reform of the French clergy in the seventeenth century.

No Catholic religious order, however, had a greater effect on the Church
in the sixteenth century and long afterward than the Jesuits. Their founder, Ignatius of Loyola, was a practical man, a former soldier and not an
intellectual. When he underwent his adult conversion, he famously submitted to studying Latin among the young boys in Barcelona, then quickly passed on to universities at Alcalá and Salamanca in Spain, and then
Paris. In August of 1534, he and nine companions made vows at Mont-
martre and thereby opened a new epoch in Catholicism. Ignatius' method
was contained in his *Spiritual Exercises,* which is not a book of intellectual
analysis but a set of instructions for a spiritual retreat meant to bring the
story of Christ vividly to life by intense meditation on scenes from the New
Testament. And while these exercises were intended to affect the heart in
depth, they were ultimately to lead to apostolic action. In some ways, it was
argued at the time and since, the Ignatian approach contents itself with
something quite a bit lower than the mystical contemplation long thought
to be the highest goal in the Catholic tradition, but it appealed in its own

way to the vast majority of people who found contemplation beyond their capacities.

Ignatius provided an outlet for those lesser, but by no means unimportant, capacities. He and his followers took special vows of obedience to the pope. Yet the Jesuits were also famous for cultivating strong individual personalities. It was a key insight of Ignatius' that a good religious superior should recognize the particular talents with which God had endowed each individual, and seek the right circumstances suited to those talents. The order founded colleges and schools all over Italy and, later, the rest of Europe, which injected energy and spirit into Catholic education for centuries. One especially important institution, founded in 1552, was the Collegium Germanicum, which trained missionaries for work in the Protestant areas of Germany. Saint Peter Canisius, a plain man like Ignatius, undertook extensive missionary journeys all over Europe, particularly Germany, where he had much success in more than thirty years of activity outside the Lutheran core areas (Jesuits even briefly converted John III of Sweden, a conversion that might have had widespread repercussions had Roman rigidity not derailed it). A skillful organizer, Canisius trained others in the work. There were 1,100 Jesuits in German-speaking territories when he died. Christians in today's Germany, largely owing to those efforts, are evenly split between Catholics and Protestants.

The Jesuits encountered significant resistance from the established orders in Spain and Portugal, but succeeded nonetheless in recruiting hundreds of members there as well. Among those members were legendary missionaries. Saint Francis Xavier and others were soon active in India, Japan, China, and other Asian nations, to say nothing of the territories of what would become Latin America. Francis Xavier was so successful in Japan that he provoked a reaction from the feudal lords, the shoguns, who martyred three hundred thousand Japanese Catholics in persecutions at the end of the sixteenth century and the beginning of the seventeenth. Matteo Ricci (1552–1610), an Italian Jesuit, was capable of astonishing feats of memory and engaged in learned conversations with the mandarins at China's imperial court that led to numerous conversions.[24] The Jesuit *Relations*, the reports of missionaries in the field, not only documented evangelizing activities, but affected the whole culture of Europe with their accounts of hitherto undreamt-of peoples, environments, and religious practices, some of which seemed just as cultivated and devout as those more familiar. Jesuits studied these cultures carefully, noted parallels with Christian beliefs and practices, and sought to adapt their approach to cultural conditions.

Alongside these expansive and successful efforts, however, there were also unfortunate Catholic institutions of repression. The Inquisition in Spain is a notorious but often exaggerated example that recent research has put in a different light. It began, not in response to the Reformation, but in the troubled circumstances of the Reconquista, when Christian forces retook the nation after what had long been regarded by them as Muslim occupation. As one commentator rightly says, "Though few governments pursued heresy with such systematic efficiency, the great majority of educated Europeans accepted the death penalty for persistent heresy, while both interrogation under torture and witch-burning were intermittently practiced in all countries. The offense especially characteristic of Spain and Portugal would seem to lie not in cruelty and intolerance as such, but in the sinister racialism which assumed that purity of doctrine went with 'purity of blood' and that it could hence be ensured by genocidal policies."[25] Recent estimates are that three thousand people were executed after judicial processes in the three hundred years of the Spanish Inquisition, a terrible figure in modern terms, but executions for heresy or witchcraft or Catholicism took place with roughly equal frequency in Protestant lands as well.

One of the remarkable features of recent scholarship is the general agreement on how much Catholic and Protestant Europe, despite obvious differences, also resembled one another in the seventeenth century. Catholics codified their beliefs at the Council of Trent; Lutheran factions felt obliged to make peace in the Formula of Concord (1577); and Calvinists adopted common teachings in the Synod of Dort (1619);[26] all of them were motivated, it seems, by a sense of the need for consolidation. Except for a brief moment after Luther's break with Rome and except for the sectarians who basically withdrew from society (and paid a heavy price for it), Catholic and Protestant jurisdictions showed many similarities.[27] Both sides became advocates of state absolutism, when the state in question happened to be in their favor. Montaigne pointed out, quite accurately, that in France, as in the rest of Europe, religion was not the cause of strife but a pretext: "Men are the leaders here, and make use of religion; it ought to be quite the opposite." If you sifted out how many men in the French army served out of pure devotion for a religious or political position, he said, you would not be able to find even a complete company. In the period after the 1589 assassination of the Catholic King Henry III and the ascent of the Protestant Henry IV, "This proposition, so solemn, whether it is lawful for a subject to rebel and take arms against his prince in defense of religion—remember in whose mouths, this year just past, the affirmative of this was the buttress of one party, the negative was the buttress of what other party; and hear now from what quarter comes the voice and the instruction of both sides . . . ."[28]

The Thirty Years' War (1618–1648) offers a stark confirmation of Montaigne's point in the international sphere. During those years, the Holy Roman Empire and the Protestant states in Germany engaged in a terrible mutual slaughter that was even more remarkable in that the two sides did not have modern weaponry with which to kill one another. Though religious differences obviously played a large role in this conflict, religion was often manipulated for political advantage and could even be ignored when doing so was expedient. After various victories and defeats on both sides, Emperor Ferdinand III stood very close to reimposing Catholicism in Germany. Though the Thirty Years' War has rightly tarnished the reputation of warfare on behalf of religious denominationalism, it was not a purely religious conflict. The emerging nation-states of Europe were also constantly clashing with one another over territory and influence. Such conflicts, as we saw, had even resulted in the armies of the Catholic emperor sacking Catholic Rome in 1527. In the later phases of the Thirty Years' War, France became especially concerned about the growth of the Holy Roman Empire, which not only controlled Spain and the Netherlands but seemed poised to reassert control over the German principalities. That final victory would have entirely surrounded France. So at the very moment when Catholicism might have largely triumphed again in central Europe, a French statesman and cleric, Cardinal Richelieu—who was wryly called the Cardinal of the Protestant Huguenots—organized Swedish action to relieve beleaguered Protestant forces in Germany. Catholic France herself directly aided the Protestant forces. When the two sides had fought each other to bloody stalemate, the Peace of Westphalia (1648) put an end to religious wars by allowing each ruler to determine the official religion of his territory. Most did so with some accommodations or even tolerance for other faiths. Thus did some measure of tolerance emerge from the bloodiest mutual intolerance.

Catholics and Protestants, for all their differences in politics and theology, continued to share a common culture rooted in Renaissance humanism and adapted to various national and local conditions. This culture had several elements. First, it was Augustinian in its focus on human experience of the divine. In particular, Augustine's *Confessions*, which once drew little attention and seemed to be a rather typical devotional book, attracted new interest among a wide variety of people looking for some point of stability in the political and religious turbulence. In addition, Catholics and Protestants alike began searching the ancients again for philosophical guidance. Stoicism in particular appealed to many, just as it had in the years of the Roman Empire, because it seemed to offer some practical help against suffering and disorientation. Montaigne was similar to Cicero and Seneca in his relative skepticism towards systems, along with relative certainty that piety, virtuous behavior, and service to the community could withstand the acid of doubt.

It was not only the therapeutic kinds of philosophy that answered the doubts and fears of the late sixteenth and early seventeenth centuries. Plato and Aristotle made a comeback after a period of excessive deprecation, mainly because people were not content with the merely defensive measures that Skepticism, Stoicism, and Epicureanism could offer. Aristotle was misused by some to hold onto the Greek cosmology that Christians had adopted—hence the Galileo trial, despite objections by Catholics who defended scientific research. But Aristotle with his wide intellectual scope, even stripped of his cosmology, could be quite useful for thinking systematically about many other questions. In any age that began to value stability and predictability over change and innovation, some larger synthesis seemed to be called for. Though Aristotle continued to generate opposition among the scientists—Bacon and Descartes were adamantly opposed to him—he retained followers among all Christians. In particular, natural law, a basic set of principles written into the world and into the very nature of man, appealed to all sides. Francisco Suarez in Spain, Richard Hooker in England, and Hugo Grotius in Holland all advanced this notion. Cotton Mather (1663–1728), living in Puritan New England a century later, still read deeply in and relied on the Aristotelianism of Thomas Aquinas for metaphysical, ethical, and other matters.[29] As a historian of the late Renaissance has remarked, "Europe was generally reacting against the openness and freedom of the Renaissance, whose novelties were on the wane as a new chapter in the history of European culture was beginning."[30]

Renaissance and Reformation were movements of great energy, both secular and religious, if not exactly in the ways they have often been portrayed. The Renaissance did open up a space for secular studies, but there is a vast distance between believing that there are relatively secular arenas within God's Creation, as almost all Renaissance figures did, and believing that secularism is the sole form of human rationality, a stance limited even in the modern world, which has been projected back onto very different views. Similarly, the Reformation challenged Catholic corruptions and sometimes abusive medieval practices as none of the many reform movements within the Catholic Church had been able to do previously. Yet the Reformation was not the origin of freedom in the marketplace, in politics, or in thought in the sense it is often presented as having been. With rare exceptions, the Reformation leaders, like their Counter-Reformation equivalents, had religious aims in mind that, in an indirect way and sometimes cutting across their intentions, aided the emergence of modern liberties. And it is worth recalling that the compromises arrived at after exhausting the older practices were nonetheless products of the older tradition. In retrospect, the theological differences at the time of the Reformation seem less large and more part of a common Christian debate. Thus a recent assessment of that period astutely claims: "The last five hundred years of Christianity . . . will surely come to be seen in the perspective of lengthening time not as a period dominated by disunity and decline, but as an era of creative diversity, overarching unity and dynamic promise."[31]

CHAPTER 7

Enlightenments, Revolutions, Reactions

> Religious need cannot be excommunicated from
> culture by rationalist incantation. Man does not
> live by reason alone.
>
> Leszek Kolakowski[1]

O N July 17, 1794, sixteen nuns of the Carmelite community of Com-
piègne, two of them seventy-eight years old, were beheaded by order
of a French Revolutionary Tribunal as enemies of the people. The tribunal defined such enemies as "those who seek to annihilate public freedom,
whether by force or subterfuge." The women in question were cloistered religious who by the rules of their Carmelite order had no contact with the outside world. It is difficult to see how they could have been any kind of threat
to anything, except as a symbol of religious freedom. In the past, historians
have either ignored the many atrocities like this one against innocent religious believers, or separated the Terror, as the period when they occurred
came to be called, from the initial revolutionary impulse, which was often
idealized. But in 1989, the two-hundredth anniversary of the French Revolution, more evenhanded research made it plain that within months of July
14, 1789, the revolutionary government prohibited the taking of religious
vows and confiscated all church property. A few weeks before the slaughter
of the Carmelites, a Festival of the Supreme Being was staged inside the cathedral of Notre Dame de Paris itself, where Reason and Liberty had become
gods. As a noted modern historian has put it, "The Terror was merely 1789
with a higher body count."[2]

Many elements went into the massacres of the innocents that took place in the French Revolution. Several key Enlightenment figures, Voltaire most prominently, had doubts about participation by the people in government and preferred "enlightened" despots. But Voltaire's famous cry *Écrasez l'infâme* ("Destroy the wretch") must bear some responsibility for the popular passions that not only did away with religious abuses but did away with innocent religious men and women, without remorse. The same enlightened license to murder has shown up around the world in revolutions inspired by aspects of the Enlightenment ever since. Similarly, it is difficult to draw a direct line from the vastly influential Jean-Jacques Rousseau—an anti-Enlightenment thinker in crucial ways—to the revolutionaries, but his language of feeling made the language of revolution possible and his odd view of liberty as identified with the General Will "substituted a sovereignty in which liberty was not alienated, but, as it were, placed in trust."[3]

Yet even without the later history of the French and the Marxist revolutions, it is not a simple matter to form a fair judgment about religion during the Enlightenment, for several reasons. First, there were different kinds of Enlightenment in the eighteenth century, largely identifiable with specific countries: revolutionary or radical (France), moderate and skeptical (England), and—for lack of a better term—organic (America). Several recent studies have tried to weigh each of these enlightenments and compare them because of the obvious fact that the two English-speaking nations did indeed absorb some of the new influences of science and new forms of rationality, but with greater calm and without the antireligious furor that strongly marked the European continent. And this fact suggests that despite claims to be following universal reason, Enlightenment thought was deeply colored by social context. Put bluntly, where centralized power repressed social movements and new ideas, as in eighteenth-century France, the reaction against religion and other forms of authority was most radical. Where political and social conditions were more tolerant, as in England and America, Enlightenment advances managed to coexist with, even benefit from, traditional beliefs.

But this, too, oversimplifies. Recent historians have rightly argued that the period we call the Enlightenment was richer and more diverse than once thought.[4] On the religious question in particular, careful attention to various sources has led some to believe that there has been too much of an emphasis on intellectuals, rationalists, and deists as the driving force behind practices much valued by the contemporary world such as tolerance. Yet it seems that tolerance emerged in many places from practice, and that the thinkers reflected rather than inspired more pluralistic social arrangements: "there is evidence to indicate that religious toleration began to assert itself as an idea and a practical reality at the grassroots level of eighteenth-century society and that the enlightened responded to public opinion rather than created it."[5] The same sorts of research seem to show further that deism, though widespread among the major Enlightenment writers, was not a wide or deep movement in the society of the period and had limited influence on religious and political reform. So the tolerant practices that begin in the eighteenth century, where they occurred, may best be described as arising from the day-to-day behavior of various Christians—often acting to thwart one another in political groups competing for power within states still committed to an official religion, but occasionally recognizing the general benefits of mutual toleration—rather than from an abstract intellectual program.

English Liberties

The process of tolerance growing in practice is visible in England. The English church since Henry VIII had been a hybrid. Henry was "Defender of the Faith" early on, until lack of an heir and multiple wives put him at odds with Rome. Even so, the quarrel was over control, not doctrine. His daughter Mary brutally tried to reimpose Catholicism; Charles I somewhat covertly, and Charles II and James II more overtly, did the same. Until the 1688 Glorious Revolution (more than 140 years after Henry's death) only two monarchs, Elizabeth and James I, were solid Protestants.

Elizabeth was a skillful manipulator who kept the nation united during her long reign, when necessary by brute force. She ruthlessly repressed the Puritans, for instance. James, however, experienced uneasy relations with Parliament, not least because he asserted the divine right of kings against old medieval liberties and emerging popular power alike. The King James Bible, a translation done under his patronage, had immense influence on English-speaking people. But the Scotsman James's clumsy efforts to rule the English earned him the title "the wisest fool in Christendom." All four Stuart kings seem to have lacked a certain political savvy. Previous kings had abused power, but they did not claim divine right as the Stuarts did, in line with similar claims elsewhere in Europe. The abolition of the monasteries, whose influential abbots had once sat in the House of Lords, shifted the locus of power; three times as many laymen as bishops sat in the new house.

Troubles flared up in the 1640s during a rebellion in Scotland. Parliament arrested and eventually executed the king's chief ministers, and demanded the abolition of bishops in favor of Presbyterianism. War ensued and the Puritans under Oliver Cromwell won. Charles I himself was executed in 1649. But many of Cromwell's soldiers were opposed to all establishments of religion, Anglican or Presbyterian, and he could not impose a religion even on them. Without anyone intending it, Cromwell's Puritan Commonwealth thus tolerated a wide variety of Protestant sects. This political expediency, however, could also employ military brutality: Cromwell massacred thousands of Catholics in Ireland and Calvinists in Scotland. He later tried to placate various parties with the Instrument of Government, a guarantee of rights. In fact, however, a military government inspired by Puritan morals resulted, an unpopular system that led to the restoration of the monarchy in 1660.

Religion and Political Parties

Religion played a central role in English developments after 1660 as well, not least in the formation of political parties. Catholicism was making a comeback on the continent. Louis XIV, *Le Roi Soleil* ("The Sun King"), promoted magnificence at his court and French influence abroad. Queen Christina of Sweden abdicated, converted, and went to live in Rome. Charles II in England and his brother (later James II) not only leaned towards Catholicism more or less openly (James publicly announced his faith), but made secret arrangements with France as a way of protecting themselves against

Parliament. Within England, neither the old Anglicans nor the old Presbyterian Puritans had achieved hegemony. Supporters of the king tended to be Anglican or Catholic, and from them arose the Tories. By contrast, Puritans and other Dissenters tended, with a few exceptions, to take the side of Parliament against the king and become the Whigs.

The situation was clearly unstable and the Stuart inability to manage political factions, when it did not actually make things worse, soon came to a head. In 1673, the partisans of Anglicanism in Parliament passed the Test Act, which required officeholders to take Anglican Communion, a step clearly intended to disenfranchise Dissenters and Catholics alike. Charles II was unable to prevent this move, which was part of a larger effort to stop his family's Catholicizing tendencies. Parliament also tried to pass laws that would have kept James II from the throne. This attempt failed and James was crowned in 1685. He might have found a way to hold onto Anglican support, but instead went ahead with ignoring the Test Act and appointing Catholics, invoking James I's belief in the divine right of kings to suspend laws. When James II's son was born and baptized a Catholic in 1688, thereby setting up a Catholic succession, all parties united in Parliament to depose him. James fled to Paris and was welcomed by Louis XIV. Parliament offered the throne to his daughter Mary and her husband, the Dutch leader William of Orange. Parliament also passed a Toleration Act in 1689, which allowed Dissenters to practice their religion but not to participate in government. The Act of Settlement in 1701 stipulated that a Catholic could not be king of England. Parliament, now made up of wealthy Whig landowners, effectively became the government of England with a weak monarch.

The limited liberty that emerged from the Glorious Revolution was directly dependent on Christian interests, as well as political and economic ones, even though no one party was able to impose its will unchecked. The settlement reached owed far more to practical compromises than to political theory. John Locke advocated parliamentary government in his *Two Treatises* (1690, two years after the Glorious Revolution), as well as religious toleration along the lines of the Toleration Act in his *Letters on Toleration* (1689, the same year the act passed). So it would be difficult to say that his work or that of any other theorist had done much to prepare the way. As we have seen, the results were not directly aimed at by anyone, but rather flowed from the interactions of various Christian groups in English society under favorable circumstances. In addition, Locke himself was a liberal Christian. It was not from some Enlightenment theory or vaguely deist sentiment (true deists were few in English society in the seventeenth and eighteenth centuries)[6] that English liberties took their origins. The English Revolution was not as "moderate" as some have come to regard it in retrospect. Political and religious passions ran high, as did violence towards many groups. In their own ways, however, the British learned a lesson parallel to that of the Thirty Years' War and the Peace of Westphalia: limited toleration and political liberty were better than anything else that could realistically be expected.

The French and English Background

In most historical accounts, however, *the* Enlightenment still seems to be identified with the developments in France, including the French Revolution. Historians disagree sharply on whether the revolution was the creation of earlier "enlightened" French theorists, or an unintended consequence of their ideas, or something else. We will look at each of these possibilities, since with the exception of Rousseau, it would be difficult to draw a direct line from the major French *philosophes* to the revolution. There are other factors, among them religious ones, that may help here. And the mere fact that various forms of enlightenment existed should, at the very least, caution us against thinking that reason or rationality was universally regarded as one obvious thing in opposition to traditional Christianity in the eighteenth century. The postmodern unmasking of French rationalism as merely one among many forms of reason—not universal reason, as it frequently thought of itself—is helpful insofar as it expands, instead of debunks, our sense of what can be considered rational.

For a long time, the French experience was contrasted sharply with the English one in the eighteenth century, and with good reason. There is a greater gulf than the English Channel that separates English and French ways in this period and since. Yet there are some surprising parallels as well. To begin with, as early as the 1438 Pragmatic Sanction of Bourges, the French Catholic Church, sometimes called the Gallican Church, had declared itself largely independent of Rome. The king and the local church officials proclaimed that they would make appointments to church posts within France, that councils were superior to the pope in disputes, and in Article 6 that "Appeals to Rome are prohibited until every other grade of jurisdiction shall have been exhausted." In other words, while the pope retained some minimal and distant jurisdiction, the French kings and their church were essentially self-governing within France's borders without actually breaking from Rome, as Henry VIII did later in England. As the French state grew, this collaboration between throne and altar also grew. Yet other factors entered into this seemingly simple religious equation.

During the Reformation, as was mentioned in the previous chapter, France was virtually unaffected by Lutheranism. But Calvinism seems to have resonated with the French, perhaps because Calvin himself had been born in France and appealed instinctively to French who had shared certain experiences. In a way, the struggle between Catholics and Calvinists in France during the sixteenth century anticipated the struggles between Anglicans and Puritans in England during the seventeenth, if with a different outcome. As in England later, a large segment of the French nobility were attracted to Calvinism, partly out of pure religious motives, partly because it represented opposition to the monarchy. France in the sixteenth century was a large and fragmented power, with many feudal jurisdictions that jealously guarded liberties they had enjoyed since the Middle Ages. In some ways it resembled the Holy Roman Empire, except that the French kings were able to impose a sort of unity on their vast holdings that the Holy Roman Emperors were not. While France remained Catholic, its political interests in checking the emperor's power and expanding its own influence led it into alliances with Protestants during the Thirty Years' War and even with the Turks.

Like the English, the French were not directly involved in the Thirty Years' War until late, but by then they had already experienced their own wars of religion. The Huguenots, as the Calvinist nobles and common people were called, pushed hard for recognition and reform, just as the Calvinists had done in England. Southwestern France in particular saw the rise of Huguenot jurisdictions under the aegis of local rulers. French kings successfully resisted and contained this combined political and religious challenge until, in the latter part of the sixteenth century, the accidental death of Henry II at a tournament left the country in the hands of Catherine de' Medici and Henry's young sons. In the power vacuum, various religious and political factions sought to gain the upper hand, and outright civil war, actually a series of wars, broke out.

As historians sometimes put it, there were three Henrys who competed for power. Two of them, the Catholics King Henry III and Henry of Guise, were each killed in 1589 by members of the rival Catholic faction. At that point, Henry of Bourbon, a Protestant, converted to Catholicism, according to rumor having explained that "Paris is worth a Mass." As Henry IV, he maintained Catholic domination in the country but granted tolerance to the predominantly Huguenot areas in the 1598 Edict of Nantes, which also allowed Protestants to have fortified cities and their own means of defense. Much of Catholic France disliked this settlement and in the *parlements* of several key cities, including Paris, it was not regarded as binding law. But after its own civil wars, France had a modicum of toleration and, more importantly, a period of social peace thanks to royal decree.

Henry IV set about trying to rebuild his war-torn country, but, like his rival Henrys, he too was assassinated, this time by a fanatical Catholic in 1610. His premature death set off yet another crisis of succession. It was Cardinal Richelieu who stepped in to fill the gap, serving as an adviser to the young Louis XIII and his mother. Richelieu was relatively tolerant of the Protestants. Even when they revolted in 1627 in La Rochelle, he merely stripped them of their armies and territorial rights, but allowed them to practice their faith. Like many French leaders after him, Richelieu believed that the overriding concern in the France of his time was the power and stability of the state.

Though Richelieu was not a strongly religious person, the unification of royal and religious power in France into a growing absolutism became a central feature from his time until the French Revolution. In retrospect, it is clear that such a concentration of power could not help but cause an explosion. But for quite a while, all over Europe and the world, things looked quite different. Particularly under Louis XIV, French civilization took on worldwide importance, from Russia in the East to the Mississippi Valley in the West. It was a largely secular and courtly culture, though the Jesuit order was a highly visible influence at court, to the dismay of the Huguenots and, significantly as we shall see, some Catholics as well.

It is important to have all this in mind as we consider how the Enlightenment affected France, because the intellectual developments had effects only insofar as the social matrix allowed them to. That matrix was essential because only a small number of people were able to read Descartes, Locke, and Newton, the presumed godfathers of the French Enlightenment. All three, of course, were involved in putting knowledge on a new footing after the advance of science had essentially destroyed the classical worldview. But it is worth recalling that none of these Enlightenment precursors was a secularist. Descartes remained a Catholic, if one of a different sort than his Jesuit teachers expected; Locke remained a liberal English Christian; Newton, though more difficult to classify, was some sort of Christian Unitarian.

It has rarely been noticed, for example, that the first sentence of Descartes's *Discourse on Method* is a deliberate quotation from Montaigne's essay "On Presumption."[7] Montaigne died in 1595, before Galileo's major discoveries in astronomy. His skeptical Catholicism—technically committed to the idea that ultimate truth cannot be proved, but content that the settled faith had met the test of long utility—derived more from the religious controversies of the Reformation and Counter-Reformation and (an early indication of more to come) from the impact of the New World, a world untouched by the Bible, causing Europeans to rethink their place on earth. Descartes clearly was not content with this sort of genial passivity towards truth. He was a brilliant mathematician and, like Plato, found correspondences between the certainties of geometry and what he sought in religion.

Descartes's famous solution was to doubt everything and, in that very process, to discover an indubitable truth: that if he was mistaken in his thinking, it was in *his* thinking that the error arose. As we saw in an earlier chapter, Augustine had made the same argument in several places, but without giving it much emphasis because during his time the possibility of knowledge was not in such serious dispute as in Descartes's day. As has often been noticed, this turn to the self opened up possibilities both for radical individualism and for radical disbelief, both contrary to Descartes's intentions. He believed that reflection on the undeniable truth of his own experience could be used by others to arrive at similar conclusions and also to argue for God's creation of the world and for the truths of Catholic teaching. But there was an incoherence in this method: it sought maximum objectivity as an end by means of maximum subjectivity. And it overlooked a critique often made of such claims today: Descartes's *Cogito ergo sum* ("I think, therefore I am") already involves the speaker in the Latin language, and in a whole culture that has taught him to speak and raise certain questions. The seemingly impersonal utterance of the *Cogito* was already conditioned by inescapable social bonds that no human being can evade.

John Locke attempted something similar in his *Essay Concerning Human Understanding.* Many people today admire Locke for his stance against improper use of authority and his attempt to develop a moderate, rational, and practical empiricism. All this Locke did brilliantly. What has been less noticed, however, is the religious motivation behind Locke's labors, his attempts to promote natural law, nature's God, and, therefore, what one writer has called "the fulfillment of the divine purpose for humanity." In this, Locke forms part of a growing current in the late seventeenth and early eighteenth centuries that saw the old biblical notion of human liberty and dignity as requiring a different set of institutions, a view that would have profound and diverse influences in England, America, and France. In its way, it was parallel to Newton's goals in setting natural philosophy or science on a different footing.

Given that Locke lived through the religious turmoil associated with the Puritan Revolution and the Glorious Revolution, and that he was an active participant on the revolutionary side, it is not surprising that he felt obliged to address these issues in ways that included a religious component. Indeed,

Locke regarded a knowledge of God and of his purposes, up to a point, as more certain than the empirical knowledge we have of things in the world. Like many earlier thinkers, he believed that God was a necessary being and knowable as such, while the things of this world, about which we can only have probable knowledge, admit of less certainty. In Book IV of the *Essay,* he lays out some of the things we may know that derive from certainties about our own existence. Unlike Descartes, Locke did not believe in innate ideas and famously regarded the human mind as a *tabula rasa,* a blank slate. Yet he resembles Descartes to the extent that he believed that just as we put together simpler ideas to form a correct idea that we exist, so we may combine simple but certain notions that lead us to recognize "*That there is an eternal, most powerful, and most knowing Being. . . .* The thing is evident; and from this idea duly considered, will be easily deduced all those other attributes, which we ought to ascribe to this eternal Being."[8]

Later students of empiricism, partly because of the much more skeptical tack of David Hume, have tended to underemphasize this feature in Locke. But Locke is even quite willing to agree with Saint Paul in the opening of the Epistle to the Romans, citing the famous passage: "the invisible things of God are clearly seen from the creation of the world, being understood by the things that are made, even his eternal power and Godhead" (Romans 1:20). Powerful arguments were made during the Enlightenment and after against this view, but the strength of Locke's belief impressed many in the eighteenth century. As Voltaire—himself a sincere believer for most of his life, if a deist—observed in his *Letters Concerning the English Nation,* Locke and Newton continued to have a positive influence on religious belief in the eighteenth century, whereas followers of Descartes often turned to atheism.

Perhaps this was because Locke had also thought through the relationship of reason and revelation, and he left strong arguments for reason itself to recognize the claims of revelation in those realms where reason could not reach. Nevertheless, a properly modest reason had its role in judging the reasonableness of revelation. Locke, for example, could rightly say that we have no direct impression of angels in our minds, but when we look at the number of creatures below us and the Supreme Being above us, it is not irrational to think that a host of intermediate beings may exist on that side as well. Reason cannot reach all things, but as this one example makes clear, reason always has its own proper role in thinking about revelation. As Locke said in a vivid description of some "enthusiastic" believers that he saw during the Civil War and the Puritan Revolution, their claim to understanding by faith alone endangered revelation: "he that takes away reason to make way for revelation, puts out the Light of both, and does much what the same, as if he would persuade a Man to put out his eyes, the better to receive the light of an invisible star by a telescope."[9]

Locke's views on God, man, and understanding had political and social consequences as well. In his *Two Treatises of Government*, among the most influential texts of political philosophy, he sets out a case for a limited government that might endorse an official religion but would tolerate others and mostly concern itself with practical, secular matters. But it is not often noted that the case depends on his perception that the reason for this is not that secularism is to be preferred to belief in general; rather, the unholy mixture of the sacred and the secular has harmed both. In *The Reasonableness of Christianity*, Locke makes a point that many Protestants and Catholics alike have agreed with, then and now: "Obedience is owed first to God, then to the laws." And the very notion that the state can order people to believe is both practically and morally absurd: "no man can so far abandon the care of his own eternal salvation as to embrace under necessity a worship or faith prescribed by someone else."

Locke's *Two Treatises* begin with religious points to arrive at a proper notion of the secular. The first treatise opens with a scathing refutation and mockery of Robert Filmer, who had put forth a naked case for the divine right of kings based on the Bible. Locke skillfully dissects the silliness of using the Bible as a prop for divine right, a Renaissance invention, and concludes with a concrete observation: "of one thousand seven hundred and fifty years that [the Israelites] were God's peculiar people, they had hereditary kingly government amongst them not one third of the time; and of that time there is not the least footstep of one moment of 'paternal government,' nor the 're-establishment of the ancient and primal right of lineal succession to it '"

When he turns to present his own theory in the second treatise, Locke begins with another religious point, "that Adam had not, either by natural right of fatherhood or by positive donation from God, any such authority over his children or dominion over the world as is pretended." Locke then famously sets out a conception of a "state of nature" that modern scholars tend to see as opposed to that of the much more formidable Thomas Hobbes, who was difficult to attack directly. Hobbes's idea of the state of nature was perpetual "war of all against all." So Hobbes, too, believed in the need for an absolute ruler. Locke instead retains some older Christian elements, even as he thinks creatively about his own state of nature:

> The state of nature has a law of nature to govern it which obliges every one; and reason, which is that law, teaches all mankind who will but consult it that, being all equal and independent, no one ought to harm another in his life, health, liberty, or possessions; for men being all the workmanship of one omnipotent and infinitely wise Maker—all the servants of one sovereign master, sent into the world by his order, and about his business—they are his property whose workmanship they are, made to last during his, not another's pleasure . . . .[10]

This not only means for Locke that we are not subject to the arbitrary violence and will of another, not even a lawful sovereign; we cannot even subject ourselves to improper violence. Since we are God's property, we cannot rightly sell ourselves into slavery or commit suicide.[11]

What we may do—and this is the positive side of the Lockean vision—is consent to give up a part of our natural liberty to proper authority in order to secure the means necessary to fulfilling the divine purpose: life, liberty, health, and property.

Locke seems himself to have been involved—at least indirectly through his friendship with the Earl of Shaftesbury—in the Rye House Plot, which was a plan to assassinate King Charles II after failed attempts to block him from naming his brother, later James II, an open Catholic, to succeed him. In 1685, the year in which James became king, France revoked the Edict of

Nantes, which had granted toleration to Huguenots. That same year, Locke published his *Letter on Toleration,* arguing that anyone who would respect the rights of others (he excluded Catholics and atheists) might be tolerated within a political system, which had no powers to discern and implement religious truth anyway. It was a bold argument that had not been presented quite so starkly before by anyone, Protestant or Catholic. Locke came to it out of a sincere respect for human beings made in the image of God and, more negatively, in reaction against what seemed to him to be improper coercion by all parties. It is almost possible to see an explicit "Do unto others . . ." philosophy in his rebuke to all parties. Locke was animated by an ambitious hope that inspired many people in England and on the continent, especially in France and America, but would take no little time, even in England, to bear its full fruits.

The French Enlightenment

Despite the admiration for Locke and Newton in France and the passionate talk of liberty, equality, and fraternity, the French Enlightenment harbored within it several kinds of authoritarianism and inequality. With few exceptions, the major Enlightenment figures in France essentially set up a Church of Reason that had its own forms of intolerance, excommunication, and inquisition. Historians are divided over the question of whether the thought of the *philosophes* was among the main causes of the revolution. That is a complex question. But there is no doubt that once the revolution got started, whether following the *philosophes* or not, revolutionary leaders felt authorized to carry out executions of religious as well as political persons, to outlaw Catholic worship, and to replace existing faiths with the worship of Reason and Liberty.

The revolutionary forces intuited something that had lain partly hidden till then. The Church of Reason in the writings of Voltaire and Diderot talked a great deal about toleration, but unlike the toleration promoted by Locke, its beating heart lay in replacing the authority of Christian revelation with the authority of secular reason. Voltaire sincerely believed in a deist god, but the cult of that divinity seemed to endorse the most sneering contempt for other Christians, both Catholic and Calvinist, who made up the vast bulk of the people in France. Though it sometimes appeared as if Voltaire's venom was aimed almost exclusively at Catholicism allied with monarchy, about which he pronounced his famous *Écrasez l'infâme*, he used the same terms to refer to the Huguenots, as well as the Jansenists—the austere, anti-Jesuit, anti-tyranny, and pro-tolerance Catholics—who would play a serious role in the lead-up to the revolution.

Voltaire's contempt stemmed from the fact that he scorned all forms of revelation. Locke thought reason itself convinced us that we needed revelation. Voltaire allowed none of it, mocked all forms of biblical revelation, and particularly blamed Jews: "You [Jews] have surpassed all nations in impertinent fables, in bad conduct and in barbarism. You deserve to be punished for this is your destiny."[12] For those who agreed with this "sublime, honorable, and dear Anti-Christ," as Diderot called him, such passion was exhilarating. Others took a different view: "Is not the fanaticism of your irreligion more absurd and dangerous than the fanaticism of superstition? Begin by tolerating the faith of your fathers. You talk of nothing but tolerance, and never was a sect more intolerant."[13] It would not be unfair to say that this angry intolerance was widespread among the French *philosophes*.

Part of the denigration of everything except a certain type of reason entailed dismissiveness not only of the religion of the masses, but of the masses themselves. Where Locke and others accepted the old intuition that most men cannot reach truth by way of reason and thought this was implicitly an argument for the utility and even the necessity of revealed religion, Voltaire regarded it as a reason for cynicism. Another of Voltaire's most famous lines is: "If God did not exist, it would be necessary to invent him." And the reason was that belief in an active God who punished wrongdoers kept the *canaille* (literally "rabble" or "scum"—Voltaire's favorite term for the masses) from their natural propensities.* And they would always be like that under any system, so education to improve their condition, which church

---

*Edward Gibbon, a less haughty figure of the British Enlightenment, seems nonetheless to have been infected by a similar snobbishness. When he says, as quoted in an earlier chapter, that in ancient Rome, "To the people all gods were equally true, to the philosopher they were all equally false, and to the magistrate they were all equally useful," he not only gets the historical facts wrong, but expresses a very un-English contempt for the common people.

schools were at least trying to carry out, was not to be bothered about: "We have never pretended to enlighten shoemakers and servants; that is the job of the apostles."[14]

The natural political order in this view was not democracy but the rule of philosopher kings or, more probably, kings advised by *philosophes* like Voltaire, who would receive favorable treatment. Voltaire may have repudiated the Jesuits who taught him and may have abhorred the ways that the Catholic Church intrigued with the French king, but he seems to have wanted to preserve a strong, if enlightened, monarchy so that the forces that might try to array themselves against the rule of Reason—whether democratic or aristocratic—could be safely ignored. It was for this reason that Voltaire had no qualms about his close relationship with Frederick the Great of Prussia, and Denis Diderot became an adviser to Catherine the Great of Russia.

Diderot, coeditor of the monumental *Encyclopédie des arts, sciences, et métiers*, deserves much credit for bringing together a wealth of learning and making it available to a large reading public in a systematic and accessible form. A true intellectual entrepreneur, Diderot was able to draw in distinguished contributors of all kinds and prevent the royal censors from seriously hindering the project. For Diderot and his collaborators took virtually every opportunity to denigrate traditional Christianity, even in articles that had essentially nothing to do with that subject. This bias masquerading as neutral knowledge earned the *Encyclopédie* a passionate readership among deists and atheists, of whom Diderot was one.

Where, then, did the great French revolutionary platitudes about liberty, equality, and fraternity come from? We must look at Rousseau, who began as a contributor to the *Encyclopédie*, though the *philosophes* by and large ridiculed him. Voltaire wrote to him with characteristic high-handedness: "I have received your new book against the human race [*The Social Contract*]. Never was such a cleverness used in the design of making us all stupid." Diderot, by this time no longer a friend, called Rousseau an *anti-philosophe*. But in spite of their differences, Diderot and Rousseau shared an authoritarian idea that is usually thought of as having originated with the latter, although it began with the former in the *Encyclopédie*. In the article on "Natural Law," Diderot put forward the idea of the General Will—which most people first encounter in Rousseau's *Social Contract*. And as was the case with Rousseau's later version, Diderot made the General Will almost like a divine rule of Reason that should trump mere individual human wills. In an article of his own on "Political Economy" in the *Encyclopédie*, Rousseau mentioned a "reign of virtue" that would do the same thing, a passage Robespierre invoked at the beginning of the Terror.[15] Unfortunately, the liberty, equality, and fraternity envisaged by the revolution were inextricably bound to an imposed virtue more intrusive than anything the Christian absolutist kings had ever attempted.

For Rousseau, religion and politics were closely intertwined, and both derived from his view of what constituted the best human life. Contrary to what his immediate followers and many subsequently have believed, Rousseau did not advocate a return to the primitive life. One explanation for this mistaken impression is that in his *Discourse on the Sciences and Arts*, one of his earliest writings, Rousseau argued—as have many moralists since Socrates and the Hebrew prophets—that advances in the arts and sciences, and the human benefits they had brought on a material level, had actually harmed morals and virtue. It was not for reasons of originality that this argument struck a nerve; in fact, in addition to classical and biblical precedents, secular analysts in the tradition of civic republicanism and even Machiavelli himself had argued pretty much the same thing. Rousseau's appeal to his contemporaries, rather, lay in the way he formulated his feelings, especially in his more personal writings, about the over-refined and hypocritical civilization of the French court and the artificiality of the French Catholic Church. His preference for a simpler life in touch with nature and "natural" religion did not mean a total withdrawal from a corrupt society, just a distancing from it.

The Social Contract became an unintentional bible of sorts for the French Revolution after it had started, though before then it was little known. Rousseau was at pains here to explain why a return to the original state of nature was impossible, and why total commitment to the state and submission of the individual will to the General Will reflected the very highest morality and religiosity. It is important to understand the emotional appeal of this position, which simultaneously gave vent to the desire for escape from existing institutions, including the deadening materialist tendencies of the Enlightenment, and also held out a vision of a simpler, passionate union of people who wish to live a more authentic and meaningful life. Both "authentic" and "meaningful" are terms that would have great careers beyond the immediate influence of Rousseau, because they anticipated the basic modern search for an understanding of human nature and the world that would preserve values deriving from Christianity in spite of the eclipse of their original Christian bases.

Paradoxically, according to Rousseau, submission to the General Will is the highest and truest freedom for the individual will. Because Rousseau did not much interest himself in how this General Will was to be discerned and expressed, he left the way open to various interpretations. One tendency was to think of democratic procedures as the General Will and the voice of God, a tendency that inspired a keen sense of right and a romantic pursuit of goodness for many involved in the democratic revolutions in the late eighteenth and nineteenth centuries. But there is clearly an authoritarian or even a totalitarian tendency in these principles without the right kind of political machinery. A person who finds himself being oppressed by a regime that declares itself to be the embodiment of the voice of God (or later, the laws of history or of dialectical materialism) has no court of appeal because all the channels of justice, human and divine, have been folded into the state itself. The state, at least ideally, is regarded as expressing a will that understands the individual's good better than he understands it himself. Commentators have frequently pointed to links between this side of Rousseau and later totalitarians.

But what of religion proper? Does it really have no independent existence or offer a refuge from all the nations of men in Rousseau's system? Here, too, ambiguity exists. Rousseau clearly regarded the Catholic Church as the wrong embodiment of religion *par excellence*, but not because it was united to the state. Towards the end of *The Social Contract* he objects that the independence of the church from the state, which did not exist in the classical and other pre-Christian civilizations, is precisely what has troubled the world: "For—because of it—nobody has ever quite succeeded in finding out whom, as between ruler and priest, he was obliged to obey."[16] By comparison, says Rousseau, Mohammed had been wiser because he followed the ancient model in creating "a system that was a single whole, which is to say a good one." In other words, Rousseau sees the whole tradition of rendering to Caesar only what was his own—which had received brilliant development in Augustine, Aquinas, and other astute Christians—as fundamentally wrong.

Instead, Rousseau seems eager to promote another form of religion that has drawn fervent support as well as criticism since his time, specifically civil religion:

> The religion of the citizens, on the other hand, is established within
> a single country, and gives the latter gods and tutelary patrons of its
> very own. It has its dogmas, its rites, its outward forms of worship pre-
> scribed by law; it regards as infidel and foreign and barbaric whatever
> lies outside the single nation in which it is established; the rights it con-
> fers and the duties it imposes reach no further than *the shadows of* its
> altars. The religions of the earliest peoples were all of this second type,
> which we might call civil, or positive, divine law.

By contrast, he says of historical Christianity: "There is no word to describe the mixed and anti-social law that results from it. . . . [I]t is so obviously baneful that it would be a waste of time if I tarried to offer proofs. Anything that impairs social unity is, *from the point of view that we have just adopted,* unwholesome. So also is any institution that sets man at odds with himself."

All human experience since Rousseau's time, in fact, suggests that it is not "unwholesome" for there to be various factions and critical currents within a society, whether they are religious or secular. Indeed, it is those apparent agents of division and disunity that prevent an unhealthy kind of unity from turning into tyranny.

Rousseau is not entirely optimistic about the other two forms of religiosity he identifies. Civil religion was the religion of the ancient world, but it runs the danger of turning into theocracy, "misleads the citizens, and drowns true worship of the Divinity in empty ceremony."[17] The true worship, of course, is deism or natural religion, which Rousseau blithely asserts is real Christianity. But this religion, in his view, has no contact with the state. A Christian republic is self-contradictory, because the two terms are "mutually exclusive." And it becomes clear that for Rousseau, even the Christianity that is "the religion of mankind" is not only unhelpful but pernicious to the state: "Christianity preaches only servitude and dependence. . . . Your true Christians are born slaves." That, Rousseau repeats—along with others in his day who misread the interactions of Christianity and the Roman Empire—was why Roman virtue disappeared in the ancient world. So he turns back to civil religion and recommends that it steer as close as possible to the religion of mankind in its beliefs, while practicing tolerance in its practices.

In *Émile*, a sentimental novel he published the same year as *The Social Contract*, Rousseau included a now-famous essay, the "Profession of Faith of the Savoyard Vicar."[18] The vicar is an easygoing, broadminded Catholic priest who has come to only three dogmas after going through a period of radical doubt: God created the world, he moves it with intelligence and providence, and man is a free spiritual being—in short, the creed of deism.* All of these derive mostly from feeling, though reasons of a sort are also offered. As in *The Social Contract*, he offers a highly idealized view of nature and argues that the evils we encounter are predominantly the result of human society. Voltaire was closer to the truth when he observed after the 1755 earthquake in Lisbon, which killed tens of thousands, that it was difficult to reconcile such events with the notion of a good God exercising providence over all his Creation. The biblical religions offered arguments about why God allowed such things to happen, but did not deny their troubling nature. And they also took pains to introduce some distance between Creator and creature so as not to make God directly responsible for evil. Rousseau himself came close to believing that the existing order of nature is somehow holy. For most people, however, as they gradually recovered

---

* See the Note on Deism at the end of the present chapter.

from the hypnotic effect of the vicar's (and Rousseau's) charming statement of faith, further advances in science tended to make even more difficult the easy worship of nature's God.

But all this was quite abstract and would not have made Rousseau the influential figure he was to become. There were many thinkers with similar
views, even if all their variations on deism soon fell apart. What made Rousseau unique was the verve with which he expounded his view of God and
nature, but even more his view of human nature. There is a curious combination of analytical sobriety and con-man special pleading in that view.

Like many of his contemporaries, Rousseau starts with a reflection on
man in the "state of nature."[19] But unlike Hobbes and Locke, among others, who find man in a state of penury and conflict, Rousseau claims that
these theorists are not radical enough. In the state of nature, man had no
language because he was a wandering individual, and did not conceive of
property or family as his own or another's. He was lazy and had few wants.
His two main emotions were a desire for self-preservation and pity for others who were suffering. The latter emotion is always dependent on the former, because it is only by imagining others in a situation of distress such as
we ourselves might experience that it becomes possible for us to care about
others. Even in contemporary society, our compassion for others is rooted
in self-love (*amour de soi*), which Rousseau distinguishes from selfishness
(*amour-propre*). Selfishness grew up along with civilization and has produced limitless desires and conflicts. Prior to entering into society, human
beings may have clashed momentarily but their rare contacts with one another were really pre-moral, since self-sufficiency and compassion were the
bedrock of life.

In other words, Rousseau is able to make the claim—beginning with
himself—that all human beings are naturally good, or at least morally neutral, until they are depraved by society. It is easy to see how this appealed
to many people in the highly artificial societies of the mid-eighteenth century, particularly with the decadence that followed the death of Louis XIV
in France. In addition to the dissatisfaction with artificiality, Rousseau succeeded because of the new sensibility that he created. In a further departure

from both pagan and Christian traditions, Rousseau and his fictional characters are not at all humble about proclaiming their natural compassion and goodness, and—a new concept—their sincerity.

From the voluminous material that we possess from people who actually knew Rousseau, nothing could have been further from the truth. Men of very different kinds—Voltaire, Diderot, David Hume—all initially befriended him, even at the times when it meant some risk to themselves because he was in danger from the authorities, and later recoiled in shock at his monstrous ingratitude, egotism, and paranoia. Rousseau was one of those poor intellectuals with the gift of making the wealthy believe that he is doing them a favor by accepting their generosity. Those who did not so believe, he scorned as having harmed themselves more than him. He was the first, it seems, to have both recognized liberal guilt and known how to exploit it.[20] Rousseau's *Confessions* were a belated attempt at damage control, a reply to the major Enlightenment figures and others who publicized his seedy exploits when nothing else seemed available to stop his misrepresentations of himself and others. After rationalizing all Rousseau's faults and explaining them as the result of evils done to him, the *Confessions* ends on an aggressively self-righteous note:

> I have told the truth. If anyone knows anything contrary to what I have here recorded, though he prove it a thousand times, his knowledge is a lie and an imposture; and if he refuses to investigate and inquire into it during my lifetime he is no lover of justice or truth. For my part, I publicly and fearlessly declare that anyone, even if he had not read my writings, who will examine my nature, my character, my morals, my likings, my pleasures, and my habits with his own eyes and can still believe me a dishonourable man, is a man who deserves to be stifled.[21]

This along with his numerous other claims of being the best of men because he is compassionate and nonjudgmental would, in another person, have been enough to warn off anyone with a modicum of knowledge about human life. But the amazing thing, and difficult to explain, is that Rousseau convinced some difficult judges (Kant had his portrait hanging over his desk). That in itself was unfortunate enough, but not nearly so unfortunate as the self-righteous impulse to which he gave license in the revolutionary political movements in France and beyond. Once the universal requirements of good behavior, humility, and even ordinary decency could be dispensed with on account of purity of heart or genius, the door was open to all sorts of behaviors apparently sanctioned by nature and nature's God.

Religion and the French Revolution?

Can we say that these intellectual developments caused the French Revolution? Of course, in some sense the major Enlightenment figures made a difference in how a certain sector of French society looked at the monarchy and social conditions. But that sector was small; we have no evidence that there was a very widespread deist, much less an atheist movement in France that contributed to the revolution. There are very sound reasons to doubt whether the intellectual component was quite as important as most intellectuals, in the Enlightenment and since, would like to believe. One of the most interesting developments in social history as applied to the French Revolution has uncovered some surprising facts. The full story is too complicated—and goes too strongly against received opinion—to go into in very much detail here. But suffice it to say that it may be better to shift the main focus of our attention away from intellectuals as fomenters of revolution and towards the same kind of social forces that English speakers have long been familiar with in thinking about the English Revolution.[22] That is to say, the French Revolution, before it went into its radical phase and the atrocities of the Terror, owed no small part of its existence to the contributions of various religious factions, and in broad outline this parallels what occurred in England a century earlier. In the French case, however, the players were quite different. Calvinists had long been a minority presence in France, but though much stronger than the *philosophes* and their followers, French Huguenots had no chance of changing social arrangements unaided. The role that the Calvinists played in precipitating the English Revolution was taken in France by the Jansenists, an austere movement for a simpler and more evangelical Catholicism, which the official church hierarchy in collaboration with the Jesuit order repeatedly tried to crush.

One participant in the Jansenist movement during the seventeenth century was the brilliant mathematician and philosopher Blaise Pascal (1623–1662), who had a personal revelation and conversion experience one night. He wrote an account of this event on a small piece of paper, which was discovered sewn into his clothes at his death:

> The year of grace 1654.
>
> Monday, 23 November, feast of Saint Clement, Pope and Martyr, and of others in the Martyrology.
>
> Eve of Saint Chrysogonus, Martyrs and others,
>
> From about half past ten in the evening until half past midnight.
>
> *Fire*
>
> "God of Abraham, God of Isaac, God of Jacob," not of philosophers and scholars.
>
> Certainty, certainty, heartfelt, joy, peace,
>
> God of Jesus Christ....[23]

And so on for several dozen more lines. Pascal's mystical experience inspired his series of *Pensées* ("Thoughts"), profound reflections on what would later come to be regarded as our existential position in the world. He also wrote a savage satire on the Jesuits in his *Provincial Letters,* criticizing their highhanded treatment of Bishop Jansen.

In the eighteenth century, Jansenism occupied a similar position to the Calvinism of seventeenth-century England: within the mainstream religion, but vehemently opposed to its alliance with tyranny and cumbersome official structure. Both also had a political dimension. In 1713, the French monarchy persuaded Pope Clement XI to issue an encyclical, *Unigenitus,* condemning Jansenism. Originally, Jansenism had run afoul of Catholic authorities because it seemed, at least to some, to side with Calvinist notions of grace and predestination. Jansenists denied this interpretation and remained Catholic despite the criticism they faced. But after *Unigenitus,* the movement increasingly took on the coloration of political opposition to the official hierarchy and the monarchy. Unlike the *philosophes,* the Jansenists came to count millions among their movement—if not for theological reasons, then for political ones. A recent study estimates that *Unigenitus* alone drove a million French into the Jansenist, antiroyal camp.[24]

Over the next two decades, Jansenism developed from being a group committed to a specific theological tradition into a much larger social movement. By 1731, according to the same study, 75 percent of the police in Paris were Jansenist in the broader sense. Clerics attempting to stop this rising tide in the 1730s denied the sacraments, including anointing of the dying, to Jansenists, creating a wide popular anticlericalism among Catholics themselves in Paris. The story grows complicated here. The Parlement of Paris, one of the old medieval sources of decentralized jurisdiction, refused to allow the archbishop's ruling to go into effect. It is a reflection of the complicated relationship of church and state in France that a secular body could defy both secular and religious authorities in such fashion. As we know from Pascal, the powerful Jesuit order was not to be identified with the Catholic Church in France, and the Jansenists could try to appeal to Rome and European opinion in general against the king and the segments of the Gallican Church that were controlled by the monarch. As one scholar has observed, "astonishingly—from the perspective of traditional Enlightenment studies—royal and governmental authority was publicly challenged by its own *Parlement*, and with mass support, all united by Jansenist politico-religious ideology."[25]

Jansenists came to believe in religious toleration for themselves and for others. Their journal, *Nouvelles ecclésiastiques,* and the masses they represented put pressure on the French monarch to expel the Jesuits—an early instance of the true force of public opinion in modern states. Jansenists were among the most fervid readers of Rousseau's *Social Contract.* In addition, *Nouvelles ecclésiastiques* had its own theory of social contract[26] and rejected the view that Protestantism was naturally more compatible with a republic than Catholicism by pointing to the historical example of Venice.[27]

There is no historical evidence that deist, secular, or other Enlightenment currents exerted anything like the concrete popular influence that the Jansenists had. Concerning the large developments leading to the French Revolution, one historian has written:

it is impossible to discern the activity of any deist movement in these events—or indeed any evidence indicating that the phenomenon of the Enlightenment, as it has been traditionally conceived, led to the French Revolution. Unfortunately for the modernity hunters, the great Church-state conflicts of eighteenth-century France were fought out in a more or less traditional manner with one Christian faction pitted against another in alliance with particular lay constituencies.[28]

This is a shocking conclusion for those who believe that intellectuals and deists exerted the primary influence on the rise of French rebellions. Once it began, radical elements clearly got control of the revolution and led to the Terror; those radicals drew something from Rousseau and perhaps other figures of the French Enlightenment. But recent social history has rightly pointed to religious currents as a contributor to the demise of French tyranny. And it was broad social factors of this nature that led to the English and American revolutions.

The American Revolution

Around the time of the American Revolution, a significant minority of the Founders and the other colonists had been influenced by a moderate deism of the British sort that also retained strong elements of Christianity. Few, however, were deists properly speaking; most were out-and-out Christians. Probably the most religiously untethered of them all (the English radical Tom Paine excepted) was Thomas Jefferson, who was of a less settled disposition than his fellows on religious matters. Jefferson had been converted to a kind of Unitarian deism by the British philosopher Joseph Priestley. Though both also continued to identify themselves with elements in the Christian tradition, Jefferson predicted in his enthusiasm: "I rejoice that in this blessed country of free inquiry and belief, which has surrendered its conscience to neither kings nor priests, the genuine doctrine of one God is reviving and I trust that there is not a young man now living in the United States who will not die a Unitarian."[29] The doctrine that revived in the nineteenth century in America and Europe, however, as it had in America's First Great Awakening a few decades prior to the revolution, was traditional, indeed passionate, religious doctrine among both Catholics and Protestants, and that is still largely the case today. Unitarians, almost two hundred years later, make up a fraction of one percent on either continent. A Unitarian may well argue that the belief, though accepted by a small number, is still true. But Jefferson's error is a reminder of how deceptive the future appeared to highly intelligent people in the early nineteenth century.

In a famously expansive passage in his *Notes on Virginia*, Jefferson argued rightly against government interference in religious affairs: "The legitimate powers of government extend to such acts only as are injurious to others. But it does me no injury for my neighbor to say there are twenty gods, or no God. It neither picks my pocket nor breaks my leg."[30] Yet this vivid liberality has confused later readers about the age-old question of whether any society that is completely indifferent about the beliefs of its people will not find its pocket picked, its leg broken, and much worse. In other moods, Jefferson—like all the Founders—recognized the importance of the right sort of religion to a free republic. Even in the *Notes* he observed later: "Can the liberties of a nation be thought secure when we have removed their only firm basis, a conviction in the minds of the people that these liberties are the gift of God? That they are not violated but with his wrath?" The civil libertarians who like to cite Jefferson on the wall of separation between church and state do not pay equal attention to the Jefferson who once said that "no nation has ever yet existed or been governed without religion. Nor can be."[31]

What did Jefferson mean by this? Most accounts of the American founding emphasize the importance of Locke without discerning that the religious dimension of Locke, analyzed earlier, resonated with Americans, clergy as well as laypersons, as much as his views on secular government and tolerance. We now have ample evidence of this from recent studies of colonial-era sermons. The generation that led the American Revolution knew clearly that a secular government designed to take care of secular affairs did not mean a society in which secularism was in effect the official religion. Church and state were separated so that each could do its job better. Yet there was a certain asymmetry in the relationship. Religion protected from government intrusion can carry out its tasks quite well. A good political order without a religious presence, as Jefferson says, is impossible, because, as we saw with Virgil and Rome, reason itself informs us that reason can restrain the more destructive human passions only in a very small number of philosophers. For social order, religion is indispensable.

It is very easy to find evidence for this view in a wide variety of sources around the time of the American Revolution. Though each religious denomination was cautious about any language that would allow any one denomination a chance to direct the power of the state, all agreed with Locke's position that there was an "overlap" of religion and politics on matters of good moral behavior. This point has become obscured in the past half century or so because Locke's teaching on individual rights has more and more been misinterpreted as meaning that public authority has no jurisdiction over either the creeds or the morals of individuals. The much-vexed question of a "right to privacy," which has come into public prominence since the 1973 Supreme Court decision in *Roe v. Wade* legalizing abortion by federal judicial fiat, would not much have impressed Locke or the American Founders, who all believed that rights and *duties* were entailed by the law of nature, which came from nature's God. Most Americans know that the Declaration of Independence says "men have been endowed by their Creator with certain inalienable rights." Far fewer realize that in the very act of showing why those rights authorize the people's resistance to tyranny, it also speaks of their duty: when a "long train of abuses and usurpations evinces a design to reduce them under absolute despotism, it is their right, it is their duty, to throw off such government." That duty stems directly from the whole infrastructure of belief about God's purposes in creating human beings that comes out of a biblical tradition properly understood.

The clearest statement of the congruence between freedom and religion—almost the polar opposite of what later came to be continental European and recent American views—appears in George Washington's Farewell Address. Washington, Jefferson, and nearly all the American Founders were from one point of view men of the Enlightenment. But when Washington wrote to the Truro Synagogue in Newport, Rhode Island, he made it plain that Jews in America, like other believers, were not merely to be "tolerated," but they had the rights of all other citizens:

> All possess alike liberty of conscience and immunities of citizenship. It is now no more that toleration is spoken of, as if it was by the indulgence of one class of people, that another enjoyed the exercise of their inherent natural rights. For happily the Government of the United States, which gives to bigotry no sanction, to persecution no assistance requires only that they who live under its protection should demean themselves as good citizens, in giving it on all occasions their effectual support.

Here again, harmony between church and state depends on the state staying out of religious questions, but also on believers doing their duty as citizens by good moral behavior.

Yet Washington went even further in the Farewell Address. There, the normally reticent leader spoke in full tones about the importance of religious principle to good order:

> Of all the dispositions and habits which lead to political prosperity, religion and morality are indispensable supports. In vain would that man claim the tribute of patriotism, who should labor to subvert these great pillars of human happiness, these firmest props of the *duties* of men and citizens. The mere politician, equally with the pious man, ought to respect and to cherish them. A volume could not trace all their connections with private and public felicity. Let it simply be asked: Where is the security for property, for reputation, for life, if the sense of religious obligation desert the oaths which are the instruments of investigation in courts of justice? And let us with caution indulge the supposition that morality can be maintained without religion. Whatever may be conceded to the influence of refined education on minds of peculiar structure, reason and experience both forbid us to expect that national morality can prevail in exclusion of religious principle. [*Emphasis added.*]

Experienced eighteenth-century leaders like Washington distrusted mere speculation. They believed that religion was a spring of "popular virtue" and that without "national morality" a free system cannot survive. So when Washington invoked "reason and experience alike," he was appealing to just about every argument that his hearers might be inclined to grant as valid.

Furthermore, he spoke not only of a generalized "religion," but of "religious principle." In his cautious way, Washington, an Anglican vestryman, may have been reminding Americans of various denominations that the real energy of both religion and morals must come out of something more than a rationalized deism. That is what had happened some decades prior to the revolution, as one historian has noted:

> Deists and Unitarians were joined in embracing republicanism by Protestant theological conservatives representing the older British churches, by rambunctious promoters of the new-breed evangelicalism, by spokesmen for traditional Protestant faiths from the Continent, by Roman Catholics, and even by representatives of what was then the tiny community of American Jews.[32]

Locke himself had written a book entitled *The Reasonableness of Christianity*, not as is sometimes believed to whittle Christianity down to its most unobjectionable teachings, but to represent a truth we encountered in Virgil's *Aeneid*, that "the greater part cannot know, and therefore they must believe." Far from being a cynical comment of the kind that Gibbon made about all religion being "useful" to the magistrate, this is Locke's and Washington's view that reason itself tells us it is reasonable to recognize that man does not live by reason alone. Indeed, reason might also expect Providence to provide precisely some such remedy for natural incapacity.

Three Social Currents

After their respective revolutions, the English and the Americans went on to a relatively tranquil existence in which religion and politics found a reasonable mutual tolerance. France, however, did not. As we will see, the French went through several more decades of turmoil as they tried to solve the problem of religion and social order. Their final solution to this day begs many questions, not least whether it is possible simply to sterilize the public square of religious influence while congratulating oneself on tolerance for private religious observance. If Locke and the American Founders were right that the public realm and the religions share a common and overlapping interest in moral behavior, then France and the kinds of lay societies modeled on it appear to have adopted an expedient that cannot ultimately resist certain challenges. Can the liberties of a nation survive, as Jefferson asked, if they are not rooted in God? The three main paths that emerged from the revolutions of the Enlightenment period were religious (America), deist inclining toward skeptical (England), though with some revivals in the Victorian age, and centralizing-secularist (France), which opened a door to the ideological developments of the nineteenth and twentieth centuries.

A Note on Deism

Deism in the more moderate circles of England and America was not always distinct from some form of biblical religion, but it was not very close to orthodox Judaism or Christianity either. A main thread running through all forms of deism is that it represents the true, rational, and universal religion of mankind, of which the particular religions are offshoots. A principle of this kind necessarily bumps into certain features of revealed religion. Reflective Jews and Christians always knew that the scriptures were not mere rational statements; that was one of the reasons why they engaged the philosophical and cultural notions of whatever civilization they came into contact with. At the same time, however, they believed that revelation was superior to rationality in at least two areas: 1) many basic truths were difficult to arrive at and few people are philosophers, so by way of revelation God mercifully provided a cheat sheet for people on questions they would otherwise be unable to answer; 2) there are aspects of God that reason cannot reach but that are important for our lives in this world. Jews and Christians alike believed that God had made important communications to his people throughout salvation history, and Christians believed in particular that Jesus was a special appearance by God himself. Faith, as had been said through the centuries, was in a sense above, but not contrary to reason.

Some of the English deists tried to split the difference. The originator of deism, Lord Herbert of Cherbury, argued that natural and rational religion paralleled the Bible. John Locke and Isaac Newton inclined more towards a liberal Christianity, which is to say they accepted Jesus as a kind of messiah but wavered on the doctrines of the Trinity and the Incarnation. Locke and Newton had leanings towards the rational side of deism without, perhaps, exactly joining the club. But shortly after them, men such as John Toland and Matthew Tindal expanded on Lord Herbert's original insight with a full-blown redefinition of Christianity in deist terms. Tindal wrote a famous text, *Christianity As Old As Creation,* that tried to redefine what counted as Christian. In the words of one interpreter, it meant "The most important criterion of the genuineness of all revelation can therefore consist only in its universality, in its transcendence of all local and temporal limitations."[33] To a later view, this might seem to be saying that revelation is revelation only when it can justify itself as a certain type of eighteenth-century reason; but in its own time, it stirred many to assent.

When this current made its way to France, it found a ready audience and also became more radicalized, in the form of Cartesian rationalism and its offshoots in men such as Malebranche and Fontenelle. Where English deism operated, however badly, in a spirit of compromise with traditional Christianity, French deism was often openly anti-Christian. Diderot's *On the Sufficiency of Natural Religion* is representative of the odd mix of tolerance and sweeping dogmatism of the central French attitude. At one point he dismisses Judaism, Christianity, Islam, and paganism with all the peremptoriness of a self-important archbishop as the heretics and schismatics of the one true religion, which is felt and verified by reason within his own soul:

> The former testimony I find within myself inscribed by the hand of
> God; the latter has been written on parchment and marble by super-
> stitious people. The former I bear within myself, and I find it always the
> same; the latter lies outside myself and differs with every country and
> clime. The former brings together and unites civilized man and barbar-
> ian, Christian and heathen, philosopher and people, scholar and un-

educated, old man and child; the latter estranges father and son, arms man against man, and exposes the wise to the hatred and persecution of the ignorant and the fanatic.[34]

Of course, this universal religion was and is unknown to historians and anthropologists—an odd fact for such an allegedly clear set of truths. It does not take a postmodernist to see that what Diderot (along with Voltaire, D'Alembert, and Rousseau) was offering as pure universal reason was actually the artificial and short-lived product of a particular historical moment.

CHAPTER 8

Civilization, Culture, and Their Discontents

> ... the *democratic* movement is the heir of the
> Christian movement.... We have a different
> faith; to us the democratic movement is not only a
> form of decay of political organization but a form
> of the decay, namely the diminution, of man,
> making him mediocre and lowering his value.
>
> Nietzsche, *Beyond Good and Evil* [1]

IN many respects, the West after the French Revolution—in the "long
century" from 1789 to 1914—embraced what might be called a religion of liberty. Not surprisingly, this faith sometimes clashed with older
faiths, particularly with the Christian churches that had suffered violence
as the French Revolution turned into the Terror. Yet the religion of liberty
also drew on renewed energies in Christianity, some of which formed an integral part of the zealous populism and nationalism that arose all over the
West. German romanticism, influential from America to Russia, for example, emphasized the organic richness of particular peoples and their traditions, including religion, as opposed to French Enlightenment abstractions
about humanity and faith. In France itself, Chateaubriand's *The Genius of
Christianity*, which had already appeared in 1802 and immediately found
a wide audience, presented a kind of Rousseauan Catholicism, pointing to
the beauties of nature, art, and popular Christian practices as reflections
of spiritual truths. People as different as Adam Mickiewicz in Poland, Gi-
useppe Mazzini in Italy, and Walt Whitman in America wrote of national

unification and independence in religious terms. In the United States, religious passions helped extend republican government and inspired both sides in the Civil War. By the end of the century, even though many of the earlier protagonists in the struggle might not have thought so, it was clear to someone like Nietzsche that the growth of parliamentary democracy was a political expression of certain Christian values that clashed with his own belief in a radically "different faith."

The unprecedented and well-known material progress of the nineteenth century—which included the emergence of popular governments, broad economic growth, industrialization, the extension of railroads, global trade, the migration of large percentages of the population from the country to the cities—seemed to have ushered in a New West, completely different from the Old and promising a boundless future. This proved to be an illusion, of course. The carnage of World War I and its reprise in World War II, with the added horror of the Holocaust and the Gulag, made clear that the optimism about material progress had been mistaken. But even in its heyday, it had been seen as such by perceptive observers. A catalogue of names is telling: Blake, Wordsworth, Wilberforce, Arnold, and Newman in England; Chateaubriand, Hugo, and Baudelaire in France; Emerson, Lincoln, Hawthorne, Melville, and Adams in America; Kierkegaard, Dostoyevsky, and Tolstoy elsewhere. As different as these figures are from one another, they illustrate that a powerful religious culture, which was ambivalent about the meaning of material improvements and looked to spiritual truths to remedy some of the features of progress itself, remained very much alive. So as a corrective to the usual picture, we need a different understanding of the mixture of new and old elements in the West in the nineteenth century.*

---

*Chateaubriand provided a kind of program for the new Christian apologist, explaining in *The Genius of Christianity* why he wrote:

> [T]he Christian religion, of all the religions that ever existed, is the most humane, and the most favorable to liberty and the arts and sciences, that the modern world is indebted to it for every improvement, from agriculture to the abstract sciences—from the hospitals for the reception of the unfortunate to the temples reared by the Michael Angelos and embellished by the Raphaels. It was necessary to prove that nothing is more divine than its morality—nothing more lovely and sublime than its tenets, its doctrine, and its worship; that it encourages genius, corrects the taste, develops the virtuous passions, imparts energy to the ideas, presents noble images to the writer, and perfect models to the artist; that there is no disgrace in being believers with Newton and Bossuet, with Pascal and Racine. In a word, it was necessary to summon all the charms of the imagination, and all the interests of the heart, to the assistance of that religion against which they had been set in array.

Reaction against Revolution

The rapid and disastrous failure of the French Revolution did not, of course, put an end to aspirations for a freer social order than had been available under monarchs claiming divine right. It merely shifted those aspirations from a self-destructive radicalism to a whole spectrum of different currents: some equally radical and self-destructive, others more realistic and practical, still others uniting spiritual and political concerns in new ways. In the immediate aftermath of the revolution, Protestants but especially the Catholic Church renewed their resistance to radical democracy. Some of the opposition was the result of obstinate refusal to come to terms with modern conditions, but a good part of it stemmed from the simple fact that the revolution in France had gone mad, giving rise to a political malady not entirely cured even in the twenty-first century, the kind of unbridled and murderous political passion that the great Russian novelists sometimes called "brain fever." It is no mystery, then, why the churches in their reaction against the political turmoil strongly supported a return to authority. The revolutionaries' own violent excesses and fanciful new cults made the rise of an authoritarian figure like Napoleon, among others, inevitable. There was no other way to keep the violence, chaos, and social strife that overwhelmed France from becoming even more deadly. When Napoleon assumed power in 1799, only ten years after the start of the revolution, he restored order and brought disaffected groups back into the French system, including the Catholic Church, with which he signed a concordat in 1801.

Yet at the same time, insofar as he had any actual ideas, Napoleon viewed himself as a liberalizing despot, and his conquests over the next few years, therefore, carried with them a certain ambiguity. On the one hand, he seemed to be freeing various peoples from traditional political and religious oppression so that they could achieve their own proper national destiny and spirituality, a new phase in France's self-imposed, unique *mission civilisatrice*. On the other hand, this self-proclaimed civilizing mission quickly began to raise not only political, but cultural and religious protests against what seemed to be yet another form of tyranny, both political and intellectual. Tensions between universalism and particularism, and others stemming from them, would mark much of the history of Europe down to the nationalist debacles of World War I, the ideological struggles of World War II and the Cold War, and in some respects the struggle over globalization even today.[2]

As his enlightened despotism "liberated" one nation after another from unenlightened despotisms, Napoleon skillfully created the impression that he was bringing about a glorious age of universal human brotherhood. Eminent cultural figures as different as Beethoven, Goethe, and Hegel celebrated the early Napoleonic conquests. In a telling incident, Hegel happened to be in Jena in Germany at the moment when Napoleon passed through, and he proclaimed, "I saw the World Spirit (*Weltgeist*) seated on a horse." Since Hegel believed that the whole of human history was the unfolding of Spirit in time, this was tantamount to saying that he had seen the manifestation of God's action in history in the person of Napoleon and the French influence he represented. It was a sentiment not fated to last long as the Napoleonic empire spread in every direction. In other nations around Europe, the kind of Enlightenment that Napoleon used as a political pretext (he harbored few deep beliefs) had begun decades earlier to take on an odd profile; it was seen simultaneously as a liberation and as a threat to national values, among them the liberties and popular practices associated with religion.

Culture versus Civilization

This dichotomy appeared most sharply in German romanticism, in which the difference between culture (*Kultur*) and civilization (*Zivilisation*) took on urgent importance in the face of the expansive influence of France. "Culture" and "civilization" are often used today as virtual synonyms. But around this time in Germany, a strong and fairly cohesive movement began trying to establish a more or less clear opposition between these two notions. For figures like Herder and Fichte, leaders of German romanticism, the French Enlightenment before the revolution was already an abstract system that threatened authentic national and personal life. Nationalism had never been very strong in Germany, owing to the fragmentation of the people into a crazy quilt of small political jurisdictions. But now a sense of German particularism gained strength in opposition to Enlightenment claims to universalism, especially as Napoleon began abolishing the liberties of the old German cities and establishing a more centralized regime under French hegemony.

For the romantics, the drive towards universalism was Civilization (French), but it was bloodless in comparison with Culture (German), which consisted of the affections, customs, traditions, popular songs and tales (the Brothers Grimm were then actively collecting these), folkways, and religion of the people (*Volk*). In Herder's early formulation, the culture of the German people was of positive value, as were other particular traditions—an early and mild form of multiculturalism. In Fichte, however, the theory was developed further into a strong assertion of the importance of the *Volksgeist*, which is to say a particular Popular Spirit. Foreshadowing the German inferiority complex that gave rise to a superiority complex a century later with Nazism, Fichte even went so far as to assert the preeminent value of German culture, which had to be kept "pure" from corrupting foreign influences. Put this way, and in light of subsequent history, such as Nazi racism, his views seem quite repugnant. But they raised a legitimate issue that survives into postmodern societies: what are the respective spheres of the universal and the particular? The universal exists, but most of us live by some mixture of universal values and truths with particular ones, including religion.

In much historical writing about the nineteenth century, movements like socialism, capitalism, liberalism, Marxism, and so on bulk large. It is right that these receive careful attention because they began to occupy spaces formerly reserved for religious ideas. And paradoxically, there were still ways in which the old revolutionary idea became an ersatz religion in Europe and even in Latin America, which had its own wars of independence. Physical science, too, now formed part of this proliferation of secular activities. Even when religion was vigorous and offered plausible explanations for its beliefs in modern conditions, there was still no getting away from the fact that religion operated in a matrix of other truths that are sometimes neutral but sometimes aggressive towards the spiritual. Yet by a kind of countermovement, religiosity purified itself by its separation from fields in which it had no special competence and, instead, focused on some fundamental problems. Material progress and political reform may satisfy human nature, as a significant number of people in the nineteenth century came to believe. But it is also possible that some of the quintessential human things are in danger or are simply lost absent some belief that goes beyond such practical activities. Indeed, after the initial enthusiasm, material goods seem to have become less and less satisfying in the advanced societies, and that discontent has opened up some new vistas in the search for order and meaning.

Perhaps this is the only way to explain a curious phenomenon of the nineteenth century. Amidst all the optimism over industry and technology, a strong current of nostalgia for the Middle Ages developed all over Europe. The center of this current was in Germany, where romantics not only touted medieval organicism over modern mechanism, they converted to Catholicism and sought to use the rich heritage of symbols, popular practices, and culture to counter what they regarded as the shallow rationalism associated with France. Such feelings were hardly unique to Germany. In the 1830s, when Britain rebuilt the structures still used for Parliament today, it chose a style that was not modern, but medieval—the Gothic. It is possible to make too much of the symbolism, but it is not without significance that the "mother of Parliaments" at the time began to meet in an atmosphere that suggested the twelfth and thirteenth centuries.

As in Germany, the culture of English-speaking nations was feeling its way back to something in medieval Catholicism that was felt to be missing in the modern world. Beginning with Walter Scott in England, literature started to tout medieval subjects. The Pre-Raphaelite painters and poets in the middle of the nineteenth century, as their name implies, emphasized notions that went back before the high point of Renaissance art, seeking a simplicity and human richness that strongly contrasted with their own time. Even America felt the pull. Nathaniel Hawthorne set his *Marble Faun* in Rome precisely to evoke the richness of that most unmodern of great cities. On the verge of the twentieth century, Henry Adams wrote his famous appreciation of medieval art and culture, *Mont Saint-Michel and Chartres*.

Like religion, medievalism offered a refuge from the Enlightenment threat of rootlessness. And the same threat lies behind many modern and postmodern ways of thinking about religion as an important element in preserving personal and group identity. So it is useful to approach the religious side of the past few centuries with multiple frames of reference in mind. As one historian has rightly characterized this new function of religion:

> the nineteenth century was both the archetypal period of secularisation, and a great age of religious revival: as large numbers were alienated from the official church, religion ceased to provide a focus of social unity; but it became instead a major basis for the distinctive identity of specific communities, classes, factions, in a divided society. Many people found their loyalty to their churches intensified in the process.[3]

We will want to look more carefully at what "secularization" has meant over the past two centuries. But from the data we have, it is quite clear that religious elements underwent something of a resurgence in several countries in the nineteenth century.

Numbers Games

To take the crucial test case, France in the nineteenth century is often described as secularizing. And in the sense that certain intellectual sectors became almost exclusively populated by secularists, as they now are around the world, that may be true. But as it was common to say for some time, there were "two Frances" after the revolution: one of them was stubbornly Catholic, the other stubbornly *laïque,* but not necessarily unbelieving. Unlike other national churches, the Catholic Church in France at the time of the revolution did not hold a large portion of the arable land, only between 5 and 10 percent, but it lost all of that and even had virtually all its churches and schools closed for a time in 1794. Religious education was thus disrupted during the revolutionary years, meaning that a good part of a generation received little or no training in religion during a time of much anticlerical hostility. Yet as was proved in the twentieth century in nations struggling for far longer under official atheism in the former Soviet bloc, religious roots can survive in spite of social repression. Part of Napoleon's appeal to the French was his restoration of normal church functioning early in his rule, an especially popular move in the large rural areas outside of Paris where the Church remained strong.

After Napoleon's ultimate departure and the restoration of the monarchy in 1815, religiosity rebounded even more vigorously. In France from 1814 to 1848, for example, the number of diocesan priests rose from 36,000 to 47,000, and those over the age of sixty declined from being 42 percent of the whole to only 5.6 percent.[4] This was during a time when the nation continued to be agitated by waves of revolutionary activity. Indeed, the religious opposition to the return of radicalized forces in 1830 and 1848, as well as in 1870, to say nothing of the radical Commune of Paris in 1871—the dates that everyone who studies Western history learns to regard as key points in the struggle between progress and reaction—may have retarded the arrival of popular government; but given the direction that radicals typically took in France, it may also have prevented a Bolshevik-style regime. By 1878, just as the Third Republic was consolidating itself and definitively parting with latter-day kings and emperors, there were 130,000 female members of religious orders, 30,000 male members, and 56,000 diocesan priests. Ordinations remained fairly stable; it was not until the persecutions by socialist governments again after 1905, when religious orders were suppressed and religious were pressured to abandon education, that they showed any significant decline, and even this was not steep.[5] Jesuits, who had been suppressed in 1764, began to reconstitute themselves after the fall of Napoleon: from a low of 91 in 1815 they grew steadily to number 3,868 in 1900. Whatever else may have been going on in French society during the nineteenth century, numbers like these show that the influence of non-Christian, even anti-Catholic forces was limited to certain sectors, while in other ways the Catholic Church in France gained substantial strength. The deep secularization of France is mostly a phenomenon of the second half of the twentieth century.*

This period between the fall of Napoleon and the First World War was

---

*Granted, these numbers hide weaknesses, both moral and intellectual, that could be quite profound. Popular religion in France could be smugly bourgeois and hypocritical; no one described it more sharply than two later Catholic novelists, François Mauriac and Georges Bernanos. When Ernest Renan's *Vie de Jésus* ("Life of Jesus") appeared in 1863, with its apparatus of skeptical German biblical scholarship, it shook the faith of many French people in much the same way that Darwin's *Origin of Species* (1859) shook the faith of many in England. Today, Christian scholars of the highest intellectual ranks work with theories of biblical inter-

primarily a time of great popular spirituality in France. John Vianney (1786–1859), widely known as the Curé of Ars, was a simple priest who generated a massive following because of his manifest gifts in talking to people in the confessional. Beginning around 1830, he attracted on average 30,000 to 60,000 pilgrims a year, who sought counsel in his small and out-of-the-way village. In that year, Catherine Labouré claimed to have seen a vision of the Virgin Mary in Paris's Rue de Bac, setting off massive enthusiasm. Similar apparitions occurred at La Salette in 1846 and Lourdes in 1858, inspiring pilgrimages that are still going on today. Towards the end of the century, Thérèse Martin (1873–1897), later known as Saint Thérèse of Lisieux, though she died at an early age after a brief and quiet life as a cloistered Carmelite, touched off another wave of simple popular spirituality. Whatever questions might be raised about these phenomena, there is no denying that popular piety—what Chateaubriand had called "harmonies of religion and nature"—was alive and very vigorous indeed in the France of the nineteenth century.

Though French high culture on the whole was not particularly religious in the nineteenth century, it was not at all uniformly secular either. Some of the greatest names were either self-defining believers or outright Catholics. In the first category, there are figures such as the very influential Victor Hugo, probably most famous in English-speaking countries for his novel *The Hunchback of Notre Dame*, a contribution to the modern literature that looked back to the Middle Ages for inspiration. Hugo also wrote poetry of various kinds, satires and ballads among others, all of which displayed a sheer technical capacity that outstripped all competitors and was so popular that his funeral was one of the most memorable—and bizarre—public moments in France.[6]

As both an artist and a thinker, Hugo belonged to the first half of the

---

pretation and literary hermeneutics that have quite adequately accommodated what seemed to be knockdown arguments against biblical belief. (For a brief and readable survey of these developments, see Nicholas Boyle, *Sacred and Secular Scriptures* (South Bend, Ind.: Notre Dame University Press, 2005).) But in France at the time, such questions seemed to threaten both traditional culture and popular belief, especially since the priests who had been ordained in large numbers were predominantly sons of the more prosperous peasants or artisans, and had not received the most sophisticated or rigorous intellectual formation. They were committed men and, on the whole, morally blameless, carefully following church rules on celibacy, but they could appeal to the people only through a religion of love, not as defenders against intellectual assault.

century. A much more modern and still influential poetic current arose with the publication of Charles Baudelaire's *The Flowers of Evil.* This collection initially earned Baudelaire a prosecution on obscenity charges; but by the time of his death, he had returned to Catholicism, and it could be seen that he had done so in part by a clear analysis of the evils that attend all human life, evils that do not have a purely natural source. As he put it in the opening lines of *Au Lecteur* ("To the Reader"), the very first poem in the collection:

> Foolishness, error, greediness, and sin
>
> Work on our flesh and occupy our hearts,
>
> And we feed our amiable remorse
>
> As dirty beggars nourish their vermin.
>
> Our sins are obstinate, repentance slack;
>
> We pay heavily for our waywardness,
>
> Yet happily return to filthy paths
>
> Sure a few tears will wash away our fault.[7]

In both subject matter and style, Baudelaire stood at the head of a list of other avant-garde poets—Rimbaud and Verlaine most notably—who also found their way back to faith by acquaintance with evil.

In his *Illuminations* and *A Season in Hell,* Rimbaud wrote visionary poetry as modern and penetrating as anything produced since. He even satirized the literary etiquette on how he ought to write about his vision: "One must be absolutely modern. No hymns." His return to religion at the end of his life after Bohemian days with Verlaine is something singular, even for such a singular age. Verlaine wrote more accessible, if equally modern poems. In one sonnet, expressing his own yearnings, he takes up a medieval figure whom Wagner would also write about, the perfect Arthurian knight Parsifal:

> Parsifal has vanquished the daughters, with their gentle
>
> Babble and amusing luxuriance; despite delight
>
> Of the flesh that lures the virgin youth, tempts him
>
> To love their swelling breasts and gentle babble;
>
> He has vanquished fair Womankind, of subtle heart,
>
> Her tender arms outstretched and her throat pale;

From harrowing Hell, he now returns triumphant,

Bearing a heavy trophy in his boyish hands,

With the spear that pierced the Saviour's side!

He healed the King, and shall be himself enthroned,

As priest-king of the sacred, vital treasures.

In robe of gold he worships that sign of grace,

The unblemished vessel in which shines the Holy Blood.

—And, o those children's voices singing in the dome!

English Culture and Religion

English culture manifested a different set of reactions to French developments. Shortly after 1800, William Blake wrote in one of his notebooks:

Mock on, Mock on Voltaire, Rousseau

Mock on, Mock on: 'tis all in vain!

You throw the sand against the wind,

And the wind blows it back again.

And every sand becomes a Gem

Reflected in the beams divine;

Blown back they blind the mocking Eye,

But still in Israel's path they shine.

The Atoms of Democritus

And Newton's Particles of light

Are sands upon the Red sea shore,

Where Israel's tents do shine so bright.[8]

Blake seems not to have had a very clear notion of the obvious differences between a sneering satirist like Voltaire and a pious deist like Rousseau, or between an ancient materialist like the philosopher Democritus and the religious mathematician Sir Isaac Newton. Yet it is significant that an uneducated genius like Blake, who developed his own highly eccentric religious system and was not a defender of orthodox Christianity, entered into the cultural fray with this powerful repudiation of the kind of vague disbelief and scientism that many associated with France and the Enlightenment more generally. Strong spirits simply refused to be confined to a modern iron cage.

Blake was not alone, or the first among poets, to take this stance in England. Though one current of romanticism turned into the disbelief and self-indulgence of Shelley and Byron, another found a new vision in religious renewal. Wordsworth, the preeminent romantic poet of nature in England, felt an equally sharp reaction to the atrocities of the French Revolution and the Terror, although he had earlier seen great promise in the revolution: "Bliss was it in that dawn to be alive, / But to be young was very heaven!" And it is clear from his poetic practice as well as theory that he came to find something problematic in the eighteenth-century Reason that everyone thought at the time had come to fruition with the revolution.

As many literary critics have since remarked, a new sensibility allied with religious views grew up with romanticism. Where poetry in the eighteenth century had usually been quite prosaic and platitudinous, with romantic poetry the world and human life took on some enchantment again. Wordsworth's own beliefs were Christian, eventually orthodox Anglican. When he makes a plea about the way that nature has been lost to us in practical life, we should not mistake his solution for a call to return to the pagan:

> The world is too much with us; late and soon
> Getting and spending, we lay waste our powers:
> Little we see in Nature that is ours;
> We have given our hearts away, a sordid boon!
> The sea that bares her bosom to the moon;
> The winds that will be howling at all hours,
> And are up-gathered now like sleeping flowers;
> For this, for everything we are out of tune;
> It moves us not.—Great God! I'd rather be
> A Pagan suckled in a creed outworn;
> So might I standing on this pleasant lea,
> Have glimpses that would make me less forlorn;
> Have sight of Proteus rising from the sea;
> Or hear old Triton blow his wreathèd horn.[9]

Later writers might think that a literal return to paganism, which Wordsworth believes is a "creed outworn," would itself bring enchantment. But for him, it is merely of comparative benefit. The real thing has to come from the fuller precincts of Christianity and reinvigorate the life of the human race within Creation.

Wordsworth's friend and collaborator in this project, Samuel Taylor Coleridge, provided the intellectual formulations, partly through his familiarity with German idealist philosophy as well as German romanticism. Coleridge's approach was quite daring within the British empiricist tradition. Where Locke, Hume, and Adam Smith had largely discounted the imagination as a generally misleading fantasy, Coleridge boldly made it one of the serious powers of the mind. In a famous distinction, he asserted that imagination was akin to the original creative power by which God brought the world into being, while fantasy was the kind of associative power of joining existing things together that we see in mediocre poets and in practical thought. Coleridge went further and spoke of reason as a faculty of appreciating the necessary postulates of moral life, an appreciation that mere understanding can never achieve. In this view, the scientific understanding of the natural world is inadequate for our full existence. In other words, reason itself tells us that something besides reason, as usually conceived, is necessary to human life.

In the English-speaking world, the *locus classicus* for what is usually believed to have happened to faith during the nineteenth century, in the broadest terms, is a brief passage from Matthew Arnold's 1867 poem, *Dover Beach:*

> The sea of faith
>
> Was once, too, at the full, and round earth's shore
>
> Lay like the folds of a bright girdle furled;
>
> But now I only hear
>
> Its melancholy, long, withdrawing roar,
>
> Retreating, to the breath
>
> Of the night wind down the vast edges drear
>
> And naked shingles of the world. (Stanza 3)

A number of eighteenth-century Enlightenment figures had thought this would be a (secular) blessing for the human race in that it would free people from "superstition" and open up the possibility for the rational pursuit of such satisfactions as life in this world had to offer. Arnold, however, concludes this poem with a vision of the human race "as on a darkling plain / Swept with confused alarms of struggle and flight, / Where ignorant armies clash by night."

Yet except for certain intellectual and social sectors in some countries— England's Bloomsbury comes to mind—this has not proved to be the general experience at all. We have not entirely lost faith; we are just more uncertain about what it is and means. Arnold had actually written a more prophetic poem a dozen years earlier. In *Stanzas from the Grande Chartreuse*, he spoke of himself as a person educated in the most modern way, yet

> Wandering between two worlds, one dead,
>
> The other powerless to be born,
>
> With nowhere yet to rest my head.

The setting of the poem is significant: the great monastery of the Carthusians in the Alps, which reminded Arnold of lost faith and the unsettled human problem that remained in its absence. It would take a while for others to feel this mood quite as strongly as Arnold, but it may not be an exaggeration to say that as early as the mid-nineteenth century, the postmodern was born, with its odd feeling of being somehow "after" what is modern yet still tied to the modern, and seeking a spiritual poise that it recognizes in the religious tradition, but cannot come to terms with in its own characteristic ways of understanding. Arnold might not have been entirely surprised by the persistence and growth of Christian churches in the world since his day.

In his prose works, Arnold makes an effort to offer a solution to the pain and emptiness evident in his poetry, and that solution is culture. In *Culture and Anarchy* (1869), a classic text that skillfully sums up the nineteenth-century debate over religion and civilization, he points to "Hebraists" and "Hellenes" as the two poles to be harmonized into a full perfection if we are to flourish as human beings. He even quotes a British bishop: "First, never go against the best light you have; secondly, take care that your light be not darkness." In Arnold's Britain—and we might say in contemporary America—there is a puritanical strain, which Arnold rightly identifies with the Hebrew respect for living according to the Law. The problem for us, Arnold believed, is to cultivate what in other contexts might be called an "informed conscience," or the play of intelligence and duty that he found in the Greek tradition at its best and among subsequent inheritors of that tradition, whom he called Hellenes.

In Arnold's system, "culture" is the antidote, a robust habit of thinking vigorously about all the questions that human life throws at us. Culture is not simply identified with the Greek side of the two poles; in fact, Arnold was unusually sensitive to the things that were lacking in the Greek tradition as much as those that were present. He did not see Jewish or Christian religion as simply a moralistic contradiction of Greek rationality. Christianity in particular had in the course of history actually replaced or adapted Greek culture to its own purposes, which seemed better to people in the ancient world and had proved quite durable: "Apparently it was the Hellenic conception of human nature that was unsound, for the world could not live by it."[10]

But unsound is not the same as thoroughly discredited. In Arnold's calm vision, no portion of truth could ever be neglected by a society that wanted to achieve a full and balanced perfection, or at least such perfection as it was capable of. The classical world needed Jerusalem. Europe after the successes of Christianity needed Greece again. Our own time may ask for some new mix of the two. But we will not understand Arnold's most famous saying unless we keep in mind that for him, culture includes the full range of goods, religious and secular. Culture is "the great help out of our present difficulties; culture being a pursuit of our total perfection by means of getting to know, on all matters which most concern us, the best which has been thought and said." It was a valiant attempt and it continues on in various forms. Arnold's idea of culture, like that of the German romantics before him, can do some good. But it knows it cannot serve as a surrogate for religion, let alone replace it.

Popular Religion in Britain

Further down the social and intellectual hierarchy, the churches in Britain, uncertain how to respond to challenging new social conditions, were often accused of failing in their moral duties—especially the high Anglicans. Though partly true, this charge neglects some real facts. For instance, William Wilberforce, after his conversion to Methodism, was already active before 1800 in seeking to mitigate the circumstances of the poor who had come to the cities from the countryside. As a member of Parliament, Wilberforce was probably the single most important figure in abolishing the slave trade worldwide; he introduced a bill towards that end every year for over a decade and a half until it was finally passed in 1805. After that, transport of slaves from Africa was prohibited and the ban was enforced by the Royal Navy, then the greatest sea power in the world. Three days before Wilberforce died in 1833, another of his long-sought goals, emancipation of all slaves in British lands, was passed in Parliament.

The churches may not have had a comprehensive social theory to deal with the new conditions. Who did? But many of them found a renewed mission, as in France, less as guides to national politics and more as ministers to the people. They labored successfully, when they saw the first signs of trouble, to keep alcoholism, drugs, prostitution, illegitimacy, and various other social ills from overwhelming the new urban populations—no small contribution to Victorian life.[11] The year 1833 was also the beginning of the Oxford Movement, a reinvigoration of Anglicanism in England by a return to the Fathers of the Church, the leading Greek and Latin thinkers of the first Christian centuries. Several members of the movement—most notably John Henry Newman and Edward Manning—eventually became Catholics. Their conversions sparked a Catholic revival in England that over the next century was to include Gerard Manley Hopkins, G. K. Chesterton, Evelyn Waugh, and Graham Greene, among many others. Even the Chartists, the most radical of the English movements, attracted a fair number of nonconformist clergy who lived lives similar to those of working men.

All these activities modify the picture of the relationship between Christians and workers that was given wide currency by Karl Marx's collaborator, Friedrich Engels, in his *Condition of the Working Class in England:*

> English Socialism affords the most pronounced expression of the pre-
> vailing absence of religion among the working-men, an expression
> so pronounced indeed that the mass of the working-men, being un-
> consciously and merely practically irreligious, often draw back before
> it. But here, too, necessity will force the working-men to abandon the
> remnants of a belief which, as they will more and more clearly per-
> ceive, serves only to make them weak and resigned to their fate, obedi-
> ent and faithful to the vampire property-holding class.

Modern scholars are not convinced that this characterization of religion among Britain's working class is any more accurate than any other part of Marxist-Leninist analysis. And the end of the quotation indicates that religious belief *was* still alive among workers in Marx and Engels' day. It seems (we have no sure data) that as people moved to industrialized towns, they did—especially the men—attend church services at lower rates than did the rural populations. But this shift in churchgoing habits, if it occurred, did not necessarily mean a vast drop-off in religious belief and even less in the pervasive social influence of Christianity in nineteenth-century Britain. In 1851, a famous report by England's Horace Mann, for example, deplored the decline of churchgoing in parts of Britain. Men who had to choose between the church or chapel on the one hand and the pub on the other in their few hours off from the factories often wound up in pubs, of course. But even so, in the late 1800s, an average of about 30 percent of men and women combined in England attended church regularly, roughly the same percentage as in a highly religious country like the United States today.[12]

In terms of more general religiosity, however, this figure, like all raw numbers about church attendance, does not nearly represent the whole reality. During the Victorian period, the overwhelming majority of working-class children attended Sunday school. In working-class homes—even among those who did not go to church or chapel—prayer, Bible reading, hymn singing, and the basic Christian ethos continued as a strong presence. Much has been made of the reaction of working people against the perceived upper-class bias of the Anglican Church and the middle-class Puritan values of the Non-Conforming congregations. These resentments do seem to have had social effects, especially among the very poor. Yet at the same time, even the union and labor movements, the Chartists, and the Socialists often combined political activism with Christian belief. The long-term steadiness of Christian belief among labor leaders was remarkable. A survey done of Labor MPs in the British Parliament of 1929–1931, for instance, found that out of 249 only 8 described themselves as atheist or agnostic.[13] Figures like these after a century of alleged decline in belief suggest that Christianity remained very strong indeed in Britain and continued to shape most people's lives even if the churches had no solutions to what came to be called the workers' question.

Contrary to popular impressions, not even the Darwin controversy, for all its effects on biblical literalists, made a big dent in religiosity. Debates over accommodating modern scientific discoveries to the central truths of the Bible had been going on for centuries prior to Darwin, as they had even in earlier ages, with scientists and philosophers who themselves were believers coming forward with serious arguments about how to reconcile the two ways of truth.[14] Some British Calvinists, for instance, welcomed the apparent randomness in Darwin's theory as revealing God's free choice (like his free choice of whom to save or damn) as opposed to the mechanical deism of the eighteenth century—an odd postulate to us but historically true. Even people most often thought to have vigorously used Darwinism as a basis for unbelief turn out, on close inspection, to have been more philosophically astute than is usually supposed and somewhat reluctant to condemn all forms of faith. In a review of *The Origin of Species*, T. H. Huxley ("Darwin's Bulldog"), for instance, famously asserted: "Extinguished theologians lie about the cradle of every science as the strangled snakes beside that of Hercules; and history records that whenever science and orthodoxy have been fairly opposed, the latter has been forced to retire from the list, bleeding and crushed if not annihilated, scotched, if not slain."[15] But in less contentious circumstances, Huxley did not maintain that Darwinism proved materialism, and he worried that essential moral principles could not be reconciled with the theory—perhaps the first person who recognized the possible dangers of Social Darwinism. Indeed, he even went so far as to say that "the human race is not yet, possibly may never be in a position to dispense with" the Bible.[16] Many continued on in faith and the old Christian ethics for that very reason.

More German Consequences

When the Enlightenment really took hold in Germany, it had a double effect. On the one hand, it produced two true geniuses, Kant and Hegel, who may be compared to the greatest philosophers of any age. Each developed a detailed rational system that in its rigor and daring cannot help but evoke admiration. In addition, each had a religious side: Kant came from a German Pietist background and Hegel from a Lutheran one. Kant's attempts to stake out the limits of reason and, therefore, the true place for faith brought fresh thought to an old truth. Hegel's notion of Universal Spirit was a brilliant effort to reconcile the sense of historical development with personal religious truths.

But the rigorous and helpful contributions of these outstanding minds were outstripped by the much less rigorous and quite deleterious influence of another German, who claimed to have stood Hegel on his head by making matter, not Spirit, the determinant of human history. People born after 1989 will find it increasingly hard to believe how potent Marxist commitment was for small enclaves in the mid-nineteenth century and for much larger swaths of public opinion in the twentieth, not only in the former Soviet Union and its allies, but even for elites in Africa, Asia, and South America, and no small numbers of people in western European nations such as France, Italy, and Germany. This is all the more difficult to comprehend because this ersatz religion, which claimed to be "scientific" while also appealing to emotions rarely manifest in real science, erred universally both in its analysis of and in its predictions about what would happen in capitalist countries. In this, Marxism was the first and the chief of several gods born in the nineteenth century that failed.

One of the dangers of supposedly scientific theories of human societies, as Edmund Burke first recognized in his analysis of the French Revolution, is that they advance simple, clear, and distinct ideas that are quite persuasive without being true. Among other fundamentally wrong "scientific" theses, which Marx nevertheless put forward with a fiercely unscientific hatred, was the notion that workers were producing excess value that owners were "expropriating." He based this theory on two others. First, that there was an Iron Law of wages by which workers would be squeezed more and more by employers until, inevitably, they revolted. (In reality, shortly after *The Communist Manifesto* appeared, workers' wages began to rise—a fact that Marx carefully excluded in the second edition). Today, of course, workers in capitalist countries enjoy greater prosperity than their counterparts in any other system. Marx also mistakenly believed in the "labor theory of value," which posited that the workers' efforts added worth to products that employers, again, siphoned off to their own purposes. This should have been obviously false on its face. A lucky swing of a pick in a diamond mine or a chance discovery of a seam of gold ore may be worth far more than items produced through considerable effort and skill. Even in normal manufacturing, a product has only the value that buyers are willing to pay for it, which can vary widely within a population and over time. The only reason these very dubious theories seemed like revolutionary bedrock to Marxist believers was that they justified hatred of bourgeois societies and gave sanction to the "inevitable" revolution ahead, after which, even more implausibly, religion and the state, both mere bourgeois instruments of repression in the Marxist view, would wither away. That passionate desire for revolution, whatever the facts, lay behind the vehemence and even violence with which the Communist gospel was preached.

Secularization and the American Case

One common way of portraying the nineteenth century is as the great age of secularization, the period in which churches were disestablished and religious institutions generally lost their hold over various secular activities and, to some extent, over the people as well. There is obvious evidence that this is true. The Catholic Church in France, for example, grew in the number of clergy but never regained its pre-revolutionary status. The Papal States, a political entity that extended across the middle of the Italian peninsula and over which popes had ruled for centuries, simply disappeared in the unification of Italy. Even in America, the individual states that possessed established churches one by one abandoned them. Viewed from the perspective of institutional arrangements, it would appear that the nineteenth century was simply a period of decline in the public influence of religion.

History rarely presents purely linear developments, however, since many different things occur simultaneously. During this same period, for example, personal commitment to religion could become more intense, partly as a result of the independence that religious bodies now had from worldly activities. Even as churches were being disestablished in America during the first half of the nineteenth century, a second Great Awakening of religious enthusiasm was under way. According to one estimate, Methodists in the United States grew from 14,000 around the time the American Constitution was being written to over a million (served by more than 11,000 preachers) in 1844.[17] In England at roughly the same time, the Oxford Movement re-energized Christian thought within Anglicanism, while evangelicals played a conspicuous public role in social reform; and Methodists grew from 92,000 in 1801 to 489,000 in 1850.

It is revealing to compare the religious history of the United States in the 1800s with a country like France. As we have seen, France experienced various Catholic revivals during the century even as its Catholic and *laïque* halves grew further apart. The French story is usually told as one of religious decline. In the United States at the same time, there were both similarities and differences, of course, but here the increasing separation of church and state is rarely regarded as evidence of religious decline. This bears some careful attention because what counts as religious vitality frames the phenomena.

The early religious history of the United States is often mistakenly presented as a search for religious liberty. It is true that the Puritans and other refugees sought religious liberty in the New World, but liberty for themselves as corporate bodies to set up social and political structures that would reflect what they believed was God's desired human order. There was something like the separation of church and state—as later formulated in the Constitution of the United States—in colonial Rhode Island and Virginia, and there were some early attempts at toleration in Maryland and Pennsylvania. But almost all of the former thirteen colonies at the time of the ratification of the U.S. Constitution had tests for public office. State establishment of religion was common and persistent. The last state to give it up was Massachusetts in 1833. The First Amendment to the Constitution was a check on the *federal* government's power to regulate religion. The individual colonies were jealous of their own settlements and did not want to cede control over religious matters to a new and unpredictable national government. But perhaps the most surprising thing about this history is that in spite of disestablishment of various kinds over the whole period, the several main religious bodies in the United States not only survived, they flourished; and by indirect means they had a powerful influence on American society.

The Methodists are perhaps the central part of this story. John Wesley's movement stimulated several waves of revivals in both Britain and the United States, including a major new wave in the early 1800s. Wesley and George Whitefield were largely responsible for what is called the First Great Awakening, which not only sparked a personal form of religion, but also aroused the colonists' enthusiasm for liberty in ways that the more staid and established churches could not. In *Common Sense,* Thomas Paine, though hardly an evangelical Christian, uses some of the scriptural passages that the Methodists had invoked to good effect for his own revolutionary purposes:

> Near three thousand years passed away from the Mosaic account of the creation, till the Jews under a national delusion requested a king. Till then their form of government (except in extraordinary cases, where the Almighty interposed) was a kind of republic administered by a judge and the elders of the tribes. Kings they had none, and it was held sinful to acknowledge any being under that title but the Lord of Hosts. And when a man seriously reflects on the idolatrous homage which is paid to the persons of Kings, he need not wonder, that the Almighty,

ever jealous of his honor, should disapprove of a form of government
which so impiously invades the prerogative of heaven.[18]

Locke, a Christian, had used similar arguments against Filmer; but for
Paine—a skillful polemicist whose attachment to Christianity was always
uncertain and seems eventually to have evaporated—to use an argument
such as this at a delicate moment testifies, at the very least, to the power of
religious arguments for liberty in America.

That influence did not end with the revolution in 1776. John Wesley had
sent the preacher Francis Asbury to America about five years earlier. Asbury is said to have traveled about 300,000 miles and visited every one of
the colonies at a time when travel was quite difficult. (Later Methodist "cir-
cuit riders" played no small part in the settlement of the frontier areas.) By
the time he died in 1816, there were 2,000 Methodist ministers in America, a hundred times that many laypeople, and around 2,700 churches. The
momentum Asbury created kept going at an incredible pace. According to
reliable estimates, as the Civil War began almost 20,000 Methodist churches had sprung up, until, as one historian put it, "there were almost as many
Methodist churches as United States Post offices."[19]

A similar sort of revivalism appeared in other denominations and is often
linked to broad social developments in what historians call the Second Great
Awakening. Like the Methodists, Baptists experienced explosive growth,
with over 12,000 churches in existence by the beginning of the Civil War.
Such currents were sometimes connected with prominent institutions.
Timothy Dwight, as president of Yale, directed students into careers as
public evangelists; two of his most famous students, Lyman Beecher and
Nathaniel W. Taylor, acquired national reputations. But revival meetings
typically had more of an emotional than an intellectual cast; and while
theologically conservative, in social terms they might be progressive—vast
public events that stirred up largely rural populations. Several women rose
to prominence as preachers with this movement. Elleanor Knight, Julia
Foote, and Rebecca Miller made national names for themselves, and Harriet
Livermore preached to the U.S. Congress in 1827, the first woman to do so.[20]
Overall, the effects of these groups were to stimulate the creation of popular

associations and strengthen already existing American beliefs that religious liberty, not state activity, should energize American life.

Popular associations were dedicated to missions, ministering to enslaved Africans, temperance, abolition, and a host of other aspects of American society. Merely to describe their activities, however, gives no sense of the scope of their influence. One historian notes that "The annual budgets for some of these associations equaled those of the country's largest businesses."[21] This was the America that Tocqueville described so vividly as composed of private associations that looked to one another for whatever they needed, and looked with suspicion on the powers of government:

> The citizen of the United States is taught from infancy to rely upon his own exertions in order to resist the evils and the difficulties of life; he looks upon the social authority with an eye of mistrust and anxiety, and he claims its assistance only when he is unable to do without it. . . . Societies are formed to resist evils that are exclusively of a moral nature, as to diminish the vice of intemperance. In the United States associations are established to promote the public safety, commerce, industry, morality, and religion.[22]

Religious belief did not always directly translate into social policy. The Baptists, for instance, split painfully over the question of slavery. Southern Baptists under the leadership of South Carolina's Richard Furman believed that the Bible authorized it. Northern Baptists were influenced by Rhode Island's Francis Wayland, president of Brown University and an ardent abolitionist. (Several of the slave revolts in the early nineteenth century drew inspiration from Christian sources.) Although the Southern Baptist Convention went on to become the largest Christian denomination in America after Roman Catholicism, the Northern Baptists saw their views prevail after the Civil War. Some people regarded the inability of the Bible to provide a definitive answer on a fundamental question like slavery as proof that it did not have clear authority of any kind, much as the Catholic/Protestant splits had done in Europe. But these remained a minority in America. Most people continued to believe in God's concern for justice and therefore claimed him as support for their views before, during, and after the Civil War. In that sense, the American Civil War was a kind of religious war. Rare was the figure like Abraham Lincoln, whose religious vision grew during that conflict and who said of the two sides in his Second Inaugural Address: "Both read the same Bible and pray to the same God, and each invokes His aid against the other. It may seem strange that any men should dare to ask a just God's assistance in wringing their bread from the sweat of other men's faces, but let us judge not, that we be not judged. The prayers of both could not be answered. That of neither has been answered fully. The Almighty has His own purposes."

In his "Meditation on the Divine Will," a brief text found among his papers and not intended for publication, Lincoln reflected deeply on the mystery of the war among a people who shared the same religious faith:

> The will of God prevails. In great contests each party claims to act in accordance with the will of God. Both may be, and one must be, wrong. God cannot be for and against the same thing at the same time. In the present civil war it is quite possible that God's purpose is something different from the purpose of either party; and yet the human instrumentalities, working just as they do, are of the best adaptation to effect his purpose. I am almost ready to say that this is probably true; that God wills this contest, and wills that it shall not end yet. By his mere great power on the minds of the now contestants, he could have either saved or destroyed the Union without a human contest. Yet the contest began. And, having begun, he could give the final victory to either side any day. Yet the contest proceeds.

Here Lincoln enunciated something not typically thought to exist amidst American optimism: a deep tragic sense of the mysteries of Divine Providence. Several nineteenth-century American writers—Fennimore Cooper, Hawthorne, and especially Melville—also display it, though they have often been overshadowed by the more optimistic figures like Emerson and Thoreau. Even the expansive Walt Whitman, although claimed by the transcendentalists, touches deep tragic chords at times, especially when he, too, reflects on the war.

As the century passed, America gave birth to vigorous new religious foundations. The Seventh Day Adventists grew out of the Millerite movement with a woman at their head, Ellen White. The Mormons were founded in upstate New York under the inspiration of Joseph Smith, and then, when Smith was killed in an uprising against the new movement, they spread under the leadership of Brigham Young to Utah and Idaho. The Mormons drew many adherents and to this day are among the fastest-growing religious groups in the world. Black Americans with Richard Allen began the highly successful African Methodist Church, and black Baptists created many local congregations. By the early twentieth century, one-third of the Baptist churches in America were black, as were a quarter of the Methodist churches. Even the Catholic Church found ways to flourish on American soil by tending to the lives of its mostly immigrant members in cities, so much so that by the end of the twentieth century a sociologist wrote quite rightly that the Catholic Church in America had done better "in the climate of a religiously neutral republic that is friendly to religion than in so-called Catholic countries where it has been both privileged and persecuted."[23]

Developments within the Catholic Church

The Catholic Church itself, the institution that appeared most wedded to the *ancien régime*, underwent a transformation during this period. As we have seen in previous chapters, the Church had been in a position of vulnerability vis-à-vis secular rulers since at least Constantine. Over the centuries, it had been at times allied with and at others opposed to the secular power in an attempt to preserve the independence of the spiritual dimension, to the annoyance of kings and democrats alike. The shakeup of the secular order in the nineteenth century forced the Church to a fuller understanding of itself as a different kind of power—as the pure moral influence it was to become in the twentieth century. Napoleon had kidnapped two popes, Pius VI (1775–1799) and Pius VII (1800–1823), around the turn of the century. One died in exile in France, the other was forever wary of political powers. One of their successors, Gregory XVI, was elected in 1831, just after the revolutionary uprising the year before, and died in 1846. Gregory abhorred modern developments, even material improvements like gas lamps and railroads, the latter of which he called *chemins d'Enfer* ("paths of Hell"), a play on the French term for railroad, *chemins de fer.* He ruled the Papal States autocratically and even issued an encyclical in 1832, *Mirari vos,* that condemned efforts by Lamennais and others in France to reconcile ancient Christian notions of liberty with modern republicanism. Yet Lamennais's work contributed to the eventual emergence of Christian Democracy, both as a generalized movement and as a political party.

Gregory's successor, Pius IX, earned a historical reputation for being a reactionary who condemned notions that the pope should reconcile himself to modernity and who sought to bolster his power against the secular forces unifying Italy by having himself declared infallible at the First Vatican Council in 1870. Yet this long-ruling pope began life as a political liberal and was hailed as such by Italians and other Europeans. He welcomed technological innovations and freed Gregory's political prisoners, to great public acclaim. Count Pellegrino Rossi, a political liberal married to a Protestant, was allowed to become head of the government in the Papal States. But Pius was traumatized by an uprising in 1848 that assassinated Rossi and nearly overran the Swiss Guards protecting him in the Quirinal Palace in Rome. He escaped unscathed, was restored to power by a French army, and thereafter would not budge an inch in ceding papal power, even when Italian forces occupied Rome in 1870 and he became a "prisoner of the Vatican."

But the story of nineteenth-century Catholicism does not end with this notorious episode. Rather, it ends with Leo XIII (1878-1903), a pope seeking a renewal of Catholic thought and also promoting liberty in the process. Leo was a trained philosopher and, as pope, an advocate of the notion that Catholics should "rally" (*ralliement*) to the French republic. He also sought to stimulate the study of Thomas Aquinas, who had been relatively neglected by the Church (the impression that Aquinas is *the* Catholic philosopher dates from Leo's efforts). The pope may have seen in Aquinas what Lord Acton, a British Catholic, around the same time called Thomas's distinction in presenting "the earliest exposition of the Whig theory of the revolution," citing this:

> A king who is unfaithful to his duty forfeits his claim to obedience. It is
> not rebellion to depose him, for he himself is a rebel whom the nation

has a right to put down. But it is better to abridge his power, that he may be unable to abuse it. For this purpose, the whole nation ought to have a share in governing itself; the Constitution ought to combine a limited and elective monarchy, with an aristocracy of merit, and such an admixture of democracy as may admit all classes to office, by popular election. No government has a right to levy taxes beyond the limit determined by the people. All political authority is derived from popular suffrage, and all laws must be made by the people or their representatives. There is no security for us so long as we depend on the will of another man.[24]

This "passage" is actually a combination of various statements by Aquinas, some of which do not accord with modern republicanism in quite the way Acton suggested. But Leo, like Acton, seems to have been willing to give the case for the Christian foundations of democracy a chance and to give France after 1878 the benefit of the doubt. His opening prepared the way for further developments towards a theory of Christian democracy. In any event, on the verge of the twentieth century, the old antagonisms between faith and freedom seemed to be shifting into something quite different even in the Catholic Church: a belief that Christian teaching supported the dignity, political as well as spiritual, of every person.

Fin-de-siècle Moods

In spite of the optimism about material developments, as the twentieth century dawned there were strong doubts about the direction of civilization as well. The disillusionment produced by the First World War and the darker vision that would soon appear in writers like T. S. Eliot, Kafka, Thomas Mann, and Hemingway, and even more pessimistically in Oswald Spengler's *The Decline of the West*. Perhaps the most striking expression of this mood came from an unexpected source. The American Henry Adams made an unusual claim in *The Education of Henry Adams,* in a chapter called "The Dynamo and the Virgin": "at the Louvre and Chartres . . . was the highest energy ever known to man, the creator of four-fifths of the noblest art, exercising vastly more attraction over the human mind than all the steam-engines and dynamos ever dreamed of; and yet this energy was unknown to the American mind. . . . All the steam in the world could not, like the Virgin, build Chartres."[25] Coming from an American who believed in the value of science and technology (the dynamo) and was not consciously a religious believer, this was a bold statement.

Even more striking is a poem found sewn into Adams' clothing after his death entitled "Prayer to the Virgin of Chartres." This pessimistic scion of the old New England aristocracy looked back over the history of America and lamented:

> Crossing the hostile sea, our greedy band
>> Saw rising hills and forests in the blue;
> Our father's kingdom in the promised land!
>> —We seized it, and dethroned the father too.
>
> And now we are the Father, with our brood,
>> Ruling the Infinite, not Three but One;
> We made our world and saw that it was good;
>> Ourselves we worship, and we have no Son.

What did Adams set in opposition to this expansionism? The Virgin:

> So, while we slowly rack and torture death
>> And wait for what the final void will show,
> Waiting I feel the energy of faith,
>> Not in the future science, but in you![26]

This is not exactly a declaration of faith in what a Roman Catholic might believe about the Virgin Mary, but Adams expressed here, with a depth of knowledge about the Western past, what other cultural figures in America and elsewhere would formulate in a variety of ways: a sense of something beautiful and precious and inspiring that was missing and unlikely to be satisfactorily replaced by economics, politics, industry, and society. If man does not live by bread alone, he certainly cannot live by progress alone. The carnage of the first half of the following century would make clear with a vengeance that even the dream of progress could easily be dispelled. What might preserve the essential human things in such circumstances was much less clear.

CHAPTER 9

The God That Did Not Fail

"The twenty-first century will be
religious, or it will not be."

André Malraux

IN 1890, forty-six-year-old Friedrich Nietzsche, who had shown signs of instability for years, went irretrievably mad while walking the streets of Turin. The final crisis came when he saw a donkey being beaten by its owner and embraced the poor animal out of pity. Explanations for his madness range from the physical (syphilis) to the psychological—the eruption of unbearable psychic tensions between his rejection of Christianity with what he regarded as its soft morals, on the one hand, and his profound sense of compassion, even for a poor beast of burden, on the other. If true, the "return of the repressed" was a sudden breakthrough of something like a religious impulse in Nietzsche's embrace of the donkey, a traditional symbol of Christ, the reversal and "transvaluation" of his anti-Christian stance.[1] When Nietzsche died in 1900, that was certainly not the general understanding of his significance; but perhaps his final decade is a cautionary tale for the last century all the same.

Nietzsche's reputation grew enormously in the twentieth century and he remains one of the most influential philosophers in the modern West, not least because of his energetic efforts to provide an alternative to the "irresistible decline of faith in the Christian God."[2] More than a century after Nietzsche's death, however, the death of God has not occurred. Indeed, if current trends hold, God's return—after the passing of several ersatz religions that in retrospect appear quite mad themselves—seems well under way.

243

For many readers, Nietzsche provided much more than a brilliant explanation for what they believed was an undeniable fact: the spread of unbelief because of the realization that "God is dead." Nietzsche dramatized this in highly personal terms, touching on the melodramatic—and the mythological. Nihilism opened the way to new possibilities and new threats. In Nietzsche, Christianity and all the alternatives since the Enlightenment, including rationalism, romanticism, and science, were equally undermined by radical skepticism. Some inconsistency arises in this view, however, perhaps because Nietzsche often jotted down insights that came to him while he was out walking, without a careful working out of overall texts. In some places he passionately denounces the untruth of biblical religion in light of science. In others, he seems to suggest that science has not disproved Christianity. Rather, modern man in his *libido dominandi*—Nietzsche does not use Saint Augustine's term, but *der Wille zur Macht* (the "will to power") is a good German equivalent—has *chosen* to turn his back on God, indeed has chosen to *kill* God in order to become his own self-creation and the master of the physical world.

Reliance on the old Christian system, in Nietzsche's view, was sheer refusal to embrace life, the "slave morality" of the weak, the powerless, and the mediocre—with its tame offshoots in democracy and socialism—which needed to be subjected to the "master morality" of an aristocratic elite. This elite would not allow the resentment of the human "herd" to stop them from exploits of courage and genius. The "superman" (*Übermensch*), a well-known Nietzschean notion, seems to combine older aristocratic virtues incoherently with hard pitilessness towards the masses—no *noblesse oblige* here. Exceptional geniuses and heroes may tolerate the all-too-human, if they are allowed to create their own values and run their own lives, occupying in their own persons the place God held in the older systems.*

*In strictly philosophical terms, much of what Nietzsche argued had already appeared before. For instance, Ludwig Feuerbach (1804–1872) had contended that God and the divine attributes were merely projections of human values. In direct contradiction to the formulation in Genesis, in Feuerbach's view it is man who made God in his own image and likeness and now had to take back those "divine" attributes and become a god to himself. The segment of the culture that already inclined towards atheism came to regard these sorts of explanations of religion as the simple maturation of human thought. Marx and Engels argued that in addition to Feuerbach's "abstract man," real existing societies with their false moral, economic, and political pieties also had to be debunked and remade into embodiments of human values. Or as Karl Marx wrote in a letter: "The religion of the workers has no God because it seeks to restore the divinity of Man."

As Nietzsche's career progressed, his attacks on existing values and his boasts about himself as a kind of "anti-Christ," the title of one of his books, became increasingly unbalanced. Yet that destructive and daemonic side is precisely what thrilled and continues to thrill many followers. His last published work, *Ecce Homo,* ends with a section entitled "Why I Am a Destiny":

> I know my fate. One day my name will be associated with the memory of something tremendous—a crisis without equal on earth, the most profound collision of conscience, a decision that was conjured up *against* everything that had been believed, hallowed, so far. I am no man. I am dynamite.—Yet for all that, there is nothing in me of the founder of a religion—religions are affairs of the rabble; I find it necessary to wash my hands after I have come into contact with religious people. [3]

Despite the disavowal, someone who has read Nietzsche carefully may suspect that the "will to power" is a bid to set up something like a new religion by blowing up all rivals. Even in earlier, somewhat saner texts such as *Thus Spake Zarathustra,* Nietzsche subtly courts disciples by the very act of claiming not to. Some scholars have tried to argue that Nietzsche dramatizes in *Zarathustra* the impossibility of founding a new, radically autonomous world. [4] A plainer reading is that he tried but failed, because all efforts at radical autonomy must be self-destructive since we are not the masters of ourselves. His myth of the "eternal return," the notion that everything repeats itself at long intervals eternally in the universe—and the belief that the strong must freely accept that necessary fate—is the last of the dogmas in an anti-theology that came into being through the deliberate rejection of all the Western philosophical and theological systems. Carl Jung, a perceptive reader, declared Nietzsche a "pathological personality" because of his one-sided emphasis on total liberation from everything past, which seems to have proceeded in parallel with his madness. [5]

A Brief History of Dynamite

"After Buddha was dead, his shadow was still shown for centuries in a cave—a tremendous, gruesome shadow. God is dead; but given the way of men, there may still be caves for thousands of years in which his shadow will be shown.—And we—we still have to vanquish his shadow, too."[6] When Nietzsche proclaimed for the first time, in this passage from *The Gay Science*, that God was dead, he had the foresight to see that, even so, God's total disappearance from the world would not take place for hundreds of generations. In this, at least, his analysis was far more realistic and closer to the truth than the wishful thinking of those who are usually classified with him as the modern Masters of Suspicion: Marx, Darwin, and Freud. Since none of us will be around in thousands of years, Nietzsche's prophecy cannot be verified or falsified. His followers always have that escape from challenges. The other Masters of Suspicion have had a harder time over the past century.

Marx has fared worst because his ideas were tried, after a fashion, in the Soviet Union and its unwilling satellites; in Asian nations such as China, Cambodia, Vietnam, and North Korea; and in Cuba, along with partial or temporary experiments in other parts of Latin America and Africa—all of them, everywhere, massive failures. In 1950, about midway through what might be called the real twentieth century (from 1914 to 1989, the date when Communism collapsed in Poland), a group of former Communists published a collection of essays called *The God That Failed*,[7] which marked the first stage of disenchantment with the revolutionary faith. A Marxist might argue—many still do today—that Soviet-style Communism was only distantly related to real Marxism. This is true, but it solves only one part of a much bigger question. Marx predicted in *The Communist Manifesto* that capitalism in the advanced countries would increasingly impoverish the mass of workers, who would then simply revolt and take over the means of production. This was the "scientific" theory that was falsified by events because in no capitalist nation in the past, and none today, are workers so impoverished, nor are they likely to overthrow any market system in the foreseeable future.*

What was actually implemented from Marx's program does not inspire confidence that other parts of his analysis were any more scientific, or likely

*In a sense, Nazism performed a similar operation on Nietzsche to the one carried out by the Soviets on Marx. There are notions in Nietzsche, especially the emphasis on hardness towards the weak and the idea of an elite master class, that lent themselves to exploitation by National Socialism in a Germany that had been humiliated after World War I.

to prove useful. In fact, long before any nation had tried Marxism, several people predicted disaster if it came about. One unexpected voice, Pope Leo XIII, basing his analysis on the Christian view of the human person, argued in an 1891 encyclical:

> To remedy these wrongs the socialists, working on the poor man's envy of the rich, are striving to do away with private property, and contend that individual possessions should become the common property of all, to be administered by the State or by municipal bodies. They hold that by thus transferring property from private individuals to the community, the present mischievous state of things will be set to rights, inasmuch as each citizen will then get his fair share of whatever there is to enjoy. But their contentions are so clearly powerless to end the controversy that *were they carried into effect the working man himself would be among the first to suffer.* They are, moreover, emphatically unjust, for they would rob the lawful possessor, distort the functions of the State, and create utter confusion in the community.[8]
>
> [*Emphasis added.*]

The workers in Poland's heroic union Solidarity, who helped bring down Communism almost exactly a century later, knew what Leo meant. The pope did not uncritically side with capitalism; he noted shortcomings of the capitalist nations in dealing with the large numbers of people who had left the countryside to become industrial workers. But he did not present a radical rejection of free societies, as he did of Communism. Other religious authorities in the West were in agreement in warning that the materialist view of the person—combined with the notion that humans as material beings can be reshaped into the New Man of the Communist dream merely by a change of their social conditions, a view still widespread today—is a falsehood that inevitably leads to awful consequences.

Those were not long in coming. By most credible estimates, Communist countries killed about a hundred million people in the twentieth century. Among these, perhaps as many as several million died as a direct result of religious persecution.[9] Marx expected the state and the churches to "wither away" like a plant when its roots are cut as Communism spread. Since the workers' uprising did not materialize, Communist leaders had to help the process along—violently. The Gulag, the system of work camps for "antisocialist elements," including religious figures, produced mounds of corpses. For some reason, the Soviets concentrated religious prisoners in special camps around the Solovetski Islands, perhaps to keep them from infecting others with a non-Communist faith. But the bigger mystery remains why most people in the West at the time did not know—or did not want to know—about such antireligious persecutions. Even *The Black Book of Communism* (1999),[10] a good attempt by a group of French scholars to right some historiographic wrongs by chronicling the human rights abuses in various Communist countries, is virtually blind to violations of religious rights.

It has long been clear that this kind of blindness has something to do with sympathy for Marxism among nonbelieving Western intellectuals, sometimes shading off into complicity with Communist regimes and a willingness to concede the need to eliminate "unprogressive" elements. For all its simplemindedness, the heartfelt rejection of "Godless Communism" by ordinary Western believers was far closer to the truth during the middle decades of the twentieth century than were the sophisticated analyses of Marxism. Susan Sontag, one of the Marxist sympathizers, conceded as much in a speech at New York's Town Hall in 1982: "Imagine, if you will, someone who read only the *Reader's Digest* between 1950 and 1970, and someone in the same period who read only the *Nation* or the *New Statesman*. Which reader would have been better informed about the realities of communism? The answer, I think, should give us pause. Can it be that our enemies were right?"

This is true, of course; but such truths, periodically discovered by surprised intellectuals during the last century, have not significantly changed the attitudes of the Western intelligentsia. The less systematic, but equally materialistic secularism of our own societies sets off few alarm bells. How many people today pay attention even to the fact that Communist China, the largest state that still professes Marxism, continues to oppress its religious groups, which are extensive and growing? (By reliable estimates, there are more Christians in church on a Sunday morning in China than in all Europe.) The Chinese carefully studied the faith-based revolt by Polish workers that was the beginning of the end for the Soviet bloc and determined not to let the same thing happen in Asia. China meanwhile grows on the world stage because it allows markets, quite contrary to Marxist belief about the need for the state to own the instruments of production. But by its notably different treatment of two old "bourgeois" practices, religion and commerce, Chinese Communists have shown that they fear spiritual more than they do economic freedom. Some in the West have the same attitude.

The Freudian Flop

The case history of Sigmund Freud tells another odd morality tale from the twentieth century. He, too, enjoyed a tremendous vogue, injecting seemingly scientific terms like complex, repression, projection, and sublimation into the popular vocabulary. Until the 1970s, Freud seemed still to have a strong intellectual case and a grip on both the scientific community and a sizeable portion of the public. He popularized the idea that religion was an illusion that would disappear: "The more the fruits of knowledge become accessible to men, the more widespread is the decline of religious beliefs." But in the last quarter of the twentieth century, it was Freudianism itself that seemed to be in decline except in certain embattled psychoanalytic enclaves.

Freud's work lost ground for several reasons. Social conditions changed; people are now less exposed to authoritarian father figures in their families and strict sexual mores in the culture than was the case in the first half of the twentieth century.* There were scientific reasons as well: Freudianism does not appear any better than the many competing theories of human personality in curing neuroses—a clinical fact that argues against its status as a universal scientific truth—even when "the talking cure" goes on for years. Drugs and cognitive therapies have been more successful in eliminating suffering. More seriously, charges have been brought that Freud may have prompted false recovered memories

---

*In his native Vienna, Freud focused on neuroses, of which there appear to have been quite a few. It is no surprise that he discovered connections to religion in some of the forms those neuroses took. As far as a layman can judge the clinical studies, Freud seems to have been right that some people internalized God and morality as a suffocating superego that conflicted, more or less uncomfortably, with physical impulses, especially Eros.

of early sexual experiences, which go to the heart of the scientific claims of his method.[11]

In the end, though, it may simply be that Freud's materialist theory of the person and the world is too narrow an approach to the fullness of human existence and has come to be seen as such. He wrote famously in *Totem and Taboo:* "God is at bottom nothing but an exalted father."[12] Today, we are much more aware of irreducible complexity and would pause before declaring the entire religious history of the human race in widely varying ages and cultures to be the product of a single psychological complex. Many neurotics think of God as an exalted father, but it is a materialist assumption from a specific period in Western history that this is all there is to be said. Freud's successors and competitors—Jung, Allport, Maslow, and others after them—for all their own theoretical difficulties, at least treated the symbols and content of religion as something worthy of study, if for no other reason than because of what they say about the nature of man. Whatever truths may still survive him, Freud some time ago entered the twilight of the gods along with Marx.

Running parallel to the vogue of Freud was existentialism, a complex movement that famously involved nonbelievers of different stripes (Martin Heidegger, Jean-Paul Sartre, Albert Camus) along with believers (Gabriel Marcel, Paul Tillich, Rudolf Bultmann, Karl Jaspers).[13] Its emphasis on the anxiety of creaturely existence had deep roots in older religious figures like Augustine and Pascal, as well as more modern sources like Kierkegaard and Nietzsche. Heidegger's sense of the "thrown-ness" (*Geworfenheit*) of human life, our discovery of ourselves as having been cast into the world without knowing where we come from or where we are going, fascinated people in the West for decades, partly because—like Freud—it seemed to provide depth of meaning without religion. Another existential notion, the Abyss (the ever-present threat of annihilation), was useful in the criticism of the "inauthentic" existence that many people were believed to lead owing to their alienation from their true selves by modern society. The American businessman was said to be particularly alienated, and all the more so because he was unaware of it. In that respect, existentialism was one more tool with which to *épater le bourgeois*, though it also made more universal points as well. Heidegger also lies behind recent movements like deconstruction, a dull and convoluted matter in the hands of its French founder, Jacques Derrida, which was turned into a terrorist device against Western principles and beliefs by artists and academics in the United States.

But existentialism too started to fade in the 1970s and 1980s—as did deconstruction in the 1990s—for reasons that may still be too close for us to fully understand. Anxiety over existence seems to have given way to meaninglessness as the main complaint of postmodern society—a meaninglessness that is not the product of Sartrean "nothingness" and "absurdity," but of a bewildering array of meanings and systems—psychological, physical, philosophical, economic, political, cultural, religious—in shifting relation to one another and offering no easy way of reconciliation. It is a delicate matter to account for changes in sentiment of this kind, but that one has occurred seems undeniable. We may still lament inauthentic lives, worry about the day when death will carry us into the Abyss, and wonder how to live well and purposively in the meantime. The main religions of the world have long engaged these preoccupations. But the whole tone is different now, and acceptance of the postmodern condition of fragmentation in some cultural circles helps explain why an indifferent relativism seems to be our only truth.*

Personalism and Christian Democracy

A very different response to the situation of the West in the twentieth century emerged alongside these currents and from an unexpected quarter: Christian Democracy. We are so accustomed now to the idea that Christianity and democracy are compatible that it is sometimes difficult to appreciate why for so long they seemed to be opposed. It is even more difficult to see that the question is still not entirely settled. Indeed, many quite intelligent people from the eminent Greek philosophers to Nietzsche

---

*Some people believe Einstein's discovery that time and space are not absolutes contributed to moral and cultural relativism. Yet relativity theory, rightly understood, provides just as definite *relations* between things in the world as does Newtonian physics, if in a different way. That relativity was thought to imply relativism rather than relatedness shows that there was already a widespread view in the West that "everything is relative."

have noted how democracy usually leads to self-indulgence, chaos, and tyranny—the French Revolution pattern. Christianity, too, conflicts with certain features of democracy because some ways of conceptualizing and practicing liberty are self-refuting and self-destructive. If by democracy we mean a system that makes loud noises about the dignity of the person but cannot say why, or that aims for an ever-expanding right of doing what we want in a zone of privacy, without specifying the what, we are on the way not only to an antireligious world but to a suicidal decadence that would have raised the hackles of Homer and Hesiod, Thucydides, Plato, Aristotle, Cicero, Virgil, Augustine, Aquinas, Dante, Thomas More, Luther, Calvin, Locke, Voltaire, Rousseau, Washington, Jefferson, Kant, Hegel, Marx, Wilberforce, Lincoln, Arnold, Lord Acton, Leo XIII, Nietzsche, Freud, Heidegger, and many other great and not-so-great figures who have appeared in earlier pages. Anything that draws criticism from so many different perspectives needs to be carefully thought through. A viable form of democracy needs to be rooted in a notion of the human person as possessing both God-given rights *and* duties. Indeed, democracy finds its viability not in the wilderness of relativism but on the bedrock of some fundamental beliefs.

One broad if little-known movement that tried to make the case for a richer understanding of democracy and human society was known as personalism.* The notion of "person" was first elaborated in the West by theologians trying to explain how the three persons of the Christian Trinity could exist together while remaining one God. Modern personalism draws on biblical notions, including the *imago Dei* (creation in the image and likeness of God; see Chapter 3), and Enlightenment notions of human dignity, especially Kant's famous formulation of the categorical imperative: "Act so that you treat humanity, whether in your own person or in that of another, always as an end and never as a means only."[14] All of these elements took on greater urgency in the twentieth century precisely because collectivism and materialism threatened essential human things. If men are regarded

---

*Personalism is little known in America because we draw what might be called our personalism from native sources that are quite different from Europe's. But there is something of a convergence on this question on both sides of the Atlantic.

as merely economic units or matter, serious consequences follow: we do not worry about using matter as a means only.

Modern personalism came into existence owing to diverse religious currents. In the United States, the Protestant theologian Reinhold Niebuhr defended persons in Augustinian categories: we all have an eternal destiny and therefore all powers in the world need to be limited because all power has been corrupted by the Fall.* In France, one of personalism's most compelling exponents was the Catholic philosopher Jacques Maritain, who also spent long periods in the United States during and after World War II. French personalism incorporated elements from Communism in Emmanuel Mounier and from existentialism in Gabriel Marcel. The Jewish philosopher Henri Bergson's notion of the *élan vital* gave expression to a freedom in us that goes beyond the mechanical. Maritain encouraged the Eastern Orthodox thinker Nicholas Berdyaev to develop a personalism rooted in his own church's rich and quite different traditions. All this abstract theorizing had a concrete *raison d'être.* As persons, we all have an irreducible set of experiences and purposes that an animal, in its unselfconscious existence, or a pure spirit does not. Persons are not merely individuals, though each of us has an individual dimension. A person is related to others in community** and can never, except by a self-refuting Nietzschean drive towards self-creation, claim otherwise.

Two of the most powerful modern proponents of personalism were Jews: Martin Buber and Emmanuel Lévinas. In the 1950s, Buber famously pointed out, in a mixture of biblical, existential, and personalist insights, that the *I-It* relationship that holds for our study of the physical world should not be taken as a model for our relations with one another and with God. An *I-Thou* notion is needed, where the Thou is deliberately the familiar second-person singular form (*Du* in Buber's German). Amidst the many forms of depersonalization and analysis of human acts into biological and

---

*Niebuhr also drew an often-repeated Augustinian conclusion about the balance between liberty and responsibility: "Man's capacity for justice makes democracy possible, but man's inclination to injustice makes democracy necessary."

**Classic individualism made it appear as if we were somehow "self-made men" or autonomous. In fact, as we saw even in the case of Descartes's *Cogito,* we are inescapably bound to community, otherwise we would not learn language, philosophy, or the skills needed to ask the questions that lead to the *Cogito.*

evolutionary routines then common, Buber brilliantly explored what is irreducibly interpersonal in us, or as he put it succinctly: "All real living is meeting."[15] Lévinas, who became widely influential in the 1980s and 1990s, added a dimension that was relatively underemphasized in Buber: the way that the Law for human beings calls communities, in his case the Jewish people, into existence and constitutes them before and beyond any duties owed to the state.[16]

This communitarian side of personalism did not imply collectivism. Indeed, it shunned collectivism and individualism alike. Personalism has existed in almost all ages in one form or another, but in the first half of the twentieth century it took on added weight from the fact that it was opposed to the submersion of the individual in collectivities that had marked both Communism and fascism. Personalism could insist on the dynamic nature of persons in communities in distinction both from radical individualism (which some thought was coming to threaten the West) and from totalitarian collectivism. The political purpose here was to articulate levels and spheres of human individuality, family life, local community, region, nation, and the international order that had been telescoped by a collectivist perspective or obliterated by a narrowly individualist view. Abraham Kuyper (1837–1920), a Dutch neo-Calvinist, was a precursor in what he called "sphere sovereignty," which marked Christian Democrat governments in his country for many years. Catholic theorists contributed to and further developed a notion that several popes propounded: subsidiarity. As Pius XI put it in a passage of his 1931, *Quadragesimo Anno*, which has since become a *locus classicus* for the idea:

> It is an injustice, a grave evil, and a disturbance of right order for a larger and higher organization to arrogate to itself functions which can be performed efficiently by smaller and lower bodies. . . . Of its very nature, the true aim of all social activity should be to help individual members of the social body, but never to destroy them.

In many ways, this resembles American notions like federalism, meaning limits on central power, decentralization, and rights protected from different levels of government. This principle allows for what is sometimes called vertical pluralism. Not only different levels of government, but communities, families, and individuals are protected in the vertical hierarchy. Before the century was out, subsidiarity was sometimes invoked against the state's intrusion into family life by way of welfare systems that distort and usurp family relationships and subtly extend the power of the state.

Christian Democracy developed somewhat in parallel with personalist notions as believers came to see the need for a substantive alternative to the atheist materialism that underlay Communism and the practical materialism that was operative in many Western nations. Various strands from Western history entered into this new attempt by Christians of differing types to support democracy: medieval constitutionalism, Reformation ideas about conscience and covenant, Catholic neo-Scholastic notions of popular sovereignty, Enlightenment theories of rights, and Christian objections to practices like slavery and injustice.[17] There had been political parties of Christian inspiration in various countries going back to the nineteenth century, such as the German Center Party, which was founded in 1871 soon after German unification. After World War II, however, it was clear that new ideas were needed to overcome several different social threats in Europe. The Christian Democrat Union under the leadership of Konrad Adenauer, in alliance with Bavaria's Christian Social Union, rebuilt Germany on very different lines from those that had allowed its descent into the horrors of Nazism. As Adenauer stated:

> Christianity denies the dominance of the state and insists on the dignity and liberty of the individual. . . . This conviction would give our party strength to raise Germany from the depths. Hence the new party had to be a Christian party, and one that embraced all denominations. Protestant and Catholic Germans, indeed all who knew and valued the importance of Christianity in Europe should be able to join—and it goes without saying that this also applied to our Jewish fellow-citizens.[18]

Adenauer's idea of "Christian" democracy was clearly not a narrow sectarianism: it sought to organize all Germans who believed in human dignity on religious grounds and who knew they needed a substantive alternative to Marxism as well as Nazism. Along with two other Christian Democrats, Robert Schuman in France and Alcide De Gasperi in Italy, Adenauer put Europe on the course that led through the European Community to today's European Union. As checkered as EU history has been, including the dogged attempt to deny its religious roots in the drafts of a constitution in 2003 and 2004, Europe owes its ideological recovery from the destruction of World War II—and the ideas that brought it about—to a conscious appeal to human dignity along personalist and Christian Democratic lines, which also helped to hold off Communist parties in western Europe.

Such appeals were much in the air after World War II. As early as 1946, UNESCO (the United Nations' newly created Education, Scientific, and Cultural Organization) appointed a distinguished committee to look into drafting a kind of international bill of rights. Prominent among its members were philosophers with religious backgrounds who were fully aware of the dangers of such a document in the wrong hands. They sent out a request for suggestions to the entire globe and were surprised to find broad agreement on basic principles. Jacques Maritain played an active part in the drafting and called for an overall framework, which was initially formulated by another Frenchman, René Cassin, a Jewish lawyer and De Gaulle's chief legal adviser. Cassin suggested as the first article:

> All human beings are born free and equal in dignity and rights. They are endowed with reason and conscience and should act towards one another in a spirit of brotherhood.

How—or by whom—we had been so endowed, he did not say. Believers, of course, could answer that question as the American Founding Fathers had in the Declaration of Independence. Nonbelievers might have a harder time of it. But it is a lesson in the possibility of cooperation between believers and nonbelievers at a fairly deep level that this document could be approved only two years later as the UN Universal Declaration of Human Rights.

The process was facilitated by another remarkable figure, Charles Habib Malik, a Lebanese philosopher of Greek Orthodox background who had studied at the American University in Beirut and at Harvard. As someone who understood both East and West by the very circumstances of his birth and who possessed the language skills to communicate personally with many different participants in the deliberations, Malik was the ideal person to oversee the ratification process. After eighty-one meetings, the drafting committee came up with a text that passed without a single vote against it—testimony to Malik's diplomacy. Only five nations decided to abstain. For all the disappointments that the United Nations system has produced in the years since—indeed, it sometimes seems like one of the obstacles to true freedom and rights—it was no small feat to get the nations of the world to agree after the cataclysm of the Second World War that there was a great deal about human dignity and the nature of political life that they held in common—even if only in principle. That commonality had been developed in part under the sacred canopy of religious reflections on modern horrors.[19]

Forms of Secularization

Why then did the second half of the twentieth century, the time when these developments were under way at a European and global level, seem to coincide with secularization? Many factors, of course, contributed to that shift. Paradoxically, one of them may have been the very successes of the democratic program. The enthusiasts for democracy and universal rights paid relatively little attention to the ways in which modern democratic theory and practice may undermine the very bases of free societies. In the two decades after World War II, the West enjoyed a remarkable period of peace, Cold War tensions notwithstanding, and growing prosperity. We may still be too close to this period to know why a new revolutionary burst—perhaps the last one inspired by the old Enlightenment dream of total liberation—appeared in the West in the 1960s. The Vietnam War was one cause, but the broad social, sexual, intellectual, and political revolution can hardly be explained simply by opposition to the war. Something like the old religion of revolution flared up all over the world—astonishingly for the time, even on American college campuses—from the 1960s until the 1980s before starting to burn itself out around the time that the Soviet Empire collapsed. It was no accident—as the Soviets used to say—that the main leaders who contributed to that collapse had deep convictions about Christianity and democracy: Ronald Reagan and Margaret Thatcher among the political leaders, and Alexander Solzhenitsyn and Pope John Paul II among the leaders in the moral realm.

In the prosperous countries of the West, however, the drive of the new campus revolutionaries towards liberation—though mostly inspired by utopian fantasies and New Age spiritual currents—revealed a deeper problem. Modern liberal democracy, the kind that emphasizes rights language and individual prerogatives, is engaged in a self-contradictory enterprise. As its critics have pointed out, it cannot provide a credible justification for two of its foundational beliefs, universal human dignity and the responsible use of freedom. Moreover, making freedom without qualification the ultimate value of a whole society unleashes popular passions that eat away at virtue and the communitarian dimension of the self. Without effective brakes on these passions, democracies have had a tendency towards anarchy—even very accomplished democracies like Athens and Florence.

This is one reason why, from ancient Greece to modern times, democracy was thought of as a poor form of government, while a "mixed" regime incorporating monarchic, aristocratic, and popular elements was believed to be best. The mixed regime valued virtue and the common good as well as liberty. The American system reflects this perception in that the president has monarchic functions, the Senate aristocratic, and the House popular. But again, machinery alone, however useful, will not succeed unless the three separate orders understand the necessity of responsibility—even morality—if liberty is not to degenerate into license, producing disorder in the polity and in the citizenry. As we saw, George Washington was so concerned in his Farewell Address about religiosity and the kinds of virtue it generated because they are necessary to the well-being of popular government. Indeed, as we also found in our study of Virgil and Rome, even nondemocratic systems may fear *furor* and popular passions untutored by religion. The Leviathan of the state is a perpetual threat, but a sizeable portion of the West has forgotten that so is the Behemoth of popular passions.

It may be a slight exaggeration, but certainly in Europe and to a large extent in North America, the last half century has proceeded on the assumption that these old truths no longer apply to human communities, that we can have respect for persons without any reason for it, and that democracies can survive—will just have to survive—whatever free democratic peoples decide they want to do with their lives. These two developments, more than mere decline in religious belief, are usually what we are talking about when we claim that the modern West has undergone a process of secularization, because there has not been a precipitous decline in religious belief so much as a change in the quality of that belief and in the behavior of certain segments of Western societies.

Europeans are usually thought to have lost faith more than any other region in the West. Yet it is worth looking carefully at the European case. Though there has been some growth in outright atheism in Europe, it is much more common to find private belief without public practice, or "believing without belonging," as British sociologist Grace Davie has called it.[20] The old thesis that modernization inevitably brings secularization largely relied on assumptions derived from European institutions. The sociologist Mary Douglas described it thus: "According to an extensive literature, religious change in modern times happens in only two ways—the falling off of worship in traditional Christian churches, and the appearance of new cults, not expected to endure."[21] Church attendance has in fact declined in some places. This and the diminishment of direct political power in the hands of religious leaders has caused some observers to think that religion cannot help but become less influential in society and less urgent for individuals. This is partly true, but it makes belief into a kind of social machinery that is potent only so long as it has measurable political power or utility—a stance revealing the intrinsic bias in much sociology. Many people would say that religion shows its greatest value precisely in those moments when social questions are most distant: in a moment of temptation or doubt, in deep sorrow such as the death of a child, or when someone acutely feels the need for forgiveness. These moments cannot be eliminated by any social system or even by psychological interventions. At such times, we want answers and some alleviation of our suffering. Faith has an intellectual component, an important one. But it is not primarily material for intellectual or social analysis. If it cannot help us in these extreme circumstances, then it has lost its true power. The testimony of people throughout history, however, is that it does help. And from this perspective, it is not surprising that belief has persisted even within Europe without strong institutional attachments.

The Standard (European) Model of Secularization

Sociological surveys—the European Values Study and the International Social Survey Program most notably—have been asking questions about religious belief in Europe for decades and, therefore, offer somewhat reliable data. Individual European countries vary, probably because of differences in their recent social histories. Formerly Communist countries like Russia, for instance, still show relatively high rates of atheism (19 percent), but given that the Soviet state tried to exterminate religion through brutal means unparalleled in Western history, it is more surprising that the rate of nonbelievers after seventy years of Communism is so low. The picture is little different in most other formerly Communist countries. As one researcher summed it up in 2003, "The materialists did not drive God out of Europe."[22] If armed Communism had so marginal an effect, it is not surprising that the other forces usually thought to have battered belief—philosophical skepticism, enlightenment, revolution, evolution, science, industrialization, urbanization, depth psychology, education, all the things an intellectual takes seriously—have also had effects less extensive than once believed. The same sociologist found that Europeans with university degrees, who might be thought to have been influenced by such currents, "are generally either not less religious or only marginally so."

There is reason to think that some of our sense of religious decline reflects a generational anomaly: people born in the period between 1929 (the start of the Great Depression) and the end of World War II in certain European countries show a sharp falloff in rates of religious belief and practice. Why this happened is not clear. But since older people are usually the most frequent churchgoers, the unusual drop for that generation may explain the cavernous emptiness in many European churches at a time when those persons, now in their sixties and seventies, should form the majority of the congregations. But it is also true that the generations born after the middle of the century show a steep increase in belief that makes graphs of the percentages of believers born in each year in Europe over the twentieth century look U-shaped. As these later cohorts age, start families, and—perhaps— return to the more typical patterns, Europe itself may not look so unusual.

There are signs that this trend may be under way. In the second half of the twentieth century, there was actually an *increase* in traditional beliefs such as life after death in twelve out of twenty-two European countries.[23] About a quarter or more of those surveyed admit to mystical experience or contact with a dead loved one.[24] All of this seemingly incontrovertible evidence for the persistence of religious belief, however, can coexist quite remarkably with loss of affiliation with religious institutions. In 1998, for example, 45 percent of Britons and 47 percent of the French claimed to have no religious affiliation in the sense of a connection to a congregation. This represents a decline of about one-third in each country in the number of people with such attachments over their lifetimes. But as far as faith itself goes, most people in Europe who were raised in some specific faith have remained in it, however ambivalently: "79 percent of those raised Protestant are still Protestants as are 95 percent of Orthodox, 87 percent of the Muslims, and 85 percent of the Catholics."[25]

Furthermore, figures concerning practice and faith may seem somewhat low if we assume a prior Age of Faith in which virtually everyone believed and attended church. This seems highly questionable. As we saw in the previous chapter, churchgoing in the nineteenth century among the newly urbanized workers of England was low for men, even while belief remained high, but we have no way of knowing whether it had already been low among the same groups when they were still living on the land. One prominent student of the secularization thesis has pointed out that "during the middle ages and during the Renaissance the masses rarely entered a church."[26] It has often been noted that the Fourth Lateran Council (1215) proposed that Catholics go to confession and receive Communion at least once a year, at Easter. The very need to spell out such a discipline means that the bishops in that gathering could not count on even minimal practice. They also recommended a massive education campaign to bring the laity into more conscious participation in the faith. Studies of Oxford in the 1700s show that perhaps 5 percent of the laity received Communion in a given year. The complaints of both Catholic and Protestant missionaries during the Reformation about the ignorance and superstitions of the common people, even about things like the need to frequent the sacraments, are further clues that in the longer historical perspective, belief may be widespread even where religious knowledge, discipline, and even church attendance are not.

Nor is it the case that education, and more particularly scientific education, has dispelled modern belief. Tocqueville noticed as early as the 1840s that the belief of the major Enlightenment figures that education would foster disbelief was disproved by what he saw in America: "The facts by no means accord with their theory. There are certain populations in Europe whose unbelief is only equaled by their ignorance and debasement; while in America, one of the freest and most enlightened nations in the world, the people fulfill with fervor all the outward duties of religion."[27] This pattern persists even among American scientists. Two studies of belief among American scientists—one undertaken in 1914 and a deliberately similar one in 1997—turned up that 41.8 percent in the first case and 39.3 in the second declared belief in a personal, responsive God. Only 16.7 percent in 1914 and 14.5 percent more recently claimed to have no definite belief about a deity.[28]

Modern Growth in America and the World

The greatest difference between Europe and the rest of the world in modern times seems to lie in the fact that non-European believers are more likely both to practice their faith and to think that religion is an essential participant in public discourse. The latter point has become one of the central disputes in American politics. Western elites often have as much disdain for the passionate forms of Christianity in the modern world as they do for Islamic fundamentalism. There is a serious confusion about these two very different religious currents. The term "fundamentalism" was deliberately created and adopted by a group of conservative Protestant theologians in America at the beginning of the twentieth century. The group included well-known religious figures such as William Jennings Bryan, Carl McIntyre, and J. Gresham Machen. In a series of pamphlets, they rejected what they saw as the abandonment of basic Christian beliefs on the part of Christian liberals and they identified a small number of principles that they regarded as the "fundamentals" for real Christians.[29]

The application of the term "fundamentalist" to some Muslim groups who later showed themselves prone to violence and terrorism occurred in the 1980s, and it has created the impression among people who should know better that conservative Christians and jihadists are basically akin. As Islamic expert Bernard Lewis has argued, "The Muslim fundamentalists, unlike the Protestant groups . . . do not differ from the mainstream on questions of theology and the interpretation of scripture. Their critique is, in the broadest sense, societal." In addition, the notion of jihad as armed struggle against nonbelievers "is present from the beginning of Islamic history—in scripture, in the life of the Prophet, and in the actions of his companions and immediate successors."[30] A certain type of Western intellectual thinks it clever to compare Christian leaders to the Taliban in Afghanistan, or televangelists to the ayatollahs of Iran. But simple fairness requires us to note that these are two very different phenomena with very different social aims.

Whatever opposition they may encounter in elite Western circles, traditional Christian groups of various kinds are growing rapidly all over the world in both numbers and influence. In the United States, the most rapidly growing Protestant communities are evangelical, not all politically conservative by any means, but generally tending in that direction. The Catholic Church in America shows a similar pattern: the church splits politically between conservatism on moral issues and a moderate stance on poverty, the death penalty, and war. The fastest-growing Catholic religious orders, however, are newly created orthodox groups of both men and women, or reformed older orders. For laypeople, renewal and charismatic movements virtually monopolize religious energies, especially among the young. Mainstream media naturally tend not to highlight or welcome these Christian developments. But America not only remains a strongly Christian nation, it seems to be on the verge of becoming even more so.

Indeed, demographic trends suggest that America will be Christian of a more traditional cast than in recent decades. Outright atheists accounted for only about 1.27 million people in America, or 0.4 percent of the population, in 2004; the figures for agnostics were roughly equal. Many of these people are concentrated in certain cities and professions—such as journalism—where their numbers and views may bulk larger than they in fact are. Asian immigration is largely responsible for about 2.5 million Buddhists in America and Muslims amount to perhaps 4 million. These are all large numbers in themselves, but they are dwarfed when viewed relative to American believers as a whole and to much larger demographic and immigration trends. In all likelihood, there will be about 100 million U.S. citizens of Hispanic background in 2050. A little under three-quarters of these immigrants, if current trends persist, will remain Catholic, while about 20 percent will become evangelicals, with the rest joining other Protestant churches. The vast majority of Filipino immigrants are Catholics, as are one-third of Vietnamese immigrants. More than one-half of Korean immigrants are Christians of some kind, as are Chinese-Americans. Black Haitians and Africans who come to America are largely Christian; in some areas, they account for one-third of African-American congregations. By reliable estimates, all non-Christian believers (including Jews and Muslims) in America combined constitute 5 to 7 percent of the population. These are figures comparable to Europe's, which we do not usually think of as a religiously diverse continent.

Immigrants from the developing world come with very different kinds of Christianity than those typically found in an American suburban parish. Even at home they already exert a global influence. When the Episcopal Church in America decided in 2003 to ordain an open and practicing homosexual, V. Gene Robinson, as a bishop of New Hampshire, for example, it provoked an outpouring of criticism from the Anglican Church in Africa and Asia, which is rapidly growing and much more orthodox than its American or British counterparts. (It also created a rift within the American church that is leading to a formal division.) To his credit, Robinson admitted openly that his ordination had no foundation in Christian scripture or tradition, and in his view was an indication of God's continuing revelation. The Anglicans in the developing world engaged him on precisely those points, believing that not only were such ordinations not supported by scripture, they ran directly contrary to its plain meaning. Since in the next fifty years, by all reliable estimates, only a small percentage of Anglicans will be white Europeans, while Anglicans in developing nations grow rapidly in numbers, it seems clear that certain forms of liberal Western Christianity are headed for virtual extinction.[31]

The average educated person in the West never hears anything about Christian growth around the world. Most Westerners, if asked, would probably answer that Islam is the fastest-growing faith. But as one prominent scholar of this epochal shift has written:

> far from Islam being the world's largest religion by 2020 or so . . . Christianity will still have a massive lead, and will maintain its position into the foreseeable future. By 2050, there should still be about three Christians for every two Muslims worldwide. Some 34 percent of the world's people will then be Christian, roughly what the figure was at the height of European world hegemony in 1900.[32]

These Christians will mostly not be European Christians, partly because of doctrinal drift in Europe but much more because of Europe's catastrophically low birth rates. Given that the birth differentials we noted in Chapter 4 probably helped Christianity become the main religion of the Roman Empire, the question arises whether the gloomy outlook for Europe may mean the supersession of Christianity by Islam. Condoms and abortion may do to Europe what Saladin and the scimitar could not. But even if that happens, Europe's demographic and religious suicide will be vastly offset by Christian growth in the developing world.

The type of Christianity that is emerging also portends significant global changes. New Christians are not particularly interested in the liberal Christianity of the developed nations, which to them seems weakened and corrupted by wealth. Their form of Christianity must coexist with poverty, and that fact of life will shape its responses to certain problems. These communities perform functions much closer to old-style church groups; they help one another spiritually and with practical problems. They tend to remove themselves deliberately from radical politics and focus on self-improvement, education, and incremental economic development. They feel little need to apologize for traditional moral views or a strong sense of the supernatural.

Elites in the developed world harbor some unfounded prejudices about these groups. While it is true that some of them may tend towards a creationism that denies scientific fact and a spiritualism mixed with non-Christian superstitions, by and large they show an intriguing mixture of liberating ideas linked to moral teaching. As was the case in the Roman Empire, Christian bodies in the developing world offer their own forms of liberation to women, for instance. While these are not identical with, say, what an upper-middle-class woman in New York or Paris might regard as liberation, they are quite powerful social changes. Traditional forms of *machismo* no longer apply within these Christian communities, and other traditional limitations on women—particularly neglect of female education and health—change sharply under this evangelistic influence, Protestant and Catholic. These vigorous forms of Christianity have also been a central factor in the so-called Third Wave of democratization.

While these sociological parallels with early Christianity help explain rapid religious growth and influence, the content of Christian belief—the story of Christ as Redeemer—is quite potent as well. A century ago, it was believed that people converted to Christianity for the food and other material goods that missionaries distributed or because of the other advantages it might confer on them with the colonial powers. But it has been since 1965—after European colonialism—that the missions have borne their greatest fruit, partly because of population growth, but also because of conversions to an energetic and attractive faith. It has been little noticed, but the rapidly developing countries of the Pacific Rim—all now relatively prosperous—

also form a kind of "Christian arc."[33] There are more Presbyterians, for example, in South Korea than there are in the United States.

As we saw in a previous chapter, converts in Ireland and Yorkshire in the early Middle Ages played a major role in the Christianization of Northern Europe and the re-Christianization of areas that swayed back and forth under various influences. Mass immigration from the developing world may very well produce a similar re-evangelizing effect in the United States and Europe, since many immigrants are committed Christians. Latins, Africans, and Asians may be our modern Irish and Yorkshiremen. In the United States, the primary immigration influences come from Latin America, especially southern Mexico and Central America, both strongholds of traditional Catholicism, but now of evangelical Protestantism as well. Some commentators have argued that this form of immigration will shift America for the worse towards the kinds of social and political problems typical of Latin nations over the years.[34] But it seems far more likely—since it has happened not only with other groups of immigrants but with earlier waves of Latin immigration—that Latinos will largely adapt to American public institutions while maintaining distinctive religious, cultural, and social traits. They may also reinvigorate traditional values in the public square as the liberal mainline Protestant denominations continue to decline, both through conversions to more evangelical congregations and through low fertility rates.

European Exceptionalism

Europe, as usual, presents a different and quite troubling picture. During the second half of the twentieth century, various European nations met their labor needs by allowing large numbers of Muslims, mostly from North Africa and the Middle East, to immigrate (Britain drew more from its former colonies in India and Pakistan). There are several reasons for this phenomenon, not least that immigration from central and eastern Europe, which might have blended more harmoniously with the western European nations, was cut off by the Iron Curtain during the Cold War. As a result, countries such as France, Germany, Italy, the Netherlands, and even Switzerland and the Scandinavian nations now have sizeable—and often militant—Muslim minorities. Until Islamic fundamentalism began to erupt in the late 1990s and with even more virulence after September 11, 2001, Europeans did not much want to notice the problem or do anything about it. The bombs that blew up civilians on the way to work in Madrid in 2004 and London in 2005 caused most European governments, even liberal states like the Netherlands (which notoriously witnessed the murder of the filmmaker Theo van Gogh by a Muslim who not only shot him but tried to cut off his head for blasphemy), to take vigorous action, rounding up hundreds of imams who were preaching jihad and whole networks of potential terrorist bombers.

But a basic demographic problem remains. European Christians, Jews, agnostics, and atheists have few children, so few that they are not only shrinking as a percentage of their national populations, in most cases they are shrinking in absolute numbers. Muslims have many children, so many that it may already be difficult, given sizeable Muslim minorities, for Europeans to try restricting further Muslim immigration. Meanwhile, they have often denied themselves other sources of much-needed workers. During the 2005 campaign in France to ratify the European Constitution, one of the tactics that opponents used to good effect was to point to the threat to French jobs from "Polish plumbers." In a country where socialist economic policies and lavish social benefits keep unemployment over 10 percent, any perceived threat to jobs has great resonance. But the French may have chosen to preserve their benefits at the price of their future existence.

It is true that Polish plumbers and other workers from Christian nations in eastern Europe will work for less than native-born French. But it is also true that France desperately needs skilled workers, and if it does not choose to get them from less problematic sources, it will continue to get them among populations that not only raise the specter of terrorism but force a massive shift in the nature of French society.* A sort of political correctness has inhibited this discussion, unfortunately leaving it in the hands of the European far right. In a quite concrete way, an entire European nation has

*During the French referendum on the EU Constitution it was reported that only about 300 Polish plumbers were actually working in France. The country needs about 6,000 additional plumbers, according to the French plumbers' unions themselves, but seems unable to find them among its own people, who may simply not wish to do that kind of work.

chosen not to solve a part of its labor, social, and religious problem, out of a combination of protectionism and myopia about the deepest social challenges that it faces. It may not be pleasant for any democratic country to have to pick and choose among potential immigrants on the basis of cultural and religious backgrounds. We all have thought we were open enough to absorb and respect migrants within democratic institutions. It remains to be seen whether this belief is correct—much, it needs to be said, depends on Muslims themselves—or whether religious and cultural factors may impose necessary limits on nations that do not wish to let themselves change into something very different.

This conversation is uncomfortable for us in the West because it was not so long ago that we tried to get rid of religious and racial prejudices. Indeed, until quite recently prejudice persisted against Jews and Catholics, and even now it may not be entirely overcome. The sad racial history of Europe and America, too, is a living memory. So it behooves us to go about this discussion with caution. But the discussion cannot be conducted at all if we embrace, unrealistically, a blind liberal impulse to include, or a blind conservative impulse to exclude, irrespective of the nature of what we are talking about. For a long time, Catholics were thought by Protestants to be unsuitable citizens in a democracy because they believed in the absolute authority of a foreign potentate, the pope, in matters of faith and morals. Catholic theology could be developed, however, in ways that made democratic participation not only possible for Catholics but a positive duty.

Much discussion has occurred since 9/11 about whether Islam is equally capable of a democratic opening. Many Muslims believe it is possible, but we should not move too quickly past the theological problem. Some Muslim voices in Britain before and after their own 7/7 bombings have called openly for a "restoration of the caliphate," which means a unified religious and political rule that would include England. In Turkey, which has been a secular democracy for almost a century, the army enforces a strict separation between political and religious institutions. But the natural tendency among many Turks and other Muslims, especially the growing fundamentalist movements, is to unify mosque and state, indeed to return to the traditional idea that they cannot even be conceived of as distinct. Conversations with Westerners and others encourage Muslim theologians to begin thinking in new ways about the possibilities of a Muslim theology of the sacred and the secular. And there are certainly resources within the long and rich Muslim tradition for developing such ideas. But whether it will be done—especially in the current global climate where it might bring violent reprisals—remains to be seen. Western-style secular states cannot pretend that what appears to us to be real theocratic pretensions can be easily accommodated within our institutions.

The Home Front

The claim that our own homegrown religious movements are also threatening to set up a theocracy or seeking to impose laws akin to Muslim *sharia* is a simple canard stemming from confusion about the notion of a secular society or state. A secular republic, we are often told, is what America is all about; the federal government is prohibited by the Constitution from establishing a religion and therefore religious arguments about matters in dispute in the public square have no standing. This is a curious position even historically, for as we saw earlier in the present book, all the main American Founders believed in a strong connection between religious belief and the health of the republican form of government. Today, however, under the cloak of claiming that the state is secular in the sense of neutral among religions and irreligion, the courts and lawmakers have effectively imposed a uniform *secularism* on the nation. This is as illegitimate as imposing Catholicism or Buddhism or Nietzscheanism, but mainstream elites do not see that *secularism* is not neutral, as a pluralistic, properly secular state open to various religious voices would be. Most Americans notice when a nation like France imposes *laicité*, its own term for secularism, on its citizens. In 2004, this meant that the French state forbade Muslim women to wear the traditional veil in public. (The law, written in quite broad terms, was soon after applied to a Catholic priest wearing clerical garb.) This phenomenon is familiar in the histories of Communist countries and other repressive regimes like Mexico, which used to have severe anticlerical laws. But we generally have not perceived that some otherwise respectable democratic systems have gone down similar paths.* In the United States, exaggerated emphasis on nonestablishment has come to exclude public expression of religion in several respects as well.

Most strong backers of nonestablishment argue that it does not infringe on free exercise in the least. Catholics, Protestants, Jews, Muslims, Buddhists, Rastafarians, Scientologists, and many other groups, they say, have the right to private religious practice. Most believers, however, do not think that private religious expression alone is full religious expression. Everyone admires the role of the churches in the abolition of slavery, the Reverend Martin Luther King Jr.'s courage in the civil rights movement, Mother Teresa's work with the poor in Calcutta, Oscar Romero's labors for justice in El Salvador, Desmond Tutu's in South Africa, Jaime Sin's in the Philippines, Kim Dae Jung's in South Korea, Lech Walesa's in Poland. Western elites approve of these people for their politics and will take the religion as necessary, but they get nervous very fast if religious leaders begin to exert similar influence in a country like the United States. Yet for many people, religion has public as well as private rights and responsibilities. Anything less is, by their lights, a curtailment of religious liberty. And as citizens, they have as much of a right to debate the limits of religious expression as anyone else.**

When religious believers step into public debate, of course, they have to argue by different means than when they reason among themselves. Given the wide diversity of views among American Protestants alone, they are unlikely to reach a consensus on controversial questions merely by citing scriptural texts or appealing to denominational positions. Public debates call for widely acceptable modes of reasoning. It does not invalidate such forms of reason that they may be rooted in religious worldviews any more

*In 2005, the Catholic bishop of Calgary in Canada was brought before Alberta's human rights commission (and he received death threats) for writing in a diocesan newspaper that homosexual activity is condemned by the Bible. A Swedish pastor faced a similar charge because he said the same in a sermon from the pulpit.

**As Michael Uhlmann, a brilliant analyst of constitutional questions, has pointed out, courts now not only make determinations about the law, but also about which issues shall be treated with particular parts of the law on the basis of judgments "divined from materials almost as enigmatic as the dreams Joseph was called upon to interpret for Pharaoh." He goes on to observe:

> Although the Court entertains few constitutional objections to government regulation of the economy, on almost every other subject it not only entertains but frequently invents them. Today, we have judicial deference on most matters affecting the administrative state, and judicial supremacy on essentially everything else, including religion, morals, social life, and culture.

than a person's atheism or agnosticism invalidates his or her own form of reasoning. Courts and universities have been inclined to regard religious-based rationality as biased and agnostic rationality as neutral. But by that standard, Plato and Aristotle, Locke, Jefferson, Washington, and many others are fatally unreasonable.

The God That Did Not Fail

Ancient Greece, which invented formal reasoning, already knew that reason is most itself when it knows what it does not know, and at the same time sees that what lies beyond itself may be more important, even for this world, than what falls within its grasp. Socrates and Plato and Aristotle—the most illustrious figures in those first stirrings of ideas that would profoundly shape the West—are unanimous in that belief. In the chaotic centuries after the fall of the Greek city-states, when most people lived within the uncertain social conditions of empire, the rational value of religion in maintaining order, repressing evil, and providing meaning were no less clear. The rationality that has always been operative in the West until very recently is a reason happily engaged with religion.

The wisdom of the Western faiths counsels us to appreciate that persons are immortal, civilizations are not. As counterintuitive as it is for people who think that military and economic power or intellectual and cultural dominance make civilizations strong, religion has repeatedly shown a capacity to survive the disappearance of all these props. The Jews who suffered the destruction of Israel in the first century A.D. still exist and still matter to human history. The Christians who survived the fall of Rome, the challenges of the Middle Ages, the divisions introduced by the Renaissance and the Reformation, the complications of modern democracy, science, and globalization, are likely to survive even if the West itself passes. For the moment, it is very unlikely that the West will come to an end primarily because it is still living on its religious capital: its beliefs in human dignity and the rightness of ordered liberty. These may seem like self-evident truths and mere generalities to many of us, but they are denied by threatening forces both within and outside the West.

The Western faiths have moved away in modern times from believing that they had some superior insight into the concrete workings of politics and economics. Though some critics have seen this as a tacit admission of failure, in fact it shows a better understanding of the true mission. Faith can usefully remind us or even hector us, as did the Hebrew prophets, that we have obligations to the poor and marginalized in addition to the daily task of living rightly in every particular. But it cannot offer a detailed blueprint for the course that public affairs should take any more than Isaiah could have run the kingdom of Hezekiah. The Augustinian element in Western Christianity, with its understanding that the world cannot become the Kingdom of God until the end of time, has shown its perennial wisdom with the failure of the political religions. In early 2006, when Pope Benedict XVI, a highly learned man, issued his first encyclical "God Is Love," he argued: "When we consider the immensity of others' needs, we can, on the one hand, be driven towards an ideology that would aim at doing what God's governance of the world apparently cannot: fully resolving every problem. Or we can be tempted to give in to inertia, since it would seem that in any event nothing can be accomplished."[35] The right attitude, he claimed, was to keep up hope but within the framework of the ancient truth of knowing ourselves as limited beings who fail quickest—indeed, create far worse evils—when we make an idol of reason and our own abilities.

Something similar has happened in the relationship between religion and science. The old "war between science and religion," though never as large or fairly joined as some people thought, has shifted its ground. As with politics, those religious authorities who in the past may have tried to resist scientific advances have come to a better understanding of the proper role of faith, which is to teach "how to go to heaven, not how the heavens go," as Galileo's friend Cardinal Baronio put it. Today, it is only a small slice of the population, even in advanced countries, that believes science simply explodes faith. The more worrisome problem is a general drift into scientific explanations for things that science cannot fathom, beginning with the view of the human person. An empirical anthropology would acknowledge our desire for transcendence and meaning, not merely try to explain all things human as the kinds of behaviors we discern in animals. The argument over Darwinism versus intelligent design may not be the best way to frame the debate, but there is no question that there is emerging a sense that we must assert something about human nature that is not captured by the usual Darwinism if we do not want to see religion and even human nature itself obliterated.

As we have noted, to keep democratic systems from becoming self-destructive, two things are necessary: good institutions that provide checks and balances over power and, equally important, a vision of human life that will be able to give a credible account of the democratic belief in human dignity, while pointing out that not everything people wish to do under the rubric of liberty is good for them or for a free society. Religion—specifically the Judeo-Christian tradition in the West—is quite good at that, even if it is still today often regarded as the enemy of freedom. Its capacity to inculcate high levels of virtue in ordinary people was already evident in the ancient world. We may be on the verge of seeing a similar recovery today. By contrast, the radically autonomous individual now often presented as the goal and ideal of modern democracy is in fact its most potent enemy. No popular government has been or can be built on a being of that kind.

God has not failed, and will not fail for any of the reasons usually given over the past century. He can fall into relative neglect if individuals, many individuals, fail to appreciate the true source of their own dignity and freedom. That has happened over and over in Western history. We experienced a sharp dip of that kind in the middle of the past century, but every indication we have at the moment is that religion is not only strong but growing in the twenty-first century. And no wonder. With the spectacular failure of the various inhumanities that have come into being in the last two hundred years, the many theories of man that claimed to liberate him but in fact enslaved him, the way is open once more to a new effort to bring faith and reason to bear on the difficult and complicated questions of human existence. There are no absolute guarantees in that quest, but we can be certain that, if God exists, he will not allow his people to remain without help forever.

ACKNOWLEDGMENTS

For exchanges over the years that have, mostly without their knowledge, helped shape the present volume, I would like to thank Michael Aeschliman, Dario Antiseri, Dennis Bartlett, J. Brian Benestad, Jason Boffetti, Jody Bottum, Todd Breyfogle, Grattan Brown, Michael Crofton, Jude Dougherty, Joao Carlos Espada, John Farina, Flavio Felice, Russell Hittinger, Paolo Janni, Joseph Johnston, Thomas Levergood, Leonard Liggio, James Luicer, Daniel Mahoney, George Marlin, Fr. C. J. McCloskey, Brad Miner, Virgil Nemoianu, Fr. J. Scott Newman, Michael Novak, Jose Osvaldo de Meira Penna, John Quinn, Didier Rance, Daniel Robinson, Fr. Kevin Royal, Austin Ruse, James V. Schall, S.J., Tracy Simmons, George Weigel, and Gregory Wolfe. Fr. William Stetson, as often happens with him, pointed me in the right direction at a crucial moment, in this instance towards a text by Arnold Toynbee that had already opened up certain questions I have tried to pursue further. Robert L. Wilken gave me some sage advice on the history of early Christianity. I have borrowed the epigraph (retranslated) for this volume from a book by Robert Sokolowski, but my general debts to his philosophical work are so large that by comparison this is, I hope, only a minor theft.

The Lynde and Harry Bradley Foundation provided support for some of the early research in this study. I am particularly grateful to the late Michael Joyce, then president at Bradley, and Michael Uhlmann, then vice president at Bradley and long a friend and counselor, for their confidence that this book could come to fruition. Michele and Donald D'Amour, Jim Holman, Fred Clarke, and Robert C. Odle have generously supported the Faith & Reason Institute, which has helped keep me at this task.

Peter Collier and Roger Kimball of Encounter Books have been almost preternaturally patient with a long project, and Carol Staswick made many useful editorial suggestions.

Writing a book is a premodern task that fits poorly with the rhythm of the modern world, and modern families often have to deal with the seemingly inhuman absence of the author. My children, John Paul and Natalie, tolerated this bravely, and my wife, Veronica, with the wisdom of experience.

NOTES

Introduction: The Gods That Have Failed

[1] Peter L. Berger, "The Desecularization of the World: A Global Overview," in *The Desecularization of the World: Resurgent Religion and World Politics* (Grand Rapids, Mich.: W. B. Eerdmans, 1999), p. 13.

[2] Pope John Paul II draws up a similar list in Section 1 of *Faith & Reason*, an encyclical that encourages a more vigorous use of *reason* in matters of religion.

[3] The *locus classicus* for this argument is, of course, Sigmund Freud, *The Future of an Illusion*, trans. James Strachey (New York: Norton, 1989).

[4] Nicolas Sarkozy, *La République, les religions, et l espérance* (Paris: Éditions Cerf, 2004).

[5] See Grace Davie, *Europe: The Exceptional Case: Parameters of Faith in the Modern World* (New York: Orbis, 2002).

[6] Paul Michael Zulehner, *Wie Europa lebt und glaubt: Europäische Wertestudie* (Patmos, 1993). Zulehner's work has been confirmed and expanded by the German-American sociologist Peter L. Berger in collaboration with the French sociologist Danièle Herveu-Léger. See in particular Berger's essay "*Religion und europäische Integration: Bemerkungen aus amerikanischer Sicht*," ["Religion and European Integration: Observations from America"], in *Transit: Europäische Revue*, no. 27 (2004).

[7] Dawkins made this remark in response to a question posed by the *New York Times* to a number of prominent scientists: "What do you believe that you cannot prove?" The *Times* published the responses on January 4, 2005.

[8] Cf., among others, Dean Hamer, *The God Gene: How Faith Is Hardwired into Our Genes* (New York: Doubleday, 2004).

[9] For a recent argument to the contrary: Alan Dershowitz, *Rights from Wrongs: A Secular Theory of the Origin of Rights* (New York: Basic Books, 2004). The very fact of the attempt to make this argument, however, shows that the contrary has long been assumed.

[10] See Chapter 4 in the present volume.

[11] Alexis de Tocqueville, *Democracy in America* (1835), ch. 21.

[12] E. O. Wilson, *Consilience: The Unity of Knowledge* (New York: Vintage, 1999), p. 131.

[13] Thomas Jefferson, *Note on the State of Virginia*, Q XVIII, 1782, ME 2:227.

[14] Winston Churchill, Speech to the House of Commons, June 18, 1940.

[15] See Richard Rorty, *Achieving Our Country: Leftist Thought in Twentieth-Century America* (Cambridge, Mass.: Harvard University Press, 1998).

[16] William James, *The Varieties of Religious Experience* (New York: Modern Library, 1929), p. 55 (Lecture III).

[17] Edward Rothstein, "Connections: Attack on U.S. Challenges the Perspectives of Postmodern True Believers," *New York Times*, September 22, 2001, p. A17.

[18] See Henry Kamen, *The Spanish Inquisition: A Historical Revision* (New Haven: Yale University Press, 1998).

[19] For a detailed history of the crimes committed against one Christian church, see Robert Royal, *The Catholic Martyrs of the Twentieth Century: A Comprehensive World History* (New York: Herder & Herder Crossroad, 2000).

[20] Roger Scruton, *The West and the Rest: Globalization and the Terrorist Threat* (Wilmington, Del.: ISI Books, 2002), p. 2.

[21] Peter Brown, *The Rise of Western Christendom* (London: Blackwell, 1997), p. 26.

[22] Representative Dick Durbin (D-Illinois), July 30, 2003.

[23] See their book: Arthur Koestler et al., *The God That Failed: Six Studies in Communism*, ed. Richard Crossman (New York: Harper, 1950).

Chapter 1: Greek Gifts

[1] Euripides, *The Medea*, trans. Rex Warner, in *Euripides I* (Chicago: University of Chicago Press, 1955), p. 108 (lines 1415–1419).

[2] For a well-balanced approach to this question, see David Gress, *From Plato to Nato: The Idea of the West and Its Opponents* (New York: Basic Books, 1999). Gress's title is meant to be an ironic commentary on the simplistic notion that we can draw a straight line from the Greeks to ourselves, and he tries to offer a better reading of what we did—and did not—get from the Greeks.

[3] Pierre Hadot, *Philosophy As a Way of Life: Spiritual Exercises from Socrates to Foucault*, ed. Arnold Davidson, trans. Michael Chase (Oxford: Blackwell, 1999), p. 83.

Notes

⁴ Bruce Thornton, *Greek Ways: How the Greeks Created Western Civilization* (San Francisco: Encounter Books, 2000), p. 197. The quotations are from R. W. Livingstone, *Greek Ideals and Modern Life* (1935).

⁵ Gress, *From Plato to Nato*, p. 61.

⁶ Sophocles, *Antigone*, trans. Elizabeth Wyckoff, in *Sophocles I* (Chicago: University of Chicago Press, 1954), p. 174 (lines 450–457).

⁷ Plato, *Republic* VI.504a.

⁸ Plato, *Laws* IV.716c. For an interesting commentary on these questions, see Simone Weil, "God in Plato," in her *Intimations of Christianity among the Ancient Greeks* (New York: Routledge & Kegan Paul, 1987), pp. 74–88. Weil may take Plato's mysticism too far, but there is no question that she has identified something.

⁹ E. R. Dodds, *The Greeks and the Irrational* (Berkeley: University of California Press, 1963) touched off a raft of modern countercultural interpretations of Greece based on Freud. Though Dodds' book is well worth reading, its psychologizing tendencies have not worn well.

¹⁰ Arthur Darby Nock, foreword to Martin P. Nilsson, *Greek Folk Religion* (New York: Harper Torchbooks, 1961), pp. v–vi.

¹¹ Thornton, *Greek Ways*, p. 184.

¹² Plato, *Apology* 21b, trans. Harold North Fowler, Loeb Classical Library (Cambridge Mass.: Harvard University Press, 1921), p. 81.

¹³ Arnold Toynbee, *The Greeks and Their Heritages* (New York: Oxford University Press, 1981), p. vii.

¹⁴ On this point, see Brian Tierney, *The Idea of Natural Rights* (Atlanta: Scholars Press, 1997).

¹⁵ Cf. Louise Bruit Zaidman and Pauline Schmitt Pantel, *Religion in the Ancient Greek City*, trans. Paul Cartledge (New York: Cambridge University Press, 1992), p. 13.

¹⁶ Daniel Mendelsohn, "What Olympic Ideal? How the Ancient Greeks Invented the Savage, Win-at-Any-Cost Athlete," *New York Times Magazine*, August 8, 2004, pp. 11–13.

¹⁷ Donald Kagan, *On the Origins of War* (New York: Doubleday, 1995), p. 571.

¹⁸ In the words of W. K. C. Guthrie, "a great deal in later Greek religion is only a development of Homeric ideas." *The Greeks and Their Gods* (Boston: Beacon Press, 1955), p. 117.

¹⁹ Ibid., p. 118.

²⁰ Ibid., p. 121.

[21] Nilsson, *Greek Folk Religion*, pp. 19–21.

[22] See George E. Mylonas, *Eleusis and the Eleusinian Mysteries* (Princeton: Princeton University Press, 1961).

[23] Hesiod, *Theogony, Works and Days, Shield*, trans., introduction and notes by Apostolos N. Athanassakis (Baltimore: Johns Hopkins University Press, 1983).

[24] Hesiod, *Works and Days*, p. 274.

[25] Jenny Strauss Clay, *Hesiod's Cosmos* (New York: Cambridge University Press, 2003), p. 50. Aristotle makes the comment quoted in Book A of his *Metaphysics*.

[26] The classic argument for this view, which has been weakened by more recent scholarship, is Erwin Rohde, *Psyche: The Cult of Souls and Belief in Immortality among the Greeks* (Freeport, N.Y.: Books for Libraries Press [1972]). The book was originally published in 1926.

[27] Aristotle, *De anima* A5, 411a7.

[28] Plato, *Phaedo* 70a.

[29] We know of this passage because it was quoted by the Christian philosopher Clement of Alexandria in his *Stromateis* V.109.I.

[30] Plato, *Phaedo* 98b–c.

[31] Werner Jaeger, *Paideia: The Ideals of Greek Culture*, vol. 1, *Archaic Greece: The Mind of Athens*, trans. Gilbert Highet (New York: Oxford University Press, 1965), p. 246.

[32] Ibid., p. 249.

[33] Aeschylus, *Prometheus Bound*, in *Aeschylus II*, trans. David Grene (Chicago: University of Chicago Press, 1967), pp. 150, 158.

[34] Plato, *Crito* 44a–b, quoting from Homer, *Iliad* IX.363.

Chapter 2: Roma Aeterna

[1] Virgil, *Aeneid*, trans. Robert Fitzgerald (New York: Vintage, 1981).

[2] Cf. the commentary of R. G. Austin, in P. Vergili Maronis, *Aeneidos, Liber Sextus* (Oxford: Clarendon Press, 1986), pp. 262–63.

[3] See Simone Weil, "Rome and Albania," in *Selected Essays*, trans. R. Rees (Oxford: Oxford University Press, 1961), pp. 140–42.

[4] Rémi Brague, *Eccentric Culture: A Theory of Western Civilization*, trans. Samuel Lester (South Bend, Ind.: St. Augustine's Press, 2002). The French original is *Europe, la voie romaine* (Paris: Gallimard, 1999).

[5] Quoted in Carl J. Richard, *The Founders and the Classics: Greece, Rome, and the American Enlightenment* (Cambridge: Harvard University Press, 1994), p. 54.

[6] The argument here is indebted to the brilliant and far too little known analysis in Eve Adler, *Vergil's Empire: Political Thought in the Aeneid* (Lanham, Md.: Rowman & Littlefield, 2003).

[7] James Madison, *The Federalist Papers*, No. 51.

[8] Edward Gibbon, *The Decline and Fall of the Roman Empire*, vol. 1, ed. and intro. by J. B. Bury (New York: Heritage Press, 1946), p. 61.

[9] Polybius, *Histories* VI.56 (Shuckburgh translation). This quotation and others about the religiosity of the Romans may be conveniently consulted in David Thompson, ed., *The Idea of Rome from Antiquity to the Renaissance* (Albuquerque: University of New Mexico Press, 1971).

[10] Sallust, *Histories* VI.56 (J. S. Watson translation).

[11] Sallust, *Catiline* VI (J. S. Watson translation).

[12] Sallust, *Catiline* XIII.

[13] Peter Simpson, "The Christianity of Philosophy," *First Things*, May 2001, p. 33.

[14] See Dante, *Purgatorio*, trans. Anthony Esolen (New York: Modern Library, 2003), Canto I.

[15] See Martha Nussbaum, *The Therapy of Desire: Theory and Practice in Hellenistic Ethics* (Princeton: Princeton University Press, 1994).

[16] Gibbon, *Decline and Fall*, ch. 2.

[17] Horace seems to go out of his way to mock what he thinks of as the credulity and proselytizing of the Jews. In his *Satires*, he writes: "Let Apelles the Jew believe it— / I won't" (Book I.5); and "If you can't abide it, / A large group of poets—for we number you know, / More than half the world—will come to my rescue, and then, / Like the Jews, we'll make you join us and join in our views" (Book I.4). *Satires and Epistles of Horace*, trans. Smith Palmer Bovie (Chicago: University of Chicago Press, 1959). The *Jewish Encyclopedia* says of Cicero: "the great orator, philosopher, and statesman (103–43 B.C.), often refers to the Jews in his orations, and in a tone of evident enmity. He calls them 'nations born to slavery'; and in his defense of Flaccus he says, among other things: 'While Jerusalem maintained its ground and the Jews were in a peaceful state, their religious rites were repugnant to the splendor of this empire, the weight of our name, and the institutions of our ancestors; but they are more so now, because that race has shown by arms what

were its feelings with regard to our supremacy; and how far it was dear to the immortal gods, we have learned from the fact that it has been conquered, let out to
hire, and enslaved."

[18] Quoted in Nussbaum, *The Therapy of Desire*, p. 102.

[19] On this point, see ibid., pp. 133–40.

[20] Diogenes Laertius, *Lives of the Eminent Philosophers*, with an English translation by
R. D. Hicks (New York: Heinemann, 1925), IV.43.

[21] Cicero, *De officiis*, trans. Walter Miller (Cambridge: Harvard University Press,
1990), III.116.

[22] Charles de Secondat, Baron de Montesquieu, *Considérations sur les causes de la grandeur des Romains et de leur décadence* (Paris: E. Flammarion, n.d.), p. 96.

[23] Cicero, *De officiis*, trans. Miller, III.27.

[24] "The manner is constantly and pointedly Lucretian; the matter would have excited
Lucretius' disdain," according to R. G. Austin, *Aeneidos, Liber Sextus*, p. 221.

[25] See Kenneth Quinn, "Did Virgil Fail?" in *Virgil: Modern Critical Views*, ed. Harold
Bloom (New York: Chelsea House, 1986), pp. 73–84.

Chapter 3: The Bible and Its Worlds

[1] "Longinus," *On the Sublime*, trans. W. Hamilton Fyfe (Cambridge: Harvard University Press, 1973), p. 149.

[2] Bruce Vawter, *A Path through Genesis* (New York: Sheed & Ward, 1956), p. 37.

[3] Gerhard von Rad, *Genesis: A Commentary*, trans. John H. Marks (Philadelphia:
Westminster Press, 1961), p. 55.

[4] Vawter, *A Path through Genesis*, p. 44.

[5] Von Rad, *Genesis: A Commentary*, p. 60.

[6] Ibid., pp. 63–64.

[7] For a fuller treatment of this material, see Robert Royal, *The Virgin and the Dynamo:
The Use and Abuse of Religion in Environmental Debates* (Grand Rapids, Mich.: W. B.
Eerdmans, 1999).

[8] Dietrich Bonhoeffer, *Creation and Fall: A Theological Interpretation of Genesis 1–3*,
trans. John C. Fletcher (New York: Macmillan, 1959), p. 15.

[9] David Gelernter, "Bible Illiteracy in America," *Weekly Standard*, May 23, 2005,
p. 22.

[10] The classic analysis of these differences is Mircea Eliade's *Cosmos and History: The*

Myth of the Eternal Return, trans. Willard R. Trask (New York: Harper Torchbooks, 1959).

[11] *Magna moralia*, 1208b.6. Scholars are divided about the authorship of this work, but agree it comes from the "school" of Aristotle.

[12] F. E. Peters, *The Harvest of Hellenism: A History of the Near East from Alexander the Great to the Triumph of Christianity* (New York: Simon & Schuster, 1970), p. 297.

[13] A clear overview of this phenomenon is James K. Feibleman, *Religious Platonism: The Influence of Religion on Plato and the Influence of Plato on Religion* (New York: Barnes & Noble, 1959).

[14] Cf. Antonia Tripolitis, *Religions of the Hellenistic-Roman Age* (Grand Rapids, Mich.: W. B. Eerdmans, 2002).

Chapter 4: Christian Paradoxes

[1] Richard Walzer, *Galen on Jews and Christians* (London: Oxford University Press, 1949), p. 15.

[2] David Ayerst and A. S. T. Fisher, *Records of Christianity*, vol. 1 (Oxford: Basil Blackwell, 1971), p. 181.

[3] In *Basic Writings of Nietzsche*, trans. Walter Kaufmann (New York: Modern Library, 1968), p. 193.

[4] Quoted in Robert L. Wilken, *The Christians As the Romans Saw Them* (New Haven: Yale University Press, 1984), p. 200. The material in the present chapter on Roman views of Christians is much indebted to Wilken's patient scholarship.

[5] Ernest Renan, *Marc-Aurèle et la fin du monde antique* (Paris: Calmann-Lévy, 1899), p. 589.

[6] Suetonius, *Lives of the Twelve Caesars* (Rolfe translation), *Nero* 16.

[7] Pliny, *Epistolae* 96, in *The Letters of Pliny*, trans. Betty Radice (New York: Penguin, 1963).

[8] Pliny, *Epistolae* 10.97, trans. Radice.

[9] Samuel Dill, *Roman Society from Nero to Marcus Aurelius* (New York: Meridian, 1957), p. 256.

[10] Suetonius, *Claudius* 25.

[11] Cicero, *De natura deorum*, trans. H. Rackham (Cambridge: Harvard University Press, 1972), I.14.

[12] Cf. Wilken, *The Christians As the Romans Saw Them*, p. 58.

[13] Tertullian, *Apology* 39, in *The Ante-Nicene Fathers*, vol. 3, ed. Alexander Roberts and James Donaldson (Grand Rapids, Mich.: W. B. Eerdmans, 1989).

[14] Wilken, *The Christians As the Romans Saw Them*, p. 124.

[15] Since none of Porphyry's works have survived entire, most of our knowledge of him is from quoted passages that have come down to us in other works. This passage from his *Philosophy from Oracles* (hence the reference to the oracles of Apollo) was quoted by Saint Augustine in *The City of God*, trans. Marcus Dods, XIX.23.

[16] See Rodney Stark, *The Rise of Christianity: How the Obscure, Marginal Jesus Movement Became the Dominant Religious Force in the Western World in a Few Centuries* (San Francisco: HarperCollins, 1997).

[17] Rodney Stark points out that two or three times as great a percentage of college graduates today take an interest in Zen, Yoga, and Transcendental Meditation as do non-graduates. Ibid.

[18] This was already Shirley Jackson Case's conclusion in "The Acceptance of Christianity by the Roman Emperors," *Papers of the American Society of Church History* (New York: G. P. Putnam's Sons, 1928), pp. 45–64. Quoted in Stark, *The Rise of Christianity*, pp. 10–11.

[19] Karl Marx and Friedrich Engels, *Marx and Engels on Religion* (New York: Schocken Books, 1967), p. 316.

[20] Stark, *The Rise of Christianity*, p. 86.

[21] Tacitus, *Histories* V.5.

[22] Minucius Felix, *Octavius* XXXI, in *The Ante-Nicene Fathers*, vol. 4.

[23] Ambrose, *Hexameron*, trans. John J. Savage (New York: Fathers of the Church, 1961), V.vii.19.

[24] Probably the classic book that makes this case is Adolf Harnack's *What Is Christianity?* (*Das Wesen des Christentums*), which originated as a series of sixteen lectures Harnack gave at the University of Berlin in 1899–1900. The English edition is translated by Thomas Bailey Saunders (New York: G. P. Putnam's Sons, 1901).

[25] Quoted in Robert L. Wilken, *The Spirit of Early Christian Thought* (New Haven: Yale University Press, 2003), p. 12.

[26] Ibid., p. 36.

[27] Augustine, *Confessions*, trans. Henry Chadwick (New York: Oxford University Press), I.1.

[28] From his work *First Principles*, quoted in Wilken, *The Spirit of Early Christian Thought*, p. 165.

[29] Augustine, *De moribus ecclesiae,* my translation. See the Latin text and comments on this phenomenon in Charles Norris Cochrane, *Christianity and Classical Culture: A Study of Thought and Action from Augustus to Augustine* (New York: Oxford University Press, 1968), p. 342.

[30] For references and comment, see Etienne Gilson, *The Unity of Philosophical Experience* (Dublin: Four Courts Press, 1982), pp. 155–58. Also his *The Christian Philosophy of Saint Augustine* (London: Gollancz, 1961). For the whole question of Augustine's emphasis on interiority: Philip Carey, *Augustine's Invention of the Inner Self: The Legacy of a Christian Platonist* (New York: Oxford University Press, 2000).

[31] Charles Taylor, *Sources of the Self: The Making of Modern Identity* (Cambridge: Harvard University Press, 1989), p. 133.

[32] Augustine, *The City of God,* trans. Dods, V.5. On this notion, see Jaroslav Pelikan, *The Excellent Empire: The Fall of Rome and the Triumph of the Church* (San Francisco: Harper, 1987), pp. 93–103.

[33] Wilken, *The Spirit of Early Christian Thought,* p. 199.

Chapter 5: Medieval Highs and Lows

[1] Lord Acton, "The History of Freedom in Christianity," in *Essays on Freedom and Power,* selected and with a new introduction by Gertrude Himmelfarb (New York: Meridian Books, 1962), p. 86.

[2] Norman F. Cantor, *Inventing the Middle Ages: The Lives, Works, and Ideas of the Great Medievalists of the Twentieth Century* (New York: William Morrow, 1991), p. 46.

[3] Ibid., p. 40.

[4] Edward Gibbon, *The Decline and Fall of the Roman Empire,* vol. 1, ed. and intro. J. B. Bury (New York: Heritage Press, 1946), ch. 52.

[5] Richard Fletcher, *The Barbarian Conversions: From Paganism to Christianity* (Berkeley: University of California Press, 1999), pp. 99ff.

[6] Ibid., p. 106.

[7] Ibid., p. 114.

[8] See for example *The Oxford History of Medieval Europe* (New York: Oxford University Press, 1992), pp. 50 and 325.

[9] David S. Landes, *The Wealth and Poverty of Nations* (New York: W. W. Norton, 1998), p. 8.

[10] Thomas Cahill, *How the Irish Saved Civilization* (New York: Anchor, 1996).

[11] Christopher Dawson, *The Making of Europe: An Introduction to the History of European Unity* (New York: Meridian Books, 1956), pp. 185–86.

[12] Fletcher, *The Barbarian Conversions*, p. 155.

[13] In the *Aeneid;* see Chapter 2.

[14] Fletcher, *The Barbarian Conversions*, p. 215.

[15] A classic study, though now a bit dated in its scholarship, is Charles Homer Haskins, *The Renaissance of the Twelfth Century* (Cambridge: Harvard University Press, 1927).

[16] Aquinas, *Summa contra Gentiles* II.iii.6.

[17] Quoted in David Knowles, *The Evolution of Medieval Thought* (New York: Vintage, 1962), p. 98.

[18] See Robert Sokolowski, *The God of Faith and Reason: Foundations of Christian Theology* (Washington, D.C.: CUA Press, 1995), pp. 1–11.

[19] St. Thomas Aquinas, *Summa theologica* I.xvii.1, trans. English Dominican Fathers (New York: Benziger, 1947), vol. 1, p. 246.

[20] Christopher Dawson, *Religion and the Rise of Western Culture* (New York: Image, 1991), p. 172.

[21] Erich Auerbach, *Dante, Poet of the Secular World*, trans. Ralph Manheim (Chicago: University of Chicago Press, 1974), p. 93.

[22] Aristotle, *Nichomachean Ethics* X.vii.8, trans. H. Rackham (Cambridge: Harvard University Press, 1925), p. 617.

[23] There have been numerous and ingenious attempts to claim Dante for heterodox religious and political causes. One of the most probing examinations of Dante as a possibly heretical thinker is Ernest Fortin, *Dissidence et philosophie au moyen âge: Dante et ses antécédents* (Paris: Vrin, 1981). See also his "Dante and the Rediscovery of Political Philosophy," in Ernest L. Fortin, *The Birth of Philosophic Christianity: Studies in Early Christian and Medieval Thought*, ed. J. Brian Benestad (Lanham, Md.: Rowman & Littlefield, 1966), pp. 251–68. The present writer is not convinced by these and similar arguments; Dante's work is original enough from what we can see clearly about it not to require esoteric speculations.

[24] Dante, *Purgatorio*, trans. Jean Hollander and Robert Hollander (New York: Doubleday, 2003), XVI.106–109.

[25] On this point, see Jean-Pierre Torrell, O.P., *Saint Thomas Aquinas*, vol. 1, *The Person and His Work*, trans. Robert Royal, 2nd ed. (Washington: Catholic University of America Press, 2005), pp. 191–94. Torrell cites a modern scholar saying: "Averroes was not an Averroist."

[26] This is the position of Etienne Gilson in his now old *Dante and Philosophy*, trans. David Moore (New York: Harper & Row, 1963). Advances have been made in Dante scholarship since Gilson wrote, but his exposition of these matters is still the best balanced and most complete.

[27] Dante, *Epistola* V, trans. Hollander.

[28] Dante, *Paradiso* XXX.137–138.

Chapter 6: Renaissances and Reforms

[1] For an insightful explication of the painting, see Giovanni Reale, *La "Scuola di Atene": una nuova interpretazione dell'affresco, con il cartone a fronte* (Milan: Rusconi, 1997).

[2] For a strong statement of this view, see Charles Freeman, *The Closing of the Western Mind: The Rise of Faith and the Fall of Reason* (New York: Knopf, 2004).

[3] William J. Bouwsma, *The Culture of Renaissance Humanism* (Richmond, Va.: The American Historical Association, 1973), pp. 5–6.

[4] Walter Ullmann, *Medieval Foundations of Renaissance Humanism* (Ithaca: Cornell University Press, 1993), provides a full and up-to-date review of the scholarly literature.

[5] Quoted in Charles Trinkaus, "The Religious Thought of the Italian Humanists: Anticipation of the Reformers or Autonomy?" in *The Scope of Renaissance Humanism* (Ann Arbor: University of Michigan Press, 1983), p. 246.

[6] Quoted in Paul Oskar Kristeller, *Eight Philosophers of the Italian Renaissance* (Stanford: Stanford University Press, 1966), p. 11.

[7] Augustine, *Confessions*, X. Cf. Francis Petrarch, Letter to Dionisio da Borgo San Sepolcro, in *Familiar Letters*, ed. and trans. James Harvey Robinson (New York: G. P. Putnam, 1898), pp. 307–20.

[8] A classic text about this period, much disputed over the years, is Hans Baron, *The Crisis of the Early Italian Renaissance: Civic Humanism and Republican Liberty in an Age of Classicism and Tyranny* (Princeton: Princeton University Press, 1966).

[9] For a balanced treatment of Pico, see Kristeller, *Eight Philosophers*, pp. 54–71.

[10] Philip Jenkins, *The Next Christendom: The Coming of Global Christianity* (New York: Oxford University Press, 2002), p. 30.

[11] "Introductory Letter," in Christopher Columbus, *Libro de las profecías*, trans. and ed. Delno C. West and August Kling (Gainesville: University of Florida Press, 1991), p. 79.

[12] Ibid., p. 111.

[13] Carlos Fuentes, *The Buried Mirror: Reflections on Spain and the New World* (New York: Mariner, 1999).

[14] Johan Huizinga, *The Waning of the Middle Ages: A Study of the Forms of Life, Thought, and Art in France and the Netherlands in the XIVth and XVth Centuries* (New York: Longmans, Green, 1948), pp. 172–73.

[15] Thomas à Kempis, *The Imitation of Christ*, trans. Richard Whitford, ed. and intro. Harold C. Gardiner, S.J. (New York: Image, 1955), pp. 31–32.

[16] A. G. Dickens, *Reformation and Society in Sixteenth-Century Europe* (New York: Harcourt, Brace, Jovanovich, 1975), p. 60.

[17] Richard Tarnas, *The Passion of the Western Mind: Understanding the Ideas That Have Shaped Our World* (New York: Ballantine, 1991), p. 234. Loose talk about Reformation rebelliousness aside, Tarnas's overall reading of Western intellectual history is quite brilliant and repays close study.

[18] Dickens, *Reformation and Society*, pp. 104–5.

[19] Martin E. Marty, "Which Luther?" *Christian Century*, February 10, 2004, pp. 30–31. See also his *Martin Luther* (New York: Penguin, 2004).

[20] Martin Luther, *Three Treatises* (Philadelphia: Fortress Press, 1960), pp. 106–7.

[21] For a lucid description of the factors leading to capitalist expansion see Douglass C. North and Robert Paul Thomas, *The Rise of the Western World: A New Economic History* (New York: Cambridge University Press, 1973).

[22] Dickens, *Reformation and Society*, p. 178.

[23] Cf. Fondazione Memmo, *I Borgia* (Milan: Mondadori-Electa, 2002).

[24] For a charming account of his life, see Jonathan D. Spence, *The Memory Palace of Matteo Ricci* (New York: Viking Penguin, 1984).

[25] A. G. Dickens, *The Counter-Reformation* (New York: Harcourt, Brace, & World, 1970), p. 48.

[26] Bouwsma, *The Culture of Renaissance Humanism*, p. 234.

[27] Cf. Wolfgang Reinhard, "Reformation, Counter-Reformation, and the Early Modern State: A Reassessment," in *The Counter-Reformation*, ed. David M. Luebke (Malden, Mass.: Blackwell, 1999).

[28] Michel de Montaigne, "Apology for Raymond Sebond," in *The Complete Essays of Montaigne*, trans. Donald M. Frame (Stanford: Stanford University Press, 1966), p. 323.

[29] See William J. Bouwsma, *The Waning of the Renaissance* (New Haven: Yale University Press, 2000), p. 157.

[30] Ibid., p. 245.

[31] Felipe Fernández-Armesto and Derek Wilson, *Reformations: A Radical Interpretation of Christianity and the World, 1500–2000* (New York: Scribner, 1996), p. x.

Chapter 7: Enlightenments, Revolutions, Reactions

[1] Leszek Kolakowski, *My Correct Views on Everything*, ed. Zbigniew Janowski (South Bend, Ind.: St. Augustine's Press, 2005), p. 270.

[2] Simon Schama, *Citizens: A Chronicle of the French Revolution* (New York: Vintage Books, 1989), p. 447.

[3] Ibid., p. 161.

[4] A strong and well-written case for the period as less narrow and shallow than the critics claim is Peter Gay, *The Enlightenment: An Interpretation* (London: Weidenfeld & Nicholson, 1969).

[5] S. J. Barnett, *The Enlightenment and Religion: The Myths of Modern Identity* (Manchester, UK, and New York: Manchester University Press, 2003), p. 4.

[6] See Barnett, "The English Deist Movement: A Case Study in the Construction of a Myth," in ibid., pp. 81–129.

[7] Michel de Montaigne, *Essays*, Bk. II, ch. 17. On this point see Etienne Gilson, *The Unity of Philosophical Experience* (New York: Charles Scribner's Sons, 1937), pp. 186–87.

[8] John Locke, *An Essay Concerning Human Understanding*, ed. Alexander Campbell Fraser (New York: Dover, 1959), vol. 2, pp. 309–10 (Bk. IV.x.6).

[9] Ibid., p. 431 (Bk. IV.xix.4).

[10] John Locke, *Second Treatise*, ch. II.6, in *Two Treatises of Government* (New York: Hafner, 1959), p. 123.

[11] Ibid., ch. IV.22.

[12] Arthur Hertzberg, *The French Enlightenment and the Jews* (New York: Columbia University Press, 1968), p. 301. Hertzberg is quoting from Voltaire's *Essai sur les moeurs*.

[13] Quoted in Will and Ariel Durant, *The Age of Voltaire: A History of Civilization in Western Europe from 1715 to 1756, with Special Emphasis on the Conflict between Religion and Philosophy* (New York: MJF Books, 1992), pp. 760–61.

14 Quoted in Peter Gay, *Voltaire's Politics: The Poet As Realist* (Princeton: Princeton University Press, 1959), pp. 221–22.

15 Gertrude Himmelfarb, *The Roads to Modernity: The British, French, and American Enlightenments* (New York: Knopf, 2004), p. 184.

16 Jean-Jacques Rousseau, *The Social Contract*, trans. and intro. Wilmoore Kendall (Chicago: Regnery, 1969), p. 209 (Bk. IV.8).

17 Ibid., p. 214.

18 Jean-Jacques Rousseau, *Émile, or On Education*, trans. Allan Bloom (New York: Basic Books, 1979). The "Profession" appears in Book IV of the novel. All quotations in the text are from this translation.

19 See on this subject Marc F. Plattner, *Rousseau's State of Nature: An Interpretation of the Discourse on Inequality* (Dekalb: Northern Illinois University Press, 1979).

20 Cf. Clifford Orwin, "Moist Eyes: Political Tears from Rousseau to Clinton," AEI Bradley Lecture Series, April 14, 1997.

21 Jean-Jacques Rousseau, *The Confessions*, trans. and intro. J. M. Cohen (Baltimore: Penguin Books, 1965), pp. 605–6.

22 The argument here is based on a number of recent studies, but principal among them: S. J. Barnett, *The Enlightenment and Religion: The Myths of Modernity* (Manchester: University of Manchester Press, 2003); Dale van Kley, *The Religious Origins of the French Revolution from Calvin to the Civil Constitution, 1560–1791* (New Haven: Yale University Press, 1996); William Doyle, *Jansenism: Catholic Resistance to Authority from the Reformation to the French Revolution* (London: Macmillan, 2000).

23 Blaise Pascal, *Pensées*, trans. and intro. A. J. Krailsheimer (Baltimore: Penguin, 1970), p. 309.

24 J. McManners, *Church and Society in Eighteenth-Century France* (Oxford: Clarendon Press, 1998), vol. 2, p. 364.

25 Barnett, *The Enlightenment and Religion*, p. 146.

26 See Patrick Riley, *The General Will before Rousseau: The Transformation of the Divine into the Civic* (Princeton: Princeton University Press, 1986).

27 Barnett, *The Enlightenment and Religion*, p. 156.

28 Ibid., p. 164.

29 Thomas Jefferson, Letter to Dr. Benjamin Waterhouse, June 26, 1822, in *Writings* (New York: Library of America, 1984), p. 1459.

30 Thomas Jefferson, *Notes on the State of Virginia*, Q.XVII, 1782, ME 2:221.

[31] Quoted in James H. Hutson, *Religion and the Founding of the American Republic* (Washington, D.C.: Library of Congress, 1998), p. 32.

[32] Mark A. Noll, *America's God: From Jonathan Edwards to Abraham Lincoln* (New York: Oxford University Press, 2002), p. 161.

[33] Ernst Cassirer, *The Philosophy of Enlightenment* (Boston: Beacon Press, 1955), p. 173.

[34] Quoted in ibid., p. 170.

Chapter 8: Civilization, Culture, and Their Discontents

[1] Friedrich Nietzsche, *Beyond Good and Evil*, in *Basic Writings*, trans. and ed. with commentaries by Walter Kaufmann (New York: Modern Library, 1968), pp. 306–7 (sections 202–203).

[2] On this process, see Alain Finkielkraut, *The Defeat of the Mind*, trans. and intro. Judith Friedlander (New York: Columbia University Press, 1995).

[3] Hugh McLeod, *Religion and the People of Western Europe, 1789–1989* (New York: Oxford University Press, 1997).

[4] Gérard Cholvy and Yves-Marie Hilaire, *Histoire religieuse de la France, 1800–1880* (Toulouse: Éditions Privat, 2000).

[5] See the chart in Ralph Gibson, *A Social History of French Catholicism, 1789–1914* (New York: Routledge, 1989), p. 66.

[6] Roger Shattuck, *The Banquet Years: The Origins of the Avant-Garde in France, 1885 to World War I* (New York: Vintage, 1968), pp. 4–5.

[7] Author's translation.

[8] William Blake, *Complete Writings*, ed. Geoffrey Keynes (New York: Oxford University Press, 1969), p. 418.

[9] William Wordsworth, Sonnet XXXIII, *Poetical Works* (New York: Oxford University Press, 1969), 206.

[10] Matthew Arnold, *Culture and Anarchy*, ed. J. Dover Wilson (New York: Cambridge University Press, 1961), p. 136.

[11] See Gertrude Himmelfarb, "A De-Moralized Society," in *The Demoralizing of Society* (New York: Knopf, 1995), pp. 221–57.

[12] Hugh McLeod, *Religion and Irreligion in Victorian England: How Secular Was the Working Class?* (Bangor, Wales: Headstart History Publications, 1993), p. 32.

[13] Ibid., p. 42.

[14] See Keith Thomson, *Before Darwin: Reconciling God and Nature* (New Haven: Yale University Press, 2005).

[15] T. H. Huxley, "The Origin of Species," *Darwiniana Essays* (New York: D. Appleton & Co., 1986), p. 52.

[16] Quoted in Gertrude Himmelfarb, "The Victorian Trinity: Religion, Science, Morality," in *Marriage and Morals among the Victorians and Other Essays* (New York: Vintage Books, 1987), p. 69.

[17] Nathan O. Hatch, *The Democratization of American Christianity* (New Haven: Yale University Press, 1989), p. 210.

[18] Thomas Paine, *Common Sense*, ch. 3.

[19] Mark A. Noll, *The Old Religion in a New World: The History of North American Christianity* (Grand Rapids, Mich.: William B. Eerdmans, 2002), p. 61.

[20] Ibid., p. 65.

[21] Ibid., p. 68.

[22] Alexis de Tocqueville, *Democracy in America* (1835), vol. 1, ch. 12.

[23] Michael Zöller, *Washington and Rome: Catholicism in the United States* (Notre Dame, Ind.: University of Notre Dame Press, 1999), p. 243.

[24] Lord Acton, *Essays on Freedom and Power* (New York: Meridian, 1955), p. 88.

[25] Henry Adams, *The Education of Henry Adams* (Boston: Houghton Mifflin, 1961), pp. 384–85.

[26] "Prayer to the Virgin of Chartres," in *Henry Adams: Novels, Mont Saint Michel, The Education* (New York: Library of America, 1983), pp. 1202–7.

Chapter 9: The God That Did Not Fail

[1] See José Osvaldo de Meira Penna, *Nietzsche e a Locura* ["Nietzsche and Madness"] (Rio de Janeiro: UniverCidade, 2004). This book is an amplification of three lectures given originally in English at the Carl Jung Institute in Zurich in April 2000.

[2] Friedrich Nietzsche, *On the Genealogy of Morals: A Polemic*, in *Basic Writings*, trans. and ed. with commentaries by Walter Kaufmann (New York: Modern Library, 1968), p. 526 (Aphorism 20).

[3] Nietzsche, *Ecce Homo*, in *Basic Writings*, ed. Kaufmann, p. 783.

[4] See Peter Berkowitz, *Nietzsche: The Ethics of an Immoralist* (Cambridge: Harvard University Press, 1995).

5 Carl Jung, *Jung's Seminar on Zarathustra*, ed. and abr. James L. Jarrett (Princeton: Princeton University Press, 1998), pp. 373–74.

6 Friedrich Nietzsche, *The Gay Science*, trans. with commentary by Walter Kaufmann (New York: Vintage, 1974), p. 167 (Section 108).

7 Arthur Koestler et al., *The God That Failed: Six Studies in Communism*, ed. Richard Crossman (New York: Harper, 1950).

8 Pope Leo XIII, *Rerum Novarum*, para. 4.

9 On this material, see the analyses in my *Catholic Martyrs of the Twentieth Century: A Comprehensive World History* (New York: Herder & Herder/Crossroad, 2000).

10 Stéphane Courtois et al., *The Black Book of Communism: Crimes, Terror, Repression*, trans. Jonathan Murphy and Mark Kramer; consulting editor, Mark Kramer (Cambridge, Mass.: Harvard University Press, 1999).

11 See Frederick C. Crews et al., *The Memory Wars: Freud's Legacy in Dispute* (New York: New York Review of Books, 1995).

12 Sigmund Freud, *Totem and Taboo*, trans. A. A. Brill (New York: Moffat, Yard, & Co., 1918), p. 242.

13 Two older studies still worth consulting are William Barrett, *Irrational Man: A Study in Existential Philosophy* (New York: Doubleday, 1958), which includes literary reflections; and, for a more purely philosophical approach, James Collins, *The Existentialists* (Chicago: Regnery, 1952).

14 Cf. *The Essential Kant* (New York: New American Library, 1970), p. 330.

15 Martin Buber, *I and Thou*, trans. Ronald Gregor Smith (New York: Charles Scribner's Sons, 1958), p. 11.

16 A good introduction is *The Lévinas Reader*, ed. Sean Hand (Oxford: Blackwell, 1999).

17 On these several developments, see Robert P. Kraynak, *Christian Faith and Modern Democracy: God and Politics in the Fallen World* (Notre Dame, Ind.: University of Notre Dame Press, 2002), pp. 107–64.

18 Konrad Adenauer, *Memoirs, 1945–53*, trans. Beate Ruhm von Oppen (Chicago: Regnery, 1966), p. 45.

19 For a sympathetic treatment of this history, see Mary Ann Glendon, *A World Made New: Eleanor Roosevelt and the Universal Declaration of Human Rights* (New York: Random House, 2001).

20 Grace Davie, *Religion in Britain since 1945: Believing without Belonging* (Oxford: Blackwell, 1994).

[21] Mary Douglas, "The Effect of Modernization on Religious Change," in *Religion and America: Spirituality in a Secular Age*, ed. Mary Douglas and Stephen M. Tipton (Boston: Beacon Press, 1982), p. 25.

[22] Andrew M. Greeley, *Religion in Europe at the End of the Second Millennium: A Sociological Profile* (New Brunswick, N.J.: Transaction Publishers, 2003), p. 7.

[23] Ibid., p. 23.

[24] Ibid., p. 50, chart.

[25] Ibid., p. 57.

[26] Rodney Stark, "Secularization, R.I.P.," *Sociology of Religion* 60:3 (1999), p. 255.

[27] Alexis de Tocqueville, *Democracy in America* (1935; New York: Vintage, 1956), p. 319.

[28] Stark, "Secularization, R.I.P.," p. 26, summing up the work in 1914 of James Lueba and the 1997 survey by Edward J. Larson and Larry Witham.

[29] For a basic explanation of this whole phenomenon, see Joel A. Carpenter, *Revive Us Again: The Reawakening of American Fundamentalism* (New York: Oxford University Press, 1999).

[30] Bernard Lewis, *The Crisis of Islam: Holy War and Unholy Terror* (New York: Modern Library, 1993), pp. 24, 37.

[31] Philip Jenkins, *The Next Christendom: The Coming of Global Christianity* (New York: Oxford University Press, 2002), p. 59.

[32] Ibid., p. 5.

[33] Ibid., p. 104.

[34] See in particular Samuel P. Huntington, *Who Are We? The Challenges to America's National Identity* (New York: Simon & Schuster, 2004).

[35] Pope Benedict XVI, *Deus Caritas Est*, para. 36.

INDEX